Jane Cox and Timothy Padfield

TRACING YOUR ANCESTORS

IN THE

PUBLIC RECORD OFFICE

Fourth edition

by

Amanda Bevan and Andrea Duncan

London: HMSO

© Crown copyright 1990, 1991 (Index)

First published 1981
Fourth edition 1990
Second impression 1991

ISBN 0 11 440222 1

British Library Cataloguing in Publication Data

A CIP catalogue record for this book is available from the British Library

CONTENTS

Preface

continued

4. Births, marriages and deaths of Britons overseas

continued

5. Family history before the parish registers

6. Wills and other probate records

7. Welsh genealogy

8. Scottish genealogy

9. Irish genealogy

10. Isle of Man genealogy

11. Channel Isles genealogy

continued

18. The Army

19. The Royal Navy

continued

19. The Royal Navy

20. The Royal Marines

21. The Royal Air Force

22. The Coastguard and the preventive services

23. Police forces

continued

38. Criminal trials

39. Remanded and convicted prisoners

40. Convicted prisoners transported abroad

41. Land ownership

42. Surveys of land and house ownership

43. Taxation

continued

PREFACE

This is the fourth edition of a handbook originally written by Mrs J M Cox and Mr T R Padfield; it has been extensively revised and enlarged by Dr A S Bevan and Miss A I Duncan to take into account the larger number of sources used by, and made available to, family historians over the decade since it was first published.

In the course of the successive editions, the editors have received help from many people, both Public Record Office staff and others; particular mention should be made of Mrs M K Banton, Miss G L Beech, Dr T Brass, Mr D A Burr, Dr N G Cox, Ms A Crawford, Dr D Crook, Dr M R Foster, Mr J S Fowler, Mrs E M Goode, Mr J M Guthrie, Mr D L Hendry, Dr E J Higgs, Mrs B Inglis, Mrs H E Jones, Mrs S B Lumas, Mr J F Murray, Mrs S Orton, Mr B Pappalardo, Dr J B Post, Dr N A M Rodger, Mr R F Rowley, Mr P J Seaman, Mr M P Stainton and Dr D L Thomas. Mr C R H Cooper contributed the chapter on bankruptcy, and Mr G Hood the chapter on wills.

The cover illustration shows part of a pedigree of the descendants of Eleanor Beauchamp, drawn up as evidence in a lawsuit in the late 1560s (C 47/9/18, no 100).

July 1990

An index compiled by Mrs G M Lowe has been added to this reprint of the fourth edition.

May 1991

1. Introduction

1.1 The Public Record Office and its services

The Public Record Office houses one of the finest, most complete archives in Europe, comprising the records of the central government and law courts from Domesday Book in 1086 to the present century. It is a mine of information for the family historian, but it is not the place to begin research, as the main collections of birth, marriage and death records are held elsewhere. There is, moreover, no central index of names, and the more you can discover about your family in advance the speedier and the more fruitful your researches in the public records will be.

The PRO does not undertake genealogical research. Readers have to come to the search rooms to conduct their own research, unless they are prepared to employ a record agent (see **1.4**). However, photocopies can be ordered by post if the documents are precisely identified by the applicant, giving full PRO references (as explained in the PRO information leaflet *Reprographic and Photographic Copies of Records in the Public Record Office*).

The search rooms are on two sites at present. The Public Record Office, Ruskin Avenue, Kew, Richmond, Surrey TW9 4DU (telephone: 081-876-3444) houses the records of modern government departments. Medieval and early modern records, all legal records and the census records are kept at the Public Record Office, Chancery Lane, London WC2A 1LR (telephone: 081-876-3444).

The search rooms are open to the public from 9.30 a.m. to 5 p.m., Monday to Friday, except on public holidays and during the first two weeks in October. A reader's ticket must be obtained in order to see original records, and will be issued on production of some positive means of identification, such as a banker's card, or, for foreign nationals, a passport or some other form of national identification document. At the time of writing, no ticket is needed for consultation of the census returns.

Public records are not normally made generally available until thirty years after the date of their final creation; thus a file opened in 1950 and closed in 1955 became available in 1986. Exceptions to this rule are noted in the text. Many documents which refer to individuals have much longer closure periods, to safeguard personal confidentiality: an obvious example is the census, which is closed for 100 years.

1.2 Classes and finding aids

The records held in the Public Record Office occupy some 90 miles of shelving, and the main guide to them, the *Current Guide*, is about 5,500 pages long. This book, *Tracing Your Ancestors in the Public Record Office*, concentrates on the main sources for genealogy, but there are many more which have not been mentioned. To find your own way round the records, you need to learn how they are arranged, and how to use the *Current Guide* and the class lists.

Records in the Public Record Office are divided into 'classes', reflecting as far as possible their original administrative arrangement. Each class has its own name and identifying code, and consists of individual 'pieces' (sometimes a single document, sometimes several). To order a piece, you must know its complete reference. This is made up of letters and numbers: letters (e.g. WO for War Office), class number (e.g. WO 97, for War Office, Royal Hospital Chelsea, Soldiers' Documents) and piece numbers (e.g. WO 97/341, for War Office, Royal Hospital Chelsea, Soldier's Documents, 13th Foot, Abb-Car, 1760-1854). These references can be discovered from the various finding aids in the Public Record Office.

The main kinds of finding aid are:

> *guide*: the general descriptive summary of the holdings of the PRO (see **1.3**);
>
> *handbook*: an introduction to the records of a particular department, or to a particular area of research;
>
> *transcript*: a full text, in which the abbreviations of the original manuscripts have been extended wherever this could be done with certainty;
>
> *calendar*: a précis, usually in English, full enough to replace the original documents for most purposes;
>
> *list*: a list of the pieces comprising a class of records, with dates and simple descriptions;
>
> *descriptive list*: a list with fuller indications of the contents of each document;
>
> *index*: alphabetically arranged references to people, places or subjects mentioned in the records;
>
> *catalogue*: a calendar or descriptive list containing records of similar content drawn from different groups or classes, sometimes for a special purpose such as a public exhibition.

It must be emphasised that there is no single finding aid which gives precise references to all the records.

The bibliographies in this book contain, besides works for further reading and the names of the relevant record classes, information on various aids to finding and understanding records. Not all the publications mentioned are available in the PRO; those which can be seen at Chancery Lane are marked with an *, those at Kew with a #. Some will be available for purchase in the shop at Chancery Lane and at Kew. Most can be read in the Guildhall Library, the library of the Society of Genealogists and in good reference libraries.

Unpublished finding aids are to be found in the appropriate reading rooms of the PRO unless otherwise stated.

There is a list of addresses of institutions and societies mentioned in the text, given in **48**.

1.3 Using the *Current Guide* and the lists

The PRO has two guides in everyday use. One, the *Guide to the Contents of the Public Record Office*, is very out of date but is still the major source for some of the earlier records at Chancery Lane. The other, the *Current Guide*, is updated at regular intervals to include the latest accessions and discoveries, and is gradually being extended to cover all the holdings of the PRO. Because the *Current Guide* is so large (over 5,500 pages) and is updated so frequently, it is sold in microfiche only, available from the PRO at a remarkably low price: at the PRO it can be seen in printed form.

The *Current Guide* occupies several loose-leaf volumes. Part 1 contains the administrative histories of the various government departments and courts whose records are in the PRO. Part 2 has class descriptions in alpha-numeric order of class code. Part 3 is the index to the other two parts. The easiest way to describe how to use it is by example.

Suppose you want to trace an ancestor who may have nursed at the Royal Greenwich Hospital. Start in Part 3, the index. There are several index entries for Greenwich Hospital, some followed by class code (e.g. ADM 2), others by a string of numbers. The numbers (e.g. 703/6/3) are references to Part 1, in which each department has its own three figure number, with further sub-divisions for different parts of its organisation.

Public Record Office Current Guide Part 3: Index

Greenwich, East
  see East Greenwich
GREENWICH HOSPITAL
   see for broader entries: Naval hospitals
  703/6/3
  Admiralty out-letters, ADM 2
  baptism registers, RG 8, RG 4
  burial registers, ADM 73, RG 8, RG 4
  county rolls, ADM 74
  deeds, ADM 75
  estates ledgers, ADM 70, ADM 71
  general court, ADM 67
  in-letters, ADM 65
  in-pensions and in-pensioners, ADM 65, ADM 73
  maintenance of children of naval officers, ADM 163,ADM 164
  maintenance of orphans of naval personnel, ADM 162
  marriage registers, RG 8, RG 4
  minutes, ADM 67
  miscellaneous registers, etc, ADM 73
  out-letters, ADM 66
  out-pensions and out-pensioners, ADM 6, ADM 73
  registered files, ADM 169
  registers of claims, ADM 162, ADM 163
  salary lists etc., T 47
  school ledgers, ADM 72
  service records of candidates, ADM 29
  staff pensions, ADM 165
  staff records, ADM 73
  survey and rentals, ADM 79
  treasurer's ledgers, ADM 69
Greenwich Hospital accounts
  see for broader entries: Charity Accounts; Estate Accounts

Notes on the contents and arrangement of this index, including
hints to users, are at the front of this binder.

In the Part 1 entry for 703/6/3, you will find a brief history of Greenwich Hospital.

703.6.3   ROYAL GREENWICH HOSPITAL

The Royal Greenwich Hospital was founded by Queen Mary, who
in 1694 gave the royal estate at Greenwich for a home for
superannuated seamen and marines. The foundation stone was
laid in 1696 and the first pensioners were admitted in 1705.
In 1716 the forfeited estates of Lord Derwentwater were
added to the hospital's endowments (the Northern Estates).
In addition to the in-pensioners, the hospital also maintained out-pensioners and provided pensions and allowances
for widows and orphans of seamen and marines. It also
provided for a limited number of officers. A school for the
sons of seamen was attached to the hospital. In 1829 this
school absorbed the Royal Naval Asylum for the children of
seamen, originally established by the Patriotic Fund of
Lloyds, but managed by commissioners since 1805. In 1803
the hospital took over the administration of the Chatham
Chest (6.1), which was thereupon renamed the Greenwich
Chest. After 1832 the hospital passed under the superin-
tendence of the Board of Admiralty (1.3), the civil lord
being the member with particular responsibility for its
affairs. It ceased to house in-pensioners in 1869 and since
1873 the building has become the home of the Royal Naval
College (6.4); but the hospital has continued to administer
the school, which moved to Holbrook in 1933, and to provide
out-pensions and allowances of various kinds.

The hospital's minutes are in ADM 67; correspondence is in
ADM 65, ADM 66, ADM 169; law papers are in ADM 76; accounts
are in ADM 68, ADM 69; miscellaneous records are in ADM 80.
Records relating to the hospital's estates are in ADM 70,
ADM 71, ADM 74, ADM 75, ADM 79. Records relating to
pensioners are in ADM 6, ADM 73, ADM 165, PMG 24, PMG 69-
71, WO 22, WO 23; records of widows' and orphans' pensions,
etc. are in ADM 73, ADM 162-164, ADM 166. Records relating
to staff of the hospital are in ADM 73 and ADM 165. Records
of Greenwich Hospital School are in ADM 72, ADM 73, ADM 80,
ADM 161. Late-seventeenth century newsletters, addressed
mainly to the first earl of Derwentwater, are in ADM 77,
with entry books in ADM 78. Registers of births, baptisms,
marriages and burials for the hospital and school are in
RG 4/1669-1679, further registers of baptisms and burials
in RG 8/16-18 and burials in ADM 73. See also PRO 30/26.

This provides a description of the Hospital's history, and a very brief guide to its records, with references to the various classes involved, but little indication of dates covered.

To find out more, you need to look at Part 2, the class descriptions. In fact, you could have gone there directly from Part 3, where the entries followed by letters and numbers are to classes described in Part 2. Neither Part 3 nor Part 1 made any references to nurses at Greenwich Hospital, but both mentioned staff records as being in ADM 73. The class description of ADM 73 in Part 2 is more helpful: nurses' records are mentioned at last. The class description also says that ADM 73 is kept at Kew.

Having identified the class you want to look at, you then have to find the class list to discover which particular document you want to order. You will need to do this when you get references to classes from this book, to identify exactly which piece you want.

At Kew, there are two sets of Kew class lists in the Reference Room. Other sets are also available: they are all arranged in alpha-numeric order. At Chancery Lane, class lists of Chancery Lane classes are kept in a kind of departmental/subject order: to find them you need to consult the card index in each search room which will give you a bookcase reference. There is also a very incomplete set of Chancery Lane lists at Kew, and a full set of Kew lists at Chancery Lane.

There may be several lists in one volume, or one list may cover several volumes. Most lists are numerical in rough chronological order, but some are arranged by subject and others by place. At the front of each list there should be an Introductory Note, which gives more detail about the class than Part 2 of the *Current Guide*, and often includes instructions on how to order documents.

The Introductory Note for ADM 73 gives a range of piece numbers for staff records, which saves searching through the descriptions of all 465 pieces in this class.

```
                            ADM 73


                   GREENWICH HOSPITAL REGISTERS

        The majority of these registers is concerned with four
        distinct  classes  of  person;  In-Pensioners,  Out-
        Pensioners, staff and children.

        Applications by former warrant officers, ratings and
        Marines for admission as In-Pensioners, arranged al-
        phabetically, are in pieces 1-35. They consist
        chiefly of certificates of the applicants' services
        issued by the Navy Pay Office. Though issued from
        1790, these describe services which in some cases go
        back at least forty years before. Pieces 36-69 are
        chiefly  registers  of  the  In-Pensioners  of  the
        Hospital at various dates.

        Pay books of out-pensions form pieces 95 to 131. They
        give only the name of the Out-Pensioner and the amount
        of his pension. The signatures of those who drew their
        pensions in cash appear as a receipt; the letter R
        against others stands in this case for 'Remitted' (to
        those living at a distance from the Hospital).

        Pieces 70 to 88 and 132 to 153 are lists and registers
        of the staff of the Hospital.

        The papers submitted on behalf of children applying
        for admission to the Greenwich Hospital Schools are
        arranged alphabetically in pieces 134-389. In almost
        every case they include certificates of the appli-
        cants' fathers' services. Registers of the children
        admitted are in pieces 390-449.




        October 1984
```

In the class list of ADM 73, pieces 83 to 88 look as though they might be useful in this search. The lettercode **ADM**, the class number **73**, and the piece number **83** are the items of information which will be needed for ordering the first of these documents via the computer. Then the real search can begin.

ADMIRALTY - GREENWICH HOSPITAL
REGISTERS, &c.

Reference		ADM 73

ADM 73	Date	Description
78	1830-1843	Establishment Book
79	1843-1845	Ditto
80	1845-1852	Ditto
81	1852-1863	Ditto
82	1865-1869	Muster Book of Servants
83	1704-1864	General Entry Book of Nurses
84	1766-1863	Entry Book of Nurses
85	1783-1863	Register of Nurses
86	1847-1865	Register of Nurses and Servants
87	1704-1772	Alphabetical List of Nurses
88	1772-1864	Ditto
89	1800-1801	Register of Children at Clarence House
90	1844-1868	Register of the In-Pensioners' Children's Schools

1.4 Assistance with your search

The Public Record Office does not undertake genealogical research itself. If you wish someone to do a full search on your behalf, names of professional record agents may be supplied but the arrangement between yourself and the agent will be of a purely private nature and the PRO can accept no responsibility for any aspect of the arrangements made between record agents and their clients. The Association of Genealogists and Record Agents will also put you in touch with a researcher accredited to the Association.

If you have sound reasons for believing that your family is armigerous (entitled to bear a coat of arms), enquire of the officer-in-waiting at the College of Arms. The College has many pedigrees relating to non-armigerous families among its collections and officers will undertake research into these. Scotland and Ireland have their own heraldic authorities.

There is a network of family history societies throughout the British Isles, most of which publish journals. These organisations can be extremely helpful in providing professional guidance and contact between family historians. A list of family history societies and like bodies appears in the journal of the Federation of Family History Societies, the *Family History News and Digest,* published twice yearly. The Federation of Family History Societies (FFHS) publish a number of excellent guides to different kinds of records, as do the Society of Genealogists.

The Society of Genealogists also has a very good genealogical library and a number of very useful indexes. It is open free to members and to anyone else on a daily fee-paying basis. The Guildhall Library in London is a public library with an excellent genealogical collection.

The Historical Manuscripts Commission will provide information on the whereabouts of private papers and manorial documents.

The addresses of all these libraries and other institutions can be found in **48**.

1.5 *Tracing Your Ancestors in the Public Record Office*

Although every effort has been made to make this book as accurate and informative as possible, its authors recognize that there are bound to be errors and omissions waiting to be found. If, in the course of research, you identify errors or discover useful unmentioned sources, please inform the Reference Desk staff at Kew, or the reading room staff at Chancery Lane, so that the next edition can be improved.

1.6 Tracing living persons

The Public Record Office is not the place to trace missing people. The hunt for living relatives should start with C D Rogers' very helpful book, *Tracing Missing Persons.* Under very special circumstances, the British Red Cross and the Salvation Army will undertake to trace relatives, but this is usually only to mitigate suffering. The Association of Genealogists and Record Agents will supply the name of an agent who will make a search for a fee. Tracing may also be carried out through the Department of Social Security. Details of this procedure are contained in leaflet PAS 6, available from the General Register Office.

1.7 Tracing your ancestors: introductory bibliography

An * means this work can be seen at Chancery Lane: a # means it can be seen at Kew. Many of the works mentioned in this and subsequent bibliographies can be bought in the PRO shops.

Introductory reading

There are numerous general guides on the techniques of ancestor tracing. Among the best are G Pelling's, *Beginning Your Family History* (FFHS, 4th edn 1987), S Colwell's *The Family History Book* (Oxford, 1980) and A Camp's *Everyone Has Roots* (London, 1978).

The Society of Genealogists publishes an excellent quarterly journal for members, entitled *The Genealogists' Magazine*. It contains articles, book reviews, a letters' page, and details of families currently being researched. The monthly *Family Tree Magazine* has a growing readership, and has features for beginners, and for computer-literate genealogists, as well as a family historians' problem page.

Trouble shooting guides are now popular, although none of those available is perfect. The best is published by the FFHS: F C Markwell and P Saul's *The Family Historian's Enquire Within* (1988). C D Rogers, *The Family Tree Detective* (Manchester, 1983), is useful, as is T V FitzHugh's *The Dictionary of Genealogy* (Dorset, 1985).

Two reference books, that can be turned to over and over again, are D Hey's *Family History and Local History in England* (London, 1987) and R Harvey's *Genealogy for Librarians* (London, 1983). The title of the latter is misleading: it is useful for everyone interested in genealogy.

For families who appear in older printed histories, look at G W Marshall's *The Genealogist's Guide* (London, 1973)*; J W Whitmore, *A Genealogical Guide* (London, 1953); G B Barrow, *The Genealogist's Guide* (London, 1977); and *Burke's Family Index* (London, 1976). These give references to books and articles, and are arranged by surname. The Church of Jesus Christ of Latter Day Saints (the Mormon church) holds a Family Registry on microfiche and J S W Gibson has written a guide to *Unpublished Personal Name Indexes* (FFHS, 1987)*.

For Scotland and Ireland, consult B de Breffny, *Bibliography of Irish Family History and Genealogy* (Cork and Dublin, 1974); E MacLysaght, *Bibliography of Irish Family History* (2nd edn 1982); and J P S Ferguson, *Scottish Family Histories* (Edinburgh, 1986).

Surnames, their origins, meanings and locations are covered (albeit imperfectly) by P H Reaney and R M Wilson, *Dictionary of British Surnames* (London, 2nd edn 1976)*; G F Black, *The Surnames of Scotland* (New York, 1962); R Bell, *The Book of Ulster Surnames* (The Blackstaff Press, 1988); E MacLysaght, *The Surnames of Ireland* (Dublin, 1978); and T J Morgan and P Morgan, *Welsh Surnames* (Cardiff, 1985)*.

For local history, try W B Stephens, *Sources for English Local History* (Cambridge, 1981)* and P Riden, *Record Sources for Local History* (London, 1987)*. Another useful book is A Macfarlane, *A Guide to English Historical Records* (Cambridge, 1983).

Biographical dictionaries

The *Dictionary of National Biography* (London, 1909 continuing) is available at Kew and Chancery Lane, and should also be available at any good library. A useful new biographical source, which is not yet very widely known, is the *British Biographical Archive* (London, 1984 continuing). This reproduces in microfiche the contents of 310 of the most important English language biographical dictionaries (excluding the *Dictionary of National Biography*), published between 1601 and 1929. A copy can be seen at Kew, on request at the Reference Desk.

General guides to the Public Record Office

British National Archives (Government Publications Sectional List 24, last published 1984) *#
J Cox, *The Nation's Memory, A Pictorial Guide to the Public Record Office* (London, 1988) *#
Public Record Office, *Access to Public Records* (Information Leaflet) *#
Public Record Office, *Current Guide to the Contents of the Public Record Office* (revised regularly) *#
Public Record Office, *Family History in England and Wales* (Information Leaflet) *#
Public Record Office, *Guide to the Contents of the Public Record Office* (London, 1963, 1968) *#
Public Record Office, *The Public Record Office* (Information Leaflet) *#
Public Record Office, *Reprographic and Photographic Copies of Records in the Public Record Office* (Information Leaflet) *#

Directories of archive institutions

J Foster and J Sheppard, *ed., British Archives: A Guide to Archive Resources in the United Kingdom,* (London, 2nd edn 1989) *#
J S W Gibson and P Peskett, *Record Offices and How to Find Them* (FFHS, 1985) *#
Record Repositories in Great Britain (London, 8th edn 1987) *#

Missing persons

C D Rogers, *Tracing Missing Persons* (Manchester, 1986) *

2. Censuses of population

2.1 Census returns: England, Wales, Isle of Man and the Channel Islands

The census returns from 1841 onwards are the most important and useful modern genealogical source in the PRO. The returns of 1841 and 1851 (HO 107), 1861 (RG 9), 1871 (RG 10) and 1881 (RG 11) in theory include all people in England, Wales, the Isle of Man and the Channel Islands on a specific night in those years. Censuses started earlier than this, in 1801, but until 1841 censuses were simply headcounts, and did not name individuals. As the information given to the census enumerator is treated as confidential for 100 years, the 1891 census will not be open to the public until the first working day of January 1992.

Before starting a search, you need to have at least an approximate home address, or an idea of where your ancestors might have been on the night of the census (e.g. on holiday, in an institution such as a prison or a workhouse, working away from home, or on board a ship in port or within territorial waters). The 1841-1881 censuses are arranged by place, grouped in the registration districts used for the registration of births, marriages and deaths. Maps of these registration districts can be found in RG 18. They are arranged by year, and can be useful in identifying the registration districts of the smaller places that do not appear in the indexes to the census.

The 1841 census is the least satisfactory in terms of information and layout: the returns, written in pencil, record full names, ages (rounded down to the nearest five years, for adults), occupations, and whether born in the county of residence. The letters S, I and F are used to indicate if the person was born in Scotland, Ireland or Foreign Parts. From 1851, the information recorded becomes more precise and the full address, name, exact age, marital status, relationship to the head of the household, sex, occupation, parish and county of birth are all given.

There are some pitfalls in using the censuses, and interpreting the evidence is not always as straightforward as it might appear. A good general rule is, the younger the person described, the more accurate the information on age and place of birth. E J Higgs's book explains the ideas behind the compilation of the censuses, and warns against accepting their contents as literal truth.

Because the census returns are so much in demand, and the originals are so fragile, they can be seen only on microfilm. As a bonus, many microfilm copies of the returns are held locally, and a complete microfilm copy is held by the Genealogical Society of Utah. The Census Room of the PRO at Chancery Lane is used by the readers of the censuses, and contains many additional finding aids such as street indexes to towns with a population over 40,000, and some name indexes. Name indexes have been compiled for about 90% of the 1851 census, and work is progressing on the other censuses: these name indexes are produced by family history societies. Most name indexes are available on request in the Census Room and at the library of the Society of Genealogists.

The PRO, in return for a fee, will make limited searches in the census records on behalf of those unable to visit the Census Room: searches are not made in towns of over 5,000 population unless a street name is provided. Application forms and further details are available on request.

Personal information in the 1891 and 1901 censuses is not kept totally secret. Direct descendants or people acting on their behalf can apply to the General Register Office, Office of Population Censuses and Surveys (see **48.7** for the address), giving the exact address to be searched: for a fee, a search will be made by the General Register Office to establish the age and place of birth of named persons. More speculative searches will have to await the opening of these censuses at the PRO, on the first working day of the year following the hundredth anniversary of the census (1992 and 2002 respectively).

2.2 Census returns: other places

Census returns for Scotland, 1841-1891, are available at the General Register Office, Edinburgh. Census returns for Ireland, 1901-1911, are held in the Public Record Office in Dublin, and are open to inspection.

Colonial census returns, if they survived, will be kept in the appropriate national archives. However, the PRO does hold a few colonial censuses. The most well known of these are the censuses of convicts (and some free settlers) in New South Wales and Tasmania, 1788-1859 (HO 10: see **40.4** for further details). In addition, the PRO has a census of 1811 from Surinam, detailing slaves and free black and white inhabitants (CO 278/15-25); a 1715 census of the white population of Barbados (CO 28/16); and a census of the colony of Sierra Leone on 30 June 1831 (CO 267/111).

2.3 Censuses of population: bibliography and sources

[An * means this work can be seen at Chancery Lane: a # means it can be seen at Kew.]

Published works

M W Beresford, 'The unprinted Census returns for 1841, 1851 and 1861 for England and Wales', *Amateur Historian,* vol.V, pp.260-269

J S W Gibson and C Chapman, *Census Indexes and Indexing* (FFHS, 1983)

J S W Gibson, *Census Returns on Microfilm, A Directory to Local Holdings*, (FFHS, 1988) *

E Higgs, *Making Sense of the Census: The Manuscript Returns for England and Wales 1801-1901* (London, 1989) *

R Lawton, ed., *The Census and Social Structure, an Interpretative Guide to nineteenth century Censuses, for England and Wales* (London, 1978)

E McLaughlin, *The Censuses 1841-1881* (FFHS, 1986)

M Medlycott, 'Some Georgian 'Censuses': The Militia Lists and 'Defence' Lists', *Genealogists' Magazine*, vol. XXIII, pp.55-59

M Nissel, *People count: A history of the General Register Office* (London, 1987) *
Public Record Office, *Censuses of Population 1801-1881* (Information Leaflet) *#

Records

Colonial Office (at Kew)
CO 28/16: Barbados Original Correspondence; 1715 census
CO 267/111: Sierra Leone Original Correspondence; 1831 census
CO 278/15-25: Surinam Original Correspondence; 1811 census

Home Office
HO 10 Settlers and Convicts, New South Wales and Tasmania. 1787 to 1859. (At Kew.)
HO 107 Census Papers: Population Returns 1841 and 1851. (At Chancery Lane.)

General Register Office (at Chancery Lane)
RG 9   1861 Census Returns
RG 10 1871 Census Returns
RG 11 1881 Census Returns
RG 18 Reference Maps of Registrar's Districts. 1861-1921

3. Birth, marriage and death registers for England and Wales

3.1 Introduction: sources outside the PRO

In general, the Public Record Office is not the first place to look for records of birth, marriage or death in England and Wales.

Parish registers, the main source between 1538 and 1837, are kept locally, either still in the parish or in a local, county or diocesan record office. To discover the present location of the registers of a particular parish, consult *The Phillimore Atlas and Index of Parish Registers*, edited by C R Humphery-Smith. *The National Index of Parish Registers* (a multi-volume work with general volumes covering the various types of sources available for Anglican, nonconformist, Catholic and Jewish genealogy, and county volumes listing the availability of parish and other registers) is not yet complete, but is well worth consulting.

The civil registers, the main source from July 1837, are kept by the General Register Office, at St Catherine's House, Kingsway, London (see **3.12**). St Catherine's House also has separate Army registers, which include births and marriages in the United Kingdom, 1761-1924. (see **4.2** and **18.2**).

However, the PRO does have a major source for registered births, marriages and deaths in England and Wales - its very large collection of non-parochial religious registers. In addition, the PRO has a considerable holding of civil registers and other records of births, marriages and deaths of Britons abroad; see **4**. The PRO also has some regimental registers of births and marriages for Army and Militia regiments in England and Wales (see **18.3**) and for the Royal Marines (see **20.8**).

3.2 Non-parochial registers in the PRO: introduction

The non-parochial registers in the PRO (RG 4-RG 8) include several thousand Protestant nonconformist registers, seventy-seven Catholic registers, a few registers of foreign churches in England, and a number of Church of England registers from churches outside the usual Anglican parish structure.

Although the Anglican parish register was the only official place to register baptisms, marriages and burials before 1837, the existence of the many dissenting Protestant churches and the Catholic church meant that thousands of people, for reasons of conscience, refused to comply with the Anglican rites and wished to be baptised, married and buried by their own church, and to record these events in the registers of their own faith.

From 1754 to 1837, marriages had to be performed by a beneficed Anglican clergyman in order to be legal, except in the case of Quakers and Jews, both of whom were acknowledged to keep excellent marriage records. Other nonconformists, in order to ensure the legitimacy of their children, married in the Anglican church, and the event was recorded in the parish register; nonconformist registers between 1754 and 1837 record details of births/baptisms and deaths/burials only.

When civil registration was set up in 1837, nonconformist registers and some Anglican non-parochial registers were collected by parliamentary commissioners for deposit in the new General Register Office, where they were used to issue birth certificates which had the status of a legal record (now RG 4-RG 6). Another collection was made in 1857 (now part of RG 8; some were placed in RG 4). On both occasions the registers of Catholic churches and Jewish synagogues were retained by their congregations; a very few Catholic registers came in nevertheless. Other registers were later deposited in RG 8 for safe-keeping. Some of the registers date from after 1837, but they can still be useful as a complement to the civil registers; failure to use the civil registration system was not penalised until 1875.

Although these non-parochial registers were held centrally in the General Register Office from 1857, public access to them was fairly limited. A list was published in 1859, which in many ways was faulty. The registers were transferred to the PRO in 1961, and accurate lists are now available. Because of the fragile condition of the original registers, most can be seen only on microfilm, at Chancery Lane.

Not all nonconformist registers were surrendered to the General Register Office. Other nonconformist registers remained with the congregations, or the minister or priest, and still do so; yet others are in county record offices, or with the archives of the colleges and societies of the various denominations. Many, but not all, of the births and marriages in the non-parochial registers have been indexed in the *International Genealogical Index*.

3.3. The *International Genealogical Index*

If you want to trace a baptismal or marriage record from before July 1837, you would be well advised to start with the *International Genealogical Index*, known as the *IGI*. This is an index to births, baptisms and marriages worldwide. The indexes to the British Isles cover the period from the beginning of registration to 1875 (religious registration was required in England and Wales from 1538, in Scotland from 1552, and in Ireland from 1634, but few of the earliest registers survive). The indexes for England and Wales are mainly to Church of England parish registers and to nearly all the registers in RG 4 in the PRO.

The *IGI* covers the British Isles in several separate sequences; one for each English and Scottish traditional county, one each for Ireland, the Channel Islands, and the Isle of Man, and two for Wales, to cover the Welsh system of naming. The *IGI* is available at both Chancery Lane and Kew (Kew has the old edition when Chancery Lane gets a new one), but the PRO cannot provide prints from the microfiche. However, these are available from the sets of the *IGI* kept at the Guildhall Library, the Society of Genealogists and the Genealogical Library of the Church of Jesus Christ of Latter Day Saints. Local libraries and record offices may well have the local county index: see J S W Gibson's book on the *IGI*.

There are some drawbacks to the *IGI*. Its coverage is not complete, as some registers have not been included. There is no guarantee that the registers which have been covered are included in full. In addition, useful information which may appear in the register, such as age or father's occupation, is not given in the *IGI*. If you do find a likely ancestor in the *IGI*, you are strongly advised to check the register yourself. If the entry looks as if it comes from a parish register, you can usually discover the present location of the register, and the existence and whereabouts of any transcripts, from *The Phillimore Atlas and Index of Parish Registers*, edited by C R Humphery-Smith; copies are available at Chancery Lane and Kew. If the entry refers to a nonconformist chapel, then it is most probably in RG 4, and can be seen on microfilm at Chancery Lane: some of the nonconformist registers contain a lot more information than is included in the *IGI*.

3.4 Nonconformist registers

The PRO has several thousand nonconformist registers from England and Wales (RG 4, RG 6, RG 8). Nonconformist registers often served a far wider area than the traditional Anglican parish, because of the way the various denominations were organised. Nonconformity was a very widespread movement in the eighteenth and nineteenth centuries: the 1851 ecclesiastical census showed that a quarter of the population were regular attenders of nonconformist chapels.

Indications that you should investigate the nonconformist registers, and the large amounts of biographical material kept by some of the denominations, might be a long family history of nonconformity; if a post-1837 marriage took place in a nonconformist chapel or in a register office; and if a parish register has a suspiciously high number of marriages and burials of one surname, in proportion to the number of baptisms.

Conversely, known nonconformist ancestors may need to be traced back to the parish registers, for pre-conversion events, occasional conformity, and the records of marriage and burial (if there was no local nonconformist burial ground).

Having discovered a nonconformist ancestor, it is worth digging a little deeper into his or her beliefs, and the organisation and discipline of the particular denomination. D J Steel's *Sources for Nonconformist Genealogy and Family History* is extremely useful, covering archive holdings in the PRO and elsewhere, and giving extensive bibliographies. It provides detailed descriptions of the types of document available for both registration and church discipline and their likely problems, as well as brief histories of over eighteen Protestant nonconformist denominations. Another useful guide is by P Palgrave-Moore, *Understanding the History and Records of Nonconformity.* A useful general introduction to the beliefs and regional concentrations of the various nonconformist denominations is *The Geography of Religion in England*, by J D Gay.

Less extensive works can also be very useful; for Baptists, try *My Ancestors were Baptists*, by G R Breed; for Quakers, *My Ancestors were Quakers*, by E H Milligan and M J Thomas; for Methodists, *My Ancestors were Methodists,* by W Leary and M Gandy. These also give indications as to the published works available in denominational libraries such as Dr Williams's Library.

The main churches represented in the PRO's holdings are the Society of Friends or Quakers, the Presbyterians, the Independents or Congregationalists, the Baptists, the Wesleyan and other Methodists, the Moravians, the Countess of Huntingdon's Connexion, the Bible Christians and the Swedenborgians, as well as various foreign churches. The English Independent congregation of St Petersburg, Russia, also deposited its registers of births, baptisms, and burials, 1818-1840 (RG 4/4605).

With the exception of the Quaker registers (see **3.6**), nonconformist registers are in RG 4 and RG 8, largely depending on whether they were collected by the 1837 or the 1857 commission. Most are in RG 4, and have been indexed in the *IGI*; there are many fewer in RG 8, and these are not centrally indexed. However, they are exactly the same kind of registers as in RG 4, and should not be overlooked.

The registers in the PRO date from 1567 to 1970. The earliest registers belong to the foreign Protestant churches who were granted toleration in England well before any native dissent was made lawful. Registers of English dissenting congregations are very rare before active persecution stopped; the earliest English registers date from the 1640s. The last date, 1970, is something of an oddity, from the dissenting church of Cam, Gloucestershire: it is the last entry in a volume in almost constant use between 1776 and 1970 (RG 8/12C). Most of the registers come from the eighteenth and early nineteenth centuries. After 1754 they do not, in general, include marriages.

3.5 Nonconformist central registries of births

There were two nonconformist central registries, which were set up in an attempt to provide legally acceptable records of birth. Many thousands of births were recorded in these registries, which are now in the PRO at Chancery Lane.

The Protestant Dissenters' Registry at Dr Williams's Library, then in Redcross Street, London, was founded in 1742; it served the congregations of Baptists, Independents and Presbyterians in London and within a twelve-mile radius of the capital. However, parents from most parts of the British Isles and even abroad also used the registry. Almost 50,000 births were registered in it. The Register was started in 1742, with retrospective entries going back to 1716, and continued to 1837 (RG 4/4658-4665, with indexes at RG 4/4666-4676). The certificates used to compile the registers also survive (RG 5/1-161, with the same index as the registers). Parents wishing to register a birth had to produce two parchment certificates signed by their minister and by the midwife and one or two other people present at the birth, giving the name and sex of the child, the name of the parents, the name of the mother's father and the date and place (street, parish and county) of birth. After 1828, paper certificates were required instead, which had to be signed by the parents as well; these signatures made them more acceptable as legal proof. On receipt of the two certificates, the registrar entered all the details, except the address of birth, in the register, filed one of the certificates (now in RG 5) and returned the other to the parents with his certificate of registration.

The Wesleyan Methodist Metropolitan Registry, founded in 1818 at 66 Paternoster Row, London, provided for the registration of births and baptisms of Wesleyan Methodists throughout England, Wales and elsewhere, independently of any congregational records. Over 10,000 children were registered here. The registers continued till 1838, with retrospective registration of births going back to 1773 (RG 4/4677-4679, with an index at RG 4/4680). One of two original certificates submitted by the parents was entered in the register and filed (RG 5/162-207, indexed by RG 4/4680), and the other was marked as entered and was returned to the parents. The certificates and the register entry have the name and sex of the child, the name and address of the father, the name of the mother and of both her parents, the date and place of birth, and the name of the Wesleyan circuit, with the signature (or name, in the register) of the parents, the witnesses to the birth, and the baptising minister.

3.6 Quaker registers

The records and registers of the Society of Friends, or Quakers, 1613-1841, are very full, and in excellent order. However, to understand and use them properly, you do need to understand the rather complicated administrative structure of the Society. This is explained in *My Ancestors Were Quakers* by E H Milligan and M J Thomas, and also in D J Steel's *Sources for Nonconformist Genealogy and Family History*; the latter includes a full discussion of Quaker birth, marriage and death registers and practices.

These registers are now in the PRO, arranged by (county) Quarterly Meeting and by

Monthly Meeting, together with original birth and burial notes, and original marriage certificates and copies, 1656-1834 (RG 6). There are also a few registers and other records, 1761-1840, at RG 8/81 and 87-89. The list of RG 6 is still the one published in 1859: it has been criticized by Steel and others, because little attempt had been made to identify the registers of earlier meetings that had been taken over by other meetings. However, a guide to the boundaries of the Quarterly Meetings, with any changes up to 1855, which was sent by the Society of Friends to the Registrar General in 1855 specifically to overcome this problem, and was apparently mislaid, has now been found (tucked inside a sheaf of marriage certificates). A transcript of it is (at last) to be found at the beginning of the list.

Quaker birth certificates were signed by witnesses at the birth, who also had to give their own residence. The marriage certificates were signed by a large number of witnesses, not all of whom were Quakers. Some of the witnesses were identified as relatives. Marriage between two Quakers, conducted according to the Quaker usage, was accepted as legal from 1661, and was exempted from Lord Hardwicke's Marriage Act in 1753.

Outside the PRO, there are indexes to (or rather alphabetical digests of) the registers, made in 1840-1842 and 1857, which are kept at Friends House Library, Euston Road, London NW1 2BJ: these can be consulted for a fee. Duplicate digests were also made, and sent to the county-based Quarterly Meetings in place of their registers. For more information on their present location, and on Quaker records in general, consult *My Ancestors Were Quakers*.

3.7 Catholic registers

For various reasons, only seventy-seven Catholic churches surrendered their registers to the commissioners in 1837; they are now in RG 4. Of these, 44 came from Yorkshire, 13 from Durham, 10 from Northumberland, 2 from Lincolnshire and 1 each from Cumberland, Dorset, Hampshire, Lancashire, Nottinghamshire, Oxfordshire, Warwickshire and Westmorland: however, some may have been personal to the priest, and thus cover events in other places as well. Most date from the mid or late eighteenth century, but there are two or three dating from the late seventeenth century.

For the location of other Catholic registers, see the county volumes of the *National Index of Parish Registers,* and *Sources for Roman Catholic and Jewish Genealogy and Family History*, by D J Steel and E R Samuel. The latter also discusses the information in the registers.

3.8 Registers of foreign churches in England

The registers of several foreign churches are in RG 4, listed separately except for those of the Scottish churches, which are included in the county lists; there are also a few in RG 8. Most are Huguenot (French and Walloon Protestant) registers, from the several churches of London, 1599-1840, and from Bristol 1687-1807, Canterbury

1590-1837, Norwich 1595-1752, Plymouth 1692-1807, Southampton 1567-1779 and Thorpe-le-Soken 1684-1726 (in RG 4); Huguenot registers from Dover, 1646-1731, are in RG 8/14. The Huguenot Society has published most of these registers. The other foreign registers are all from London; they are those of the French Chapel Royal 1700-1754, the Dutch Chapel Royal 1689-1754, the German Lutheran Chapel Royal 1712-1836, the German Lutheran churches 1694-1853, and the Swiss church, 1762-1839, all in RG 4.

Two later French registers came from the French Episcopal Church of the Savoy, in Bloomsbury, London, 1843-1900 (RG 8/34), and from the Reformed French Church in Brighton, 1865-1879 (RG 8/94).

The registers and papers of the Russian Orthodox church in London, 1721-1927, which are mostly in Russian are at RG 8/111-304; they include registers of births, marriages and deaths.

3.9 Anglican registers in the PRO

The commissioners for non-parochial registers collected some Anglican registers as well as nonconformist registers, in both 1837 and 1857. Most of these Anglican registers came from the custody of the Consistory Court of London in 1837, and are either from abroad (see **4.3**), or relate to the so-called 'Fleet marriages' (see **3.10**).

Other Anglican registers came from Mercers' Hall, Cheapside, London (marriages, 1641-1754, and burials, 1640-1833, RG 4/4436) and from the chapels royal at St James's Palace, Whitehall and Windsor Castle, 1647-1709 (RG 8/110). Some of the later registers of the chapels royal, 1755-1880, were deposited directly in the PRO (PRO 30/19/1), but others remain in the custody of the Chapel Royal, St James's Palace: ask at Chancery Lane for more details. In addition, the PRO has marriage licences for marriages in the Chapel Royal, Whitehall (not royal marriages), 1687-1754 and 1807 (RG 8/76-78). There are also some odd registers elsewhere in the PRO's holdings. Among the PRO's own records are the registers of the Rolls Chapel, Chancery Lane, 1736-1892, with gaps (PRO 30/21/3/1). Another Anglican oddment is the long series of registers from the Dockyard Church of Sheerness, Kent, covering 1688-1960 (ADM 6/429-433 and 438).

However, the bulk of the reputable Anglican registers in the PRO came from the military, naval and charitable hospitals, as non-parochial registers. The birth, marriage and death registers of Greenwich Hospital (including the Royal Naval Asylum and the Royal Hospital Schools) cover 1705-1864 (RG 4/1669-1679 and RG 8/16-18): those of the Army's Chelsea Hospital cover 1691-1856 (RG 4/4330-4332, and 4387). Although Greenwich Hospital and Chelsea Hospital were Navy and Army institutions, these registers appear to include local inhabitants as well. For details of other Army registers, see **4.2**, **18.2** and **18.3**. For details of Royal Marine registers, see **20.8**.

The charitable hospitals include the Foundling Hospital, London, with registers of baptisms (naturally with no details of parents), and of all too many burials, for 1741-

1838 (RG 4/4396 and 4328); they are of great human interest, but not much use to genealogists.

One of the PRO's main hospital holdings is the series of records of the British Lying-In (i.e. maternity) Hospital, Holborn, London. This was set up in 1749, and catered for the distressed poor (married women only) with special attention to the wives of soldiers and sailors. Admission was by recommendation: many women appear to have been the wives of servants, recommended by their husbands' employers. The baptismal registers, 1749-1830 (RG 8/62-66) are simply a hospital-composed list of names, parents and dates of birth and baptism until 1814, when proper Anglican baptismal registers appear, and give the parents' address. However, they are supplemented by a fascinating source, the hospital's own record of the admission of the mother and the birth, which gives the names of the parents, the occupation of the father, the age of the mother, place of settlement (place of marriage after 1849), the expected date of delivery, the date of admission, the date of delivery, the name of the child and date of baptism, the date of discharge or death, and the name of the person on whose recommendation the woman was admitted (RG 8/52-61). These hospital records cover 1749-1868, and give details of 42,008 admissions, and about 30,000 baptisms, by no means all of Londoners; one women at least came from the Cape of Good Hope, and others came from Yorkshire, Ireland, the Isle of Wight and Jersey.

Another register from a charitable institution is the marriage register of the chapel of God's House Hospital, Kingston-upon-Hull, 1695-1715 (RG 8/101).

From less charitable institutions, the prisons, there are a few records of births and burials. The Westminster Penitentiary has a register of baptisms, 1816-1871 (PCOM 2/139) and another of burials, 1817-1853 (PCOM 2/140). There is a register of deaths and inquests at the Millbank Penitentiary, 1848-1863 (PCOM 2/165): in this case, most burials were in the Victoria Park cemetery, whose records are discussed in **3.11**. For other prison records, see **39**, and for other inquests, see **37**.

3.10 Fleet marriage registers, and other marriage records

In 1753, Lord Hardwicke's Marriage Act (26 George II c.33) ruled that the only lawful marriage was one celebrated by a beneficed Anglican clergyman, in an Anglican church after banns or with a licence. An exception was made for Jews, and also for Quakers, who kept excellent records and who had an elaborate method of validating marriages, including signature of a marriage certificate by many witnesses: (see **3.6**). As a result, nonconformists had to marry in the Anglican church; Catholics generally continued to marry in their own church.

However, Lord Hardwicke's Marriage Act was not aimed directly at preventing nonconformist marriages, but at preventing clandestine Anglican ones. Before it came into effect in 1754, unbeneficed and sometimes unscrupulous clergymen were able to make a living by performing marriages on request, in places exempt from ecclesiastical jurisdiction. One of the most popular of these was the Fleet Prison and its precincts in London; the registers kept by the presiding ministers are known as

Fleet registers (RG 7). The report of the 1837 commissioners on non-parochial records on the Fleet marriages is worth quoting at length.

'The generality of them were celebrated by Clergymen of low character, some at the Chapel of the Fleet, others at various taverns and other places within the precincts of the Fleet and King's Bench Prisons, and the Mint in Southwark. These Registers were, in some instances, in the keeping of the Ministers who performed the ceremony, and they were also often kept by the proprietors of the houses or taverns in which the marriages happened to have taken place. After the door was closed against marriages of this description by the operation of the Marriage Act (in 1754), it appears, that a clerk of one of the Fleet Ministers collected a number of them together, and opened an office, where reference might be had to them. Another office for the deposit of these registers was opened in another part of the town; but in 1813 the great bulk of them came into the hands of a private individual, of the name of Cox, from whom the Government purchased them in 1821, and, by the direction of Lord Sidmouth, then Secretary of State for the Home Department, they were deposited in the Registry of the Consistorial Court of London. We apprehend that by far the greater number of the Registers of the Marriages celebrated within the precincts of these several places are comprised in this collection. There are, however, exceptions; for two of the Fleet Registers are known to be in the possession of a professional gentleman in Doctors' Commons, a third has found its way into the Bodleian Library at Oxford. [Now Rawlinson Ms.360.]
'The Chapel at May Fair was built about 1730, and Marriages took place there under the same circumstances with those in the places above referred to. Many of the Registers of this Chapel formed a part of the purchase made by the Government in 1821, the remainder are preserved in the church of St George, Hanover Square'.

These registers from the Fleet and King's Bench Prisons, the Mint and the May Fair Chapel, 1694-1754, are now in the PRO (RG 7); in addition, there are two volumes covering 1726-1735 which were brought into court as evidence (PROB 18/50).

The information in the Fleet registers should be treated with extreme caution, as the dates given are unreliable (particularly before 1714), and names or indeed whole entries may be fictitious. The Fleet registers have entries from over the whole country, but with more from London and the home counties; about 200,000 marriages are thought to have been celebrated there. The Fleet was frequented for marriages and for some baptisms by craftsmen and sailors in general; professionals and the aristocracy went to the more salubrious May Fair Chapel instead. Such clandestine marriages could result in prosecution, and there are records of many such cases among the ex officio Act Books of the Commissary Court of London in the Guildhall Library, and in the records of the Consistory Court of London in the Greater London Record Office. For more information see 'The Rise and Fall of the Fleet Marriages' by R L Brown, or the chapter on clandestine marriages in D J Steel's *Sources of Births, Marriages and Deaths before 1837 (I)*.

There is an index to Fleet marriages for Sussex, south-west Kent and south-east Surrey, arranged chronologically within parish of residence of bride and groom; an index cross-referring to the bride's surname is in preparation.

Other marriage indexes are to more regular unions. The Pallot Index, covering the years c.1780-1837, includes marriages from most established churches in London and extracts from nonconformist registers; it is held by the Institute of Heraldic and Genealogical Studies, who will search it for a fee. The Boyd Marriage Index, available at the Society of Genealogists and the Guildhall Library, has a 12% coverage of English marriages between 1538 and 1837; the PRO has odd volumes of the Boyd Index at Chancery Lane, covering grooms, 1538-1625 and 1726-1800, and brides, 1575-1600 (A-S only), 1601-1625, 1751-1775 (E-R only) and 1776-1800.

There are some marriage licences for the Chapel Royal, Whitehall, 1687-1754 and 1807 in RG 8/76-78, but in general the PRO is not the place to look for these documents. See J S W Gibson's book, *Bishops' Transcripts and Marriage Licences*.

3.11 Burial grounds

Although the nonconformist registers do include details of deaths and burials, burials were usually in the parish churchyard, and noted in the parish register, until nonconformist burial grounds were established. Some of these were small and local, such as the Protestant Dissenters' Burial Ground at Great Dunmow, Essex, 1784-1856 (RG 4/597) or the Dissenters' Ground at Boston, Lincs, 1789-1856 (RG 4/24-25). However, nonconformists also established large burial grounds or cemeteries for dissenters; this practice later spread to all denominations.

The main cemetery records in the PRO are those of the following:

· Bethnal Green Protestant Dissenters' Burying Ground, or Gibraltar Burying Ground, 1793-1837 (RG 8/305-314);
· Bunhill Fields Burial Ground, City Road, London, 1713-1854 (RG 4/3974-4001, 4288-4291 and 4633, with indexes at RG 4/4652-4657): other records, including an alphabetical list of persons buried, 1827-1854, are kept in the Guildhall Library;
· Bunhill Burial Ground or Golden Lane Cemetery, London, 1833-1853 (RG 8/35-38);
· Victoria Park Cemetery, Hackney, London, 1853-1876 (RG 8/42-51; each volume is arranged in letter order);
· South London Burial Ground, East Street, Walworth, London, 1819-1837 (RG 4/4362);
· Southwark New Burial Ground, London, 1821-1854 (RG 8/73-74);
· Necropolis Burial Ground in Everton, Liverpool, for all denominations, 1825-1837 (RG 4/3121).
For information on the location of other London burial records, see *Greater London Cemeteries and Crematoria*, by P S Wolfston.

Also worth consulting are the records of the removal of tombs and gravestones from churchyards, cemeteries and burial grounds of all denominations (including some Jewish ones), in order to develop the land for some other purpose (RG 37). These are modern records of the actual removals and reinterments, but the tombs and gravestones themselves date from 1601 to 1980, with most coming from the later eighteenth and the nineteenth centuries. The files usually include a list of names, where these were discoverable, and frequently contain transcripts of the monumental inscriptions. They also indicate the place of reinterment.

3.12 Births, marriages and deaths after 1837

Civil registration of births, marriages and deaths started in England and Wales on 1 July 1837. These records are not held by the PRO, but by the General Register Office, at St Catherine's House, 10 Kingsway, London WC2B 6JP. Searchers are not permitted to look at the original records, and no information is available except in the form of a copy certificate, which must be purchased. A copy certificate, which takes a minimum of 48 hours to prepare, can be applied for in person, or by post. The certificates of births, marriages and deaths are filed separately, and reference to them is by quarterly indexes which are open for inspection. The public search room is open from 8.30 a.m. to 4.30 p.m., Monday to Friday. Microfilm copies of the birth, marriage and death indexes (1837-1980) may be purchased from the General Register Office. They are available for search in many of the branch libraries of the Church of Jesus Christ of Latter Day Saints and at Salt Lake City.

Failure to find a birth, marriage or death in the indexes may be for these reasons:

· Before 1875 there was no penalty for non-registration and there may be omissions in the birth and death registers; marriages were usually registered by the officiating clergyman or registrar. Try the parish and non-parochial registers after 1837.
· Before 1927 there was no formal adoption procedure and there is no record of the birth of the adopted child under the name by which he or she was known.
· There may have been a clerical error when the entry in the local registrar's register was transferred to the central register.
· Some people were known by a christian name which was not the first forename on their birth certificate.
· The child may not have been named by the date of registration. Entries under the sex of the infant are given at the end of each surname section.
· In the nineteenth century approximately 10% of marriages took place after the birth of the first child.
· A birth or marriage may have been registered by the Army: see **4.2** and **18.2**.

It may be worth checking the Registrar General's correspondence on births, marriages and deaths, 1874-1985, at Kew (RG 48). These papers include files on individual cases of difficulty, but some are closed for 50 or 75 years.

Announcements of many births, marriages and deaths may be found in local newspapers held in public libraries and in the British Library newspaper collection at Colindale. For more details, see J S W Gibson's book *Local Newspapers 1750-1920*.

Registers of births on Lundy Island, in the Bristol Channel, were treated as foreign registers, and are in the PRO, in RG 32-RG 35, indexed by the general indexes in RG 43. Some records from the Channel Islands were treated the same way.

3.13 Adoption

Certificates of any adoption in England and Wales since 1 January 1927 may be obtained from the Registrar General. They show the date of the adoption, the name of the child adopted, and the full name and address of the adoptive parents. For information as to how to obtain a birth certificate, the adopted person should apply to the General Register Office (CA section): the address is in **48.7**.

Before 1927 there was no system of legal adoption and it is usually extremely difficult to trace private arrangements. Some charities, such as Barnardos, arranged adoptions, and may conduct searches for a fee. See the book by G Stafford, *Where to Find Adoption Records*.

3.14 Divorce

Before 1858 (except in Scotland) true divorce was rare and expensive, and achieved by private bill in the House of Lords. There was only one divorce bill before 1670. The PRO has a very few of these private acts for divorce, in C 89 and C 204, but they should be available at the House of Lords Record Office.

The church courts could decree a legal separation, known as divorce *a mensa et thoro* (i.e. from board and bed), but the parties had to undertake not to remarry. In order to remarry, the marriage had to be declared null from the beginning, on the grounds of want of ability to marry (e.g. a pre-contract to marry another, or want of consent to the marriage: for example, if the parties were under age and therefore incapable of consenting). This total dissolution of a marriage was described as a divorce *a vinculo matrimonii* (from the bond of matrimony). These uncommon procedures were abolished in 1754. Records of the proceedings in the church courts, which are deposited in diocesan record offices, are largely unindexed and can be extremely difficult to interpret.

Appeals from ecclesiastical courts in matrimonial cases went to the High Court of Delegates between 1532 and 1832, and to the Judicial Committee of the Privy Council from 1833 until 1858: the records of both of these courts are in the PRO, Chancery Lane. Copies of the proceedings of the lower, ecclesiastical, courts for 1609-1834 are in DEL 1 (indexed in DEL 11/7), and for 1834-1858 in PCAP 1. The cases as presented to the appeal courts are in DEL 2, DEL 7 and PCAP 3: judgements are included. These records have been relatively little used, but they can be very informative.

After 1858, all divorce cases were heard by the new Court for Divorce and Matrimonial Causes, until 1873, when the Probate, Divorce and Admiralty Division of the Supreme Court took over. Divorce files, 1858-1937 are in J 77, with a 75 year closure: the indexes, 1858-1958 (J 78) have the usual 30 year closure. Permission to consult individual case papers in the files which are still closed under the 75 year closure may be obtained from the Principal Registry of the Family Division at Somerset House (address in **48.7**). The Principal Registry also has records of divorces since 1938, and will search them for a fee.

3.15 Births, marriages and deaths in England and Wales: bibliography and sources

[An * means this work can be seen at Chancery Lane: a # means it can be seen at Kew.]

Published works

G R Breed, *My Ancestors were Baptists* (Society of Genealogists, 1988) *

British Agencies for Adoption and Fostering, *Where to Find Adoption Records* (1988)

R L Brown, 'The Rise and Fall of the Fleet Marriage', in *Marriage and Society*, ed. R B Outhwaite (London, 1981)

W Leary and M Gandy, *My Ancestors Were Methodists* (Society of Genealogists, 1982) *

Dr Williams's Trust, *Nonconformist Congregations in Great Britain: A list of histories and other material in Dr Williams's Library* (London, 1973) *

Factsheet on Tracing the Natural Parents of Adopted Children (FFHS, 1987)

J D Gay, *The Geography of Religion in England* (London, 1971)

General Register Office, *Abstract of Arrangements respecting Registration of Births, Marriages and Deaths in the UK and other Countries of the British Commonwealth of Nations, and in the Irish Republic* (London, 1952) *#

J S W Gibson, *Bishops' Transcripts and Marriage Licences* (FFHS, 2nd edn 1985) *

J S W Gibson, *Local Newspapers 1750-1920* (FFHS, 1987) *

J S W Gibson, *Marriage, Census and other Indexes for Family Historians* (FFHS, 1988) *

J S W Gibson, 'Marriage Licences, Bonds and Allegations', *Family History,* vol. V, no 25 NS, no 1, pp.7-32

J S W Gibson and M Walcot, *Where to Find the International Genealogical Index,* (FFHS, 1985) *

A Horstman, *Victorian Divorce* (London, 1985)

C R Humphery-Smith, *The Phillimore Atlas and Index of Parish Registers* (Chichester, 1984) *#

International Genealogical Index, compiled by the Church of Jesus Christ of Latter Day Saints (also known as LDS and Mormons) * #

O R McGregor, *Divorce in England* (London, 1957)

E McLaughlin, *St Catherine's House* (FFHS, 1985) *

H Mellor, *London Cemeteries: Illustrated Guide and Gazetteer* (Godstone, 1985)

E H Milligan and M J Thomas, *My Ancestors Were Quakers* (Society of Genealogists, 1983) *

National Index of Parish Registers (Society of Genealogists, 1968 continuing). For individual volumes, see the works listed under D J Steel *

M Nissel, *People Count, A History of the General Register Office* (London, 1987) *

P Palgrave-Moore, *Understanding the history and records of Nonconformity* (2nd edn, Norwich, 1989) *

Parliament, *Report of the commissioners appointed to inquire into the state, custody, and authenticity of registers or records of births or baptisms, deaths or burials and marriages, in England and Wales other than parochial registers* (London, 1838: parliamentary paper presented to both Houses) *

Parliament, *Report of the commissioners appointed to inquire into the state, custody and authenticity of certain non-parochial registers or records of births or baptisms, deaths or burials, and marriages in England and Wales (1857)* (London, 1858: parliamentary paper presented to both Houses) *

Public Record Office, *Records of Births, Marriages and Deaths* (Information Leaflet) * #

G Stafford, *Where to Find Adoption Records* (London, 1985) *

D J Steel and others, *Sources of Births, Marriages and Deaths before 1837 (I)* (National Index of Parish Registers, vol. I, 1968) *

D J Steel, *Sources for Nonconformist Genealogy and Family History* (National Index of Parish Registers, vol. II, 1973) *

D J Steel and E R Samuel, *Sources for Roman Catholic and Jewish Genealogy and Family History* (National Index of Parish Registers, vol. III, 1974) *

M Walcot, 'English Marriage Indexes', *Genealogists' Magazine*, vol. XIV, pp. 204-208

E Welch, 'Nonconformist Registers', *Journal of the Society of Archivists*, vol. II, pp. 411-417

P S Wolfston, *Greater London Cemeteries and Crematoria* (Society of Genealogists, 1985) *

Unpublished finding aids

Boyd Marriage Index, 1536-1837; Society of Genealogists and the Guildhall Library: there is an incomplete copy at Chancery Lane (see **3.10**).

Fleet Marriage Index for Sussex, south-west Kent and south-east Surrey. *

Pallot Index to marriages in London, c.1780-1837: Institute of Heraldic and Genealogical Studies.

Society of Genealogists: transcripts of parish registers.

Records

Admiralty (at Kew)
ADM 6/429-433, 438: registers of the Dockyard Church, Sheerness, Kent,1688-1960

Chancery (at Chancery Lane)
C 89 *Certiorari* Bundles, (Rolls Chapel Series). Henry VIII to 1800
C 204 *Certiorari* Bundles (Petty Bag Office Series). James I to 1764

High Court of Delegates (at Chancery Lane)
DEL 1 Processes. 1609-1834
DEL 2 Cause Papers. c.1600-1834
DEL 7 Case Books. 1796-1834
DEL 11/7: alphabetical index to DEL 1

Supreme Court of Judicature (at Chancery Lane)
J 77   Principal Probate Registry: Divorce Files. 1858-1935. Most pieces closed for 75 years.
J 78   Principal Probate Registry: Indexes to Divorce Files. 1858-1958

Judicial Committee of the Privy Council (at Chancery Lane)
PCAP 1 Privy Council Appeals Processes. 1834-1879. (Last date of 1858 for divorce and matrimonial cases.)
PCAP 3 Privy Council Appeals Case Books. 1834-1879. (Last date of 1858 for divorce and matrimonial cases.)

Prison Commission (at Kew)
PCOM 2 Prison Records, Series I. 1770-1940

Public Record Office
PRO 30/21/3/1: register of the Rolls Chapel, 1736-1892. (At Chancery Lane.)

Prerogative Court of Canterbury (at Chancery Lane)
PROB 18/50 contains two Fleet marriage registers, 1726-1735

General Register Office (split between Chancery Lane and Kew)
RG 4 General Register Office: Registers of Births, Marriages and Deaths surrendered to the 1837 and 1857 Non-Parochial Registers Commissions. 1567-1858. (At Chancery Lane.)
RG 5 General Register Office: Birth Certificates from the Presbyterian, Independent and Baptist Registry and the Wesleyan Methodist Metropolitan Registry. 1742-1840. (At Chancery Lane.)
RG 6 General Register Office: Society of Friends' Registers and Certificates of Births Marriages and Deaths. 1613-1831. (At Chancery Lane.)
RG 7 General Register Office: Registers of Clandestine Marriages and of Baptisms in the Fleet Prison, the King's Bench Prison, the Mint and the May Fair Chapel. 1667-c.1777. (At Chancery Lane.)
RG 8 General Register Office: Registers of Births, Marriages and Deaths surrendered to the 1857 Non-Parochial Registers Commission, and other registers and church records. 1646-1970. (At Chancery Lane.)
RG 32 Miscellaneous Foreign Returns. 1831-1958. (At Chancery Lane.)
RG 33 Miscellaneous Foreign Registers and Returns. 1627-1958. (At Chancery Lane.)
RG 34 Miscellaneous Foreign Marriages. 1826-1921. (At Chancery Lane.)
RG 35 Miscellaneous Foreign Deaths. 1830-1921. (At Chancery Lane.)
RG 37 General Register Office: Removal of Graves and Tombstones. 1923-1988. Most pieces in this class are open immediately: the dates of the information are c.1601-1980. (At Chancery Lane.)
RG 43 Miscellaneous Foreign Returns of Births, Marriages and Deaths: indexes. 1627-1955. (At Chancery Lane.)
RG 48 Registration of Births, Deaths and Marriages: Correspondence and Papers. 1874-1985. This class includes files about individual cases of difficulty: some pieces are closed for 50 or 75 years. (At Kew.)

4. Births, marriages and deaths of Britons overseas

4.1 Introduction

There are considerable numbers of sources available within Britain for births, marriages and deaths of Britons in other countries and at sea, but they are scattered between the various General Register Offices, the PRO, the Guildhall, the Society of Genealogists and elsewhere. Records in the Guildhall, the Society of Genealogists and some other places, and in the Foreign Office records at Kew are included in G Yeo's invaluable book, *The British Overseas*, which lists the sources country by country: however, it does not include the overseas registers at the General Register Office, St Catherine's House (see **4.2**), nor some of the records at Chancery Lane. This present chapter lists only the indexes at St Catherine's House (**4.2**) and the holdings of the PRO at Kew and Chancery Lane (**4.7**). As a result, you may need to consult both Yeo and this book in order to get full information on what is available for a particular country. A copy of Yeo's book can be seen at both Kew and Chancery Lane.

One general point is that, in the case of British colonies, registration records were and are kept locally, and you will need to enquire in the country concerned: Yeo provides the addresses for the official holdings. There are microfiche copies of the indexes to the Australian registers, 1790-c.1900, at the Society of Genealogists. After 1940 (births) and 1950 (marriages and deaths) you may find something in the registers kept by the United Kingdom High Commissions in colonies and ex-colonies: these are kept at St Catherine's House (**4.2**).

The sections of the *International Genealogical Index* (see **3.3**) relating to records of births, baptisms and marriages in countries other than Britain are available for consultation at the Society of Genealogists and at the Genealogical Library of the Church of Jesus Christ of Latter Day Saints.

An exception to the general rule of colonial records being held in those countries is provided by pre-independence India. Records of British and European baptisms, marriages and burials in India (including former parts of India which are now Bangladesh, Burma and Pakistan, and places on the Indian Ocean, such as Aden) for 1698-1948, with a partial continuation to 1968, are at the India Office Library and Records. There are also some Indian records in the PRO and at St Catherine's House. Some other exceptions are listed in **4.7**.

Religious records of baptisms, marriages and burials in foreign countries are either still held locally (especially if there was a formal church organisation), or were returned to the Bishop of London. Most of the latter have since been deposited in the Guildhall Library, where there is a very extensive collection called the Bishop of London's International Memoranda (see Yeo for further details): some, originally sent to the Bishop for safe-keeping, were later deposited in the General Register

Office and have now been passed on to the PRO (RG 32-RG 35).

Statutory civil registration of English (and Welsh) citizens in foreign (*not* colonial) countries began in 1849, under the Consular Marriages Act. Civil registration of Scots abroad began in 1860, and of the Irish abroad in 1864. Since then, the Foreign Office has returned registers of births, marriages and deaths, compiled at its embassies and consulates, to the General Register Offices of England (St Catherine's House), Scotland, Ireland (1864-1921) and Northern Ireland (from 1922); the full addresses are given in **48.7** and **48.8**.

With so many statutory and non-statutory registers, returns and copies being sent first to one place and then to another, it is not surprising that considerable duplication and confusion exists. Where the PRO has duplicates of registers at St Catherine's House, it may be worth going to the trouble of using the indexes there and then discovering the PRO reference in order to browse in the whole register at the PRO, rather than buying a single copy certificate: if you are looking for someone who lived in a close-knit British community abroad, you may find all kinds of clues as to the life they led and the people they knew.

4.2 Registers at St Catherine's House

There is a numerous collection of odd registers at the General Register Office, St Catherine's House, some from overseas and some (the regimental registers of births and marriages) partly from this country as well. They are not included in Yeo's book. The other General Register Offices of Scotland and Ireland were also supposed to receive similar information. Public access is only to the index; you cannot see the register, but have to purchase a copy of the particular certificate you want. The indexes available at St Catherine's House are as follows:

Armed forces

1761-1924 *Indexes to Regimental Registers of Births*
These include events in the United Kingdom and abroad (from c.1790). The indexes are arranged alphabetically, giving name, place, year and regiment. There are also marriage registers, but these are not indexed and cannot be inspected: see **18.2** for more information.

1796-1880 *Index to [Army] Chaplains' Returns of Births; and Marriages; and Deaths*
These all relate to events abroad. The index gives name, place and a date range of 2-3 years.

1881-1955 *Indexes to Army Returns of Births; and Marriages; and Deaths*
These all relate to events abroad. The indexes give name, station and date. From 1920, entries relating to the Royal Air Force are included.

1956-1965 *Indexes to Service Departments Registers of Births; and Marriages*
These relate to Army, Navy and Air Force births and marriages abroad. The indexes give name, station and year.

For events after 1965, see the *Indexes to the Registers of Births, Marriages and Deaths Abroad*, which start in 1966.

Armed forces: war deaths

1899-1902 *Index to Natal and South Africa Forces*
1914-1921 *Index to Army Other Ranks' War Deaths*
1914-1921 *Index to Army Officers' War Deaths*
1914-1921 *Index to Naval War Deaths*
1939-1948 *Index to Army Other Ranks' War Deaths*
1939-1948 *Index to Army Officers' War Deaths*
1939-1948 *Index to Naval War Deaths*
1939-1948 *Index to RAF All Ranks' War Deaths*
1939-1948 *Index to Indian Services' War Deaths*

Civilians

1849-1965 *Indexes to Consular Registers of Births; and Marriages; and Deaths*
The indexes are arranged alphabetically within a range of five or so years; no closer indication of date is given. Deaths were not registered with consuls until 1859. The indexes include name and consul's registration district: from 1906, the spouse's name is given in the marriage index, and the age in the death index.

These are the statutory consular registers, kept as a result of the 1849 Act. Among the Foreign Office embassy and consular records at Kew are the duplicates kept by the consulates. It may be worth using the index at St Catherine's House, and then looking at the duplicate registers at Kew: this would save the cost of buying the wrong certificate if the index is not sufficiently precise. However, the reference given in the index at St Catherine's House does not apply to Kew. You will need to match up the place of registration with the right consulate, and then find that consulate's records from **4.7**.

1837-1965 *Indexes to Marine Registers of Births; and Deaths*
These give name and year of English and Welsh births and deaths at sea; after 1875, the name of the ship is given as well. The age is given for deaths. From 1837 to 1874 they relate to events occurring on British merchant and naval ships; from 1875, to other ships carrying passengers to or from the United Kingdom as well.

1941-1965 *Indexes to Protectorates of Africa and Asia: Registers of Births*
The registers for 1895-1957, and the indexes up to 1940, are in the PRO, Chancery Lane.

1940-1981 *Indexes to UKHC Registers of Births Abroad 1950-1965; and Marriages; and Deaths*
These registers were kept in colonies and ex-colonies by the United Kingdom High Commissions. Although the birth registers start in 1950, they do include a few births from the 1940s.

1947-1965 *Index to Air Registers of Births; and Deaths*
The index gives name, age (for deaths), place and year of births and deaths occurring in civil aircraft in flight.

1956-1965 *Index to Miscellaneous Foreign Registers of Births, Marriages and Deaths*
   The index gives name, place and year. Most of the entries appear to be from the Gulf States, Singapore etc.

Armed Forces and Civilians

1818-1864 *Index to Registers of Births, Marriages and Deaths in the Ionian Islands.*
   The index is to a military register, a civil register, and a chaplain's register. It gives names only. See also **4.7**, under **Greece**.

1966-1987 *Indexes to Registers of Births Abroad; and Marriages Abroad; and Deaths Abroad*
   These registers took over from the Air, Consular, Marine, Miscellaneous, and Services series, and apparently from the marriage and death sections of the United Kingdom High Commission series. The birth indexes give name, mother's maiden name, place of registration and date or year of birth. The marriage registers include the spouse's surname. The death registers give age.

4.3 Foreign registers in the PRO

The holdings of the PRO overlap the registers in St Catherine's House in many respects; the PRO has duplicates of most of the consular returns (see **4.2**), and also has a number of regimental registers, and records of births, marriages and deaths at sea. There are some unique sources as well, particularly the miscellaneous non-statutory registers deposited by the General Register Office in the PRO (RG 32 - RG 36, with indexes in RG 43).

The embassy and consular records of the Foreign Office at Kew often contain duplicates of the statutory registers sent in to the General Register Office from 1849 onwards, and also contain earlier records. Although they do not cover the whole range of registers at St Catherine's House, there are some Foreign Office registers which appear to be unique. Even when they duplicate the St Catherine's House registers they have the considerable advantage that you can browse through them, if they are over 30 (in some cases 50) years old. At the time of writing it is unclear if the Foreign Office registers include references to the Scots and Irish; it may be worth investigation. For details of the various registers, listed by country, see **4.7**.

Among the records of the Foreign Office there is a 46 volume series of consular correspondence on marriages abroad, covering 1814-1905, split between FO 83 and FO 97, with a register and index for 1814-1893 at FO 802/239. This series includes information on some individual marriages. Also in FO 83 are covering despatches to certificates of marriages abroad giving the names of the parties, 1846-1890; general correspondence and circulars on consular marriages; and acknowledgements of receipt of certificates by the Bishop of London's Registry.

References to similar correspondence can be traced in the Foreign Office card index for 1906-1919, and in the printed index for 1920-1957; both these indexes are in the Reference Room at Kew. However, many of the documents they refer to no longer exist.

The other main source in the PRO is at Chancery Lane. This is the collection of miscellaneous non-statutory registers and records, 1627-1958 (RG 32-RG 36, largely indexed in RG 43), which used to be in the General Register Office until 1977. They relate to the births, baptisms, marriages, deaths and burials abroad, and on British and foreign ships, of British subjects, nationals of the colonies, of the Commonwealth, or of countries under British jurisdiction. Some foreign nationals are also included. The indexes, in RG 43, are kept on the open shelves at Chancery Lane. References, by country, are given in **4.7**; however, this includes only the most well-represented countries in RG 32-RG 36, and there are many others besides (e.g. Uruguay and Gibraltar). You should check in the indexes in RG 43 even if the country you are interested in does not appear in **4.7**, or if it does with a wrong date-range.

As many of these records appear to partly duplicate the records in the Guildhall, it is worth checking Yeo's book to find out which place has the more complete collection; the list in **4.7** indicates whether Yeo gives references to other sources outside the PRO. Records at the Guildhall, as at the PRO, are produced directly to the public, sometimes on microfilm.

Other records of births, marriages and deaths abroad occur elsewhere among the public records; these are included in **4.7**. Two possible sources that are not listed in **4.7** are the Protestant Dissenters' Registry at Dr Williams's Library, and the Wesleyan Methodist Metropolitan Registry; both of these registered births abroad as well as in the United Kingdom. For more details, see **3.5**.

4.4 Registers of births, marriages and deaths at sea

Records of births, marriages and deaths at sea are available in the records of the Registrar General of Shipping and Seamen, at Kew. There are registers of births, marriages and deaths of passengers, 1854-1890 (BT 158); of deaths of British nationals, 1875-1888 (BT 159); and of births of British nationals, 1875-1891 (BT 160). These are, by and large, the duplicates of the marine registers in St Catherine's House (**4.2**), except that they also contain the information sent to the General Register Offices of Scotland and Ireland as well. It may be useful to use the indexes at St Catherine's House before browsing in the BT records at Kew.

At Chancery Lane, there are registers of marriages aboard naval ships, 1842-1889 (RG 33/156, indexed in RG 43/7). These often appear to be the marriages of people living in places where other methods of obtaining a valid British marriage may have have been difficult, such as the Cayman Islands. Deaths of British citizens on board French ships, 1836-1871, are in RG 35/16 (in French); deaths on board Dutch ships, 1839-1871, are in RG 35/17 (in Dutch): both are allegedly indexed by RG 43. Later records are held by the Registrar General of Shipping and Seamen, Llantrisant Road, Cardiff CF5 2YS.

4.5 Commonwealth War Graves, and other burial grounds

The Commonwealth War Graves Commission has details of servicemen who died overseas and on ships in the two World Wars, and can often supply detailed information. You should write to the Information Officer, Commonwealth War Graves Commission, 2 Marlow Road, Maidenhead, Berks SL6 7DX.

For details of military graves other than for the two World Wars, contact the Ministry of Defence, PS4(CAS)(A), Room 1012, Empress State Building, London SW6 1TR.

The British Association for Cemeteries in South Asia (BACSA) is a voluntary organisation which deals with the preservation, conversion and registration of European cemeteries in South Asia, and in particular those that were formerly administered by the East India Company, and the British government in India. It compiles records of both civilians and soldiers, and produces a twice-yearly magazine, *Chowkidar*. For more information, contact The Secretary, BACSA, 76½ Chartfield Avenue, Putney, London SW15 6HQ: a stamped addressed envelope would be appreciated.

4.6 Births, marriages and deaths of Britons overseas: bibliography and sources

[An * means this work can be seen at Chancery Lane: a # means it can be seen at Kew]

Published works

General Register Office, *Abstract of Arrangements Respecting Registration of Births, Marriages and Deaths in the United Kingdom and the Other Countries of the British Commonwealth of Nations, and in the Irish Republic* (London, 1952) *#
G Yeo, *The British Overseas, A Guide to Records of Their Births, Baptisms, Marriages , Deaths and Burials Available in the United Kingdom* (London, 2nd edn 1988) *#

Unpublished finding aids

For the indexes to the registers at St Catherine's House, see **4.2**
RG 43: indexes to most of RG 32-RG 36, and to RG 4/4605, on the open shelves at Chancery Lane. Some entries relate to registers still at St Catherine's House.

Records

For a list of records of births, marriages and deaths overseas, arranged by country, see **4.7**

Registrar General of Shipping and Seamen (at Kew)
BT 158 Registrar General of Shipping and Seamen: Registers of Births, Deaths and Marriages of Passengers at Sea. 1854-1890. On microfilm.

BT 159   Registrar General of Shipping and Seamen: Registers of Deaths at Sea of British Nationals. 1875-1888. On microfilm.

BT 160   Registrar General of Shipping and Seamen: Registers of Births at Sea of British Nationals. 1875-1891. On microfilm.

Foreign Office (at Kew)

Records of births, marriages and deaths, kept in the archives of the various British consulates and embassies, are listed in **4.7**, by country. The place given in that list is the consulate of registration, not the actual place of birth, marriage or death.

FO 83 and FO 97: these include a series of consular correspondence on marriages abroad, 1814-1905, with an index at FO 802/239.

General Register Office (at Chancery Lane)

RG 32   Miscellaneous Foreign Returns. 1831-1958

RG 33   Miscellaneous Foreign Registers and Returns. 1627-1958

RG 34   Miscellaneous Foreign Marriages. 1826-1921

RG 35   Miscellaneous Foreign Deaths. 1830-1921

RG 36   Registers and Returns of Births, Marriages and Deaths in the Protectorates of Africa and Asia. 1895-1950

RG 43   Miscellaneous Returns of Births, Marriages and Deaths: Indexes. (Covering dates of information, 1627-1955.)

See **4.7** for further information, listed by place.

4.7 Conspectus of records in the PRO of births, marriages and deaths overseas

African Protectorates

births 1911-1946; marriages 1912-1935; deaths 1911-1946	RG 36

Algeria

deaths 1840-1871	RG 35/14-15
deaths 1871 and onwards	RG 35/20-44

Angola

Luanda: births 1865-1906; marriages 1871-1928; deaths 1859-1906	FO 375/1-4

Argentina

	(see Yeo)
Buenos Aires: marriages 1826-1900	FO 446/3-6, 28-30

RG 32 - RG 36 are largely indexed by RG 43

Ascension Island   (see Yeo)

       baptisms/births from 1858-1861 and onwards   RG 32

       deaths from c.1858 and onwards   RG 35

Austria   (see Yeo)

       deaths c.1831-1920   RG 35/20-44

       Vienna: marriages 1883-1891   FO 120/6970

       Vienna: baptisms 1867-1886 and onwards   RG 32

Belgium   (see Yeo)

       deaths 1831-1871   RG 35/1-3

       deaths 1871-1920   RG 35/20-44

            (including *Belgian Congo*)

       military deaths 1914-1920   RG 35/45-69

            (not indexed in RG 43)

       Antwerp: baptisms and burials 1817-1852;   RG 33/1-2
       marriages 1820-1849

       Antwerp: baptisms and burials 1831-1836,   RG 33/155
       1841-1842; marriages 1832-1838, 1841-1842

       Antwerp: baptisms 1840 and onwards   RG 32

       Brussels: marriages 1816-1890   RG 33/3-9

       Ghent: marriages 1849-1850   RG 33/9

Bermuda   (see Yeo)

       naval dockyard baptisms and burials   ADM 6/434-
       1826-1946   436,439

Brazil   (see Yeo)

       Bahia: marriages 1816-1820   RG 33/155

       Maranhão: marriages 1844   RG 33/155

       Parà: births and deaths 1840-1841   RG 33/155

       Rio de Janeiro: marriages 1809-1818   RG 33/155

       Rio de Janeiro: births 1850-1859   FO 743/11

       Rio de Janeiro: baptisms 1850 and onwards   RG 32

       Rio de Janeiro: marriages c.1850 and onwards   RG 34

       Rio de Janeiro: burials 1850 and onwards   RG 35/20-44

       São Paulo: births 1932; marriages 1933   FO 863/1-2

Brunei

       births 1932-1950   RG 36

Bulgaria   (see Yeo)

       Plovdiv: births 1880-1922; deaths 1884-1900   FO 868/1-2

       Rustchuk: births 1867-1908; deaths 1867-1903   FO 888/1-2

       Sofia: births 1934-1940   FO 864/1

       Varna: births 1856-1939; deaths 1851-1929   FO 884/1-5

RG 32 - RG 36 are largely indexed by RG 43

Burma

    Rangoon: marriages 1929-1945   RG 33/10

China   (see Yeo)

    births, marriages and deaths 1869-1876   FO 681/1

    Amoy: births 1850-1950; marriages 1850-1949;   FO 663/85-95
    deaths 1850-1948
        (see also **China** FO 681/1)

    Canton: births 1864-1865, 1944-1950; marriages   FO 681/2-9
    1865, 1943-1949; deaths, 1865, 1944-1950
        (see also **China** FO 681/1)

    Changsha: births 1905-1941; marriages 1906-   FO 681/10-12
    1936; deaths 1906-1933

    Chefoo: births 1861-1943; marriages 1872-1940;   FO 681/13-22
    deaths 1861-1942

    Chengtu: births 1902-1915; marriages 1904-1924;   FO 664/3-5
    deaths 1904-1926

    Chinanfu (Tsinan): births and marriages 1906-   FO 681/23-27
    1935; deaths 1906-1931, 1937

    Chinkiang: births 1865-1866, 1899-1926;   FO 387/4-5,
    marriages 1865-1866, 1896-1959; deaths   7-11
    1865-1866, 1889-1927
        (see also **China** FO 681/1)

    Chungking: births 1888-1951; marriages 1891-   FO 681/28-34
    1949; deaths 1891-1950

    Darien: births and marriages 1907-1940;   FO 681/35-88
    deaths 1910-1940

    Foochow: births 1858-1866,1905-1944;   FO 665/3-8
    marriages 1909-1942; deaths 1858-1866,
    1921-1945
        (see also **China** FO 681/1)

    Hankow: births 1863-1951; marriages 1869-1949;   FO 666/2-22
    deaths 1861-1950
        (see also **China** FO 681/1)

    Ichang: births 1879-1938; marriages 1881-1937;   FO 667/2-6
    deaths 1880-1941 (damaged by fire)

    Kuikiang: births 1866-1929; marriages 1872-   FO 681/39-45
    1928; deaths 1863-1929
        (see also **China** FO 681/1)

    Kunming: births 1949-1951; deaths 1950   FO 668/2-3

    Kwelin: births 1942-1944; deaths 1943   FO 681/46-47

    Mukden: births and deaths 1949 (date of   FO 681/48-49,
    registration); marriages 1947-1948   79-80

    Nanking: births 1930-1948; marriages 1929-1949;   FO 681/50-53
    deaths 1930-1947

    Newchang: births, marriages and deaths between   FO 681/1
    1869 and 1876

RG 32 - RG 36 are largely indexed by RG 43

China continued

Ningpo: births 1858; marriages and deaths 1856-1858	FO 670/2-4
(see also **China** FO 681/1)	
Peking: births 1911-1914; deaths 1911-1913 (date of registration)	FO 564/13-14
(see also **China** FO 681/1)	
Shanghai: births 1856-1864; marriages 1851; deaths 1851-1864	FO 672/1-3
Shanghai: marriages 1852-1951	RG 33/12-20
Shanghai, Union Church: marriages 1869-1951	RG 33/21-32
(see also **China** FO 681/1)	
Shantung Province: marriages 1912-1914	RG 33/33
Swatow: births 1864-1865, 1947-1949 (date of registration); marriages 1865; deaths 1864-1865	FO 681/54-56
(see also **China** FO 681/1)	
Taku: births 1862-1875; deaths 1871-1875	FO 673/9-10
Tengyueh: births 1904-1941; marriages 1913-1941; deaths 1906-1941	FO 681/60-62
Tientsin: births 1864-1951; marriages 1862-1952; deaths 1863-1952	FO 674/297-327
(see also **China** FO 681/1)	
Tsingtao: births 1911-1950; marriages 1923-1949; deaths 1921-1951	FO 675/7-10
Wei-hai-wei: births 1899-1929; marriages 1905-1940; deaths 1899-1929, 1938-1941	FO 681/63-71
Wei-hai-wei: births, marriages, deaths 1899-1930	RG 33/34
Wei-hai-wei: births, marriages,deaths 1899-1930	RG 36
Wei-hai-wei: index to births, marriages and deaths 1899-1930	RG 43/19
Whampoa: births and deaths 1865	FO 681/72-73
(see also **China** FO 681/1)	
Yunanfu: births 1903-1948; marriages 1904-1949; deaths 1903-1950	FO 681/74-78

Colombia   (see Yeo)

marriages 1824-1827	RG 33/155
births 1853-1924; deaths 1858-1927	FO 736/2-3

Denmark   (see Yeo)

deaths 1842-1872	RG 35/4
Copenhagen: marriages 1853-1870	FO 211/236
Copenhagen: marriages 1853-1874	RG 33/35
Copenhagen: baptisms 1866-1870; marriages and burials 1869-1870 and onwards	RG 32
For Danish colonies, see **West Indies**	

RG 32 - RG 36 are largely indexed by RG 43

Ecuador

    Guayaquil: births, marriages and deaths   FO 521/2
    1879-1896

Falkland Islands   (see Yeo)

    births and baptisms 1853 and onwards   RG 32
    marriages 1854 and onwards   RG 34
    burials 1854 and onwards   RG 35/20-44

Finland   (see Yeo)

    Helsinki: births 1914-1924   FO 753/19
    Helsinki: deaths 1924   FO 768/5
    Kristinestad: deaths 1928   FO 756/1
    Raahe (Brahestad): deaths 1930   FO 755/1
    Tampere: births 1906-1923; deaths 1909-1934   FO 769/1-2
    Turku (Abo): births 1928; deaths 1929   FO 754/1-2
    Vyborg: births 1924-1931; deaths 1929-1937   FO 751/1-3

France   (see Yeo)

    deaths 1831-1871   RG 35/8-10,
                                          12-13

    military deaths 1914-1920   RG 35/45-69
        (not indexed in RG 43)
    Boulogne: baptisms and burials 1815-1896;   RG 33/37-48
    marriages 1829-1895
        (index at RG 33/161)
    Calais and St Omer: baptisms 1817-1878;   RG 33/50-55
    marriages 1818-1872; burials 1819-1878
        (index at RG 33/49)
    Dieppe: births 1872-1892; deaths 1871-1894   FO 712/1-3
    Le Havre: baptisms, marriages and burials   RG 33/56-57
    1817-1863
    Le Tréport: births 1917-1926; deaths 1899-1929   FO 713/1-2
    Nantes: marriages 1851-1867   FO 384/1
    Paris: baptisms, marriages and burials 1784-1789,   RG 33/58-77
    1801-1809, 1815-1869; marriages 1869-1890
    Paris: deaths 1846-1852   RG 35/11
    Paris: marriages 1935-1937   FO 630/1
    Rouen: baptisms 1843-1844   RG 33/78
    French colonies (Cochin China, Guadeloupe,   RG 35/16
    Guyana, Haiti, India, Martinique, Mexico,
    New Caledonia, Réunion, Saigon, Shanghai,
    Senegal, Society Islands): deaths 1836-1871

        (See also **Algeria, Réunion, Madagascar** and **West Indies**)

RG 32 - RG 36 are largely indexed by RG 43

Germany　　　　　　　　　　　　　　　　　　(see Yeo)

    deaths c.1831-1920　　　　　　　　　　　　RG 35/20-44

    Aachen (Aix-la-Chapelle): deaths 1925　　FO 604/7

    Bavaria: marriages 1860-1861　　　　　　FO 149/99

    Bavaria: marriages 1884-1897　　　　　　FO 601/2-6

        (see also RG 32)

    Berlin: births 1944-1954; deaths 1944-1945　FO 601/2-6

    Bremen: births 1872-1914; marriages 1893-1933　FO 585/1-5

    Bremerhaven: births 1872-1893　　　　　FO 585/1

    Bremerhaven: marriages 1903-1914　　　FO 586/1

    Cologne: births and marriages 1850-1866;　FO 155/5-11,

    deaths 1850-1866 and 1879-1881　　　　　17

    Cologne: births 1880; marriages 1920-1934　FO 604/8-10

    Darmstadt: births 1869-1898; deaths 1871-1905　FO 716/1-2

    Dresden: births, baptisms and burials 1817-1836　RG 33/79

    Dresden: births and deaths 1859-1866　RG 33/80

    Dresden: births 1901-1907; marriages 1899-1900　FO 292/4-5

    Düsseldorf: births 1873-1884; baptisms 1903-　FO 604/1-6,

    1907; marriages 1873-1878, 1893-1898;　　8

    deaths 1876-1884

    Essen: births 1922-1927　　　　　　　　FO 604/11

    Frankfurt am Main: marriages 1836-1865　FO 208/90

    Hanover: baptisms, marriages, deaths and　RG 33/81

    burials 1839-1859

    Hanover: births 1861-1866　　　　　　　FO 717/1

    Karlsruhe: births 1860-1864; deaths 1859-1864　FO 718/1-2

    Leipzig: marriages 1850-1865; deaths 1850-1860　FO 299/22

    Saxony: marriages 1850-1865; deaths 1850-1869　FO 218/3

Greece　　　　　　　　　　　　　　　　　　(see Yeo)

    Ionian Islands, Zante: baptisms, marriages,　RG 33/82

    deaths and burials 1849-1859

        (see also **4.2)**

Hawaii

    births 1848-1893　　　　　　　　　　　FO 331/59

    marriages 1850-1853　　　　　　　　　RG 33/155

Hong Kong

    deaths from enemy action in the Far East 1941-　RG 33/11

    1945, indexed in RG 43/14

        (see also **Indonesia** RG 33/132)

Hungary

    Budapest: marriages 1872-1899　　　　FO 114/1-5

RG 32 - RG 36 are largely indexed by RG 4

Indian States   (see Yeo)

    Bikaner, Eastern Rajputana, Gwalior,   RG 33/90-113
    Hyderabad, Jaipur, Madras States, Mysore,
    Punjab States, Travandrum, and other states:
    births and deaths 1894-1947 (most from 1930s
    and 1940s)

    Jammu and Kashmir, Kolhapur and Deccan   RG 33/157-158,
    states, Udaipur: births 1917-1947   159
    Srinagar: deaths 1926-1947   RG 33/159
        (indexed in RG 43/15)

Indian Sub-continent   (see Yeo)

    deaths in French India 1836-1871   RG 35/16
    deaths c.1831-1920   RG 35/20-44

Indonesia (Dutch East Indies)   (see Yeo)

    deaths 1839-1871   RG 35/17
    deaths 1871-1920   RG 35/20-44
    Borneo: births 1907; deaths 1897-1907   FO 221/2-3
    Borneo and Sarawak: deaths from enemy   RG 33/132
    action 1941-1945
    Java: births 1869-1941; baptisms 1906;   FO 803/1-3
    deaths 1874-1898 and 1912-1940
    Java: deaths 1839-1871   RG 35/20-44
    Sumatra: births and deaths 1883-1884   FO 220/12

Iran (Persia)   (see Yeo)

    births 1903-1950; marriages 1895-1950;   FO 923/1-25
    deaths 1899-1950
    Bushire: births, marriages and deaths 1849-1895 FO 560
    Isfahan: births 1829-1950; marriages 1893-1951; FO 79/34-37
    deaths 1892-1943
    Tabriz: births 1851-1932; marriages 1850-1923; FO 451/1-8
    deaths 1882-1931

Iraq (Mesopotamia)   (see Yeo)

    births, marriages and deaths 1915-1931   RG 33/133-
       (with marriages only indexes in   137
        RG 33/138-139)
    births, marriages and deaths 1915-1931   RG 36
       (indexed in RG 43/16)

Israel   see **Palestine**

Italy   (see Yeo)

    deaths 1871-1920   RG 35/20-44

RG 32 - RG 36 are largely indexed by RG 43

Italy continued

Florence: marriages 1840-1855, 1865-1871	RG 33/114-115
Florence: marriages 1856	FO 352/43
Leghorn (Livorno): births, baptisms, marriages and burials 1797-1824	RG 33/116-117
Licata: births and deaths 1871-1900	FO 720/1
Naples: baptisms, marriages and burials 1817-1822	RG 33/118
Naples: baptisms, marriages and burials 1835-1836	RG 33/155
Rome and Tuscany: baptisms and marriages 1816-1852	FO 170/6
Rome: marriages 1872-1889	RG 33/119
Sicily: births 1810-1957; deaths 1847-1957	FO 653/2-38 and FO 720/1
Turin: marriages 1858-1864	RG 33/120
Venice: marriages 1874-1947	RG 33/121

Japan (see Yeo)

Kobe: baptisms and marriages 1874-1941; burials 1902-1941	RG 33/122-126
Nagasaki: births 1864-1940; marriages 1922-1940; deaths 1859-1944	FO 796/236-238
Osaka: marriages 1892-1904	RG 33/127-130
Shimonoseki: births 1903-1921; marriages 1906-1922; deaths 1903-1921	FO 797/48-50
Tokyo: marriages 1875-1887	FO 345/34
Yokohama: marriages 1870-1874	FO 345/34

Jordan

Amman: births 1946; marriages 1927	RG 36

Kenya (East African Protectorate)

births 1904-1924 (partly indexed by RG 43/18)	RG 36

Lebanon

Beirut: marriages c.1859-1939	FO 616/5

Libya

Tripoli: marriages 1916, 1931-1940; deaths 1938-1939	FO 161/4-7

Madagascar (see Yeo)

Diego Suarez: births 1907-1921	FO 711/1
Tamatave: deaths 1935-1940	FO 714/1
Tananarive (Antananarivo): births 1865-1868	FO 710/1

RG 32 - RG 36 are largely indexed by RG 43

Malaysia   (see Yeo)
     births 1917-1949   RG 36
     births 1920-1948; deaths 1941-1945   RG 33/131-132
     Borneo: births 1907; deaths 1897-1907   FO 221/2-3
     Borneo and Sarawak: deaths from enemy   RG 33/132
     action 1941-1945
     Johore: births 1924-1931   RG 36
     Sarawak: births 1910-1948; marriages 1921-   RG 36
     1935; deaths 1910-1948

Malta   (see Yeo)
     marriages 1904-1936   FO 161/7

Mexico
     marriages 1850 and onwards   RG 34
     deaths c.1850 and onwards   RG 35/16,
                                                  20-44
     Mexico City: burials 1827-1926   FO 207/58
     Mexico City: births and deaths 1854-1867   FO 723/1-2
     Vera Cruz: births, deaths and burials 1858-1867   RG 33/140

Netherlands   (see Yeo)
     deaths 1839-1871   RG 35/17
     The Hague: baptisms 1627-1821; marriages   RG 33/83-88
     1627-1889; births 1837-1839, 1859-1894;
     deaths 1859-1907
         (these also include some church records;
         for others, see FO 259)
     Rotterdam: baptisms and marriages 1708-1794   RG 33/89

For Dutch colonies, see **Indonesia, Surinam** and **West Indies**

Norway
     Bodo: births 1888-1890; deaths 1895   FO 724/1-2
     Drammen: deaths 1906   FO 532/2
     Kragero: deaths 1895   FO 725/1
     Lofoten Islands: births 1850-1932   FO 726/1
     Oslo (Christiania): births 1850-1932; marriages   FO 529/1-14
     1853-1936; deaths 1850-1930
     Porsgrund and Skien: births 1885-1891   FO 531/2

Palestine   (see Yeo)
     births and deaths 1920-1935   RG 33/141
        (indexed in RG 43/17)
     births 1923-1948; deaths 1941-1945   RG 36
        (partly indexed in RG 43/18)

RG 32 - RG 36 are largely indexed by RG 43

Palestine continued

Jaffa: births 1900-1914	FO 734/1
Jerusalem: births 1850-1921; deaths 1851-1914	FO 617/3-5
Jerusalem: military baptisms 1939-1947	WO 156/6
Sarafand: military baptisms 1940-1946; banns of marriage 1944-1947	WO 156/7-8

Paraguay

births 1863 and onwards	RG 32
deaths 1831-1920	RG 35/20-44

Peru

	(see Yeo)
births and deaths 1837-1841; marriages 1827 and 1836	RG 33/155

Poland

	(see Yeo)
Breslau (Wroclaw): births 1929-1938; deaths 1932-1938	FO 715/1-2
Danzig (Gdansk): births 1851-1910; deaths 1850-1914	FO 634/16-18
Lodz: births 1925-1939	FO 869/1
Stettin: births 1864-1939; deaths 1857-1933	FO 719/1-2

Portugal

	(see Yeo)
deaths 1831-1920	RG 35/20-44
Azores: births, baptisms, marriages, deaths and burials 1807-1866	FO 559/1
Azores: baptisms, marriages and burials 1835-1837	RG 35/155
Azores: baptisms 1850-1857	RG 32
Azores: burials 1850-1857	RG 35/20
Cape Verde Islands: marriages 1894-1922	FO 767/6-7
Lisbon: marriages 1859-1876	FO 173/8
Oporto: baptisms, marriages and burials 1814-1874	RG 33/142
Oporto: baptisms, marriages and burials 1837	RG 33/155
Oporto: baptisms, 1835 onwards	RG 32
Oporto: marriages 1835 onwards	RG 34
Oporto: burials 1835-1844	RG 35/20

Réunion

deaths 1836-1871	RG 35/16
marriages 1864-1921	FO 322/1-2

Romania

	(see Yeo)
Braila: births 1922-1930; deaths 1921-1929	FO 727/1-2

RG 32 - RG 36 are largely indexed by RG 43

Romania continued

Bucharest: births 1851-1931; baptisms 1858-1948: deaths 1854-1929	FO 625/2-4, 6
Constanta (Kustendje): births 1866-1873	FO 887/1
Galatz: marriages 1891-1939	FO 517/1-2
Lower Danube: baptisms 1869-1907	FO 625/5
Lower Danube: marriages 1868-1914	RG 33/143
Lower Danube: burials 1869-1870	FO 786/120
Sulina: births 1861-1932; deaths 1860-1931	FO 728/1-2 and FO 886/1-2

Russia (see Yeo)

births, baptisms, and deaths 1835-1870	RG 35/18-19
births 1849-1909; marriages 1849-1861; deaths 1849-1915	FO 267/44-46
deaths 1871-1920	RG 35/20-44
Archangel: births 1849-1909; marriages 1849-1861; deaths 1849-1915	FO 267/44-46
Batum: births 1884-1921; marriages 1891-1920; deaths 1884-1920	FO 397/1-6
Berdiansk (Osipenko): marriages 1901	FO 399/1
Ekaterinburg (Sverdlovsk): deaths 1918-1919	FO 399/5
Estonia, Pernau: births 1894-1930; deaths 1894-1930	FO 339/11-12
Estonia, Tallin (Reval): births 1866-1940; marriages 1921-1939; deaths 1875-1940	FO 514/1-9
Konigsberg (Kaliningrad): births 1869-1933; marriages 1864-1904; deaths 1857-1932	FO 509/1-4
Latvia, Libau: births 1883-1932; deaths 1871-1932	FO 440/10 and FO 61/4-5
Latvia, Riga: births 1850-1910; deaths 1850-1915	FO 377/3-4
Latvia, Riga: births 1921-1940; marriages 1920-1940; deaths 1921-1940	FO 516/1-9
Latvia, Windau: births 1906-1909	FO 399/19
Lithuania, Kovno and Memel: births 1924-1940; deaths 1922-1940	FO 722/1-4
Moscow: births 1882-1918; marriages 1894-1924; deaths 1881-1918	FO 518/1-4
Nicolaiyev: births 1872-1917; deaths 1874-1915	FO 399/7-8
Novorossisk: births 1911-1920; deaths 1896-1920	FO 399/9-10
Odessa: births 1852-1919; baptisms 1893; marriages 1851-1916; deaths 1852-1919	FO 359/3-12
Poti: births 1871-1906; deaths 1871-1920	FO 399/13-14
Rostov: births 1891-1914; marriages 1904-1918; deaths 1906-1916	FO 398/1-9

RG 32 - RG 36 are largely indexed by RG 43

Russia continued

St Petersburg (Petrograd, Leningrad): baptisms 1818-1840; burials 1821-1840. Independent denomination.	RG 4/4605
(indexed in RG 43)	
St Petersburg (Petrograd, Leningrad): births, baptisms, marriages, deaths and burials 1840-1918	RG 33/144-152
(with an index for 1886-1917 in RG 33/162)	
St Petersburg (Petrograd, Leningrad): births 1856-1938; marriages 1892-1917; deaths 1897-1927	FO 378/3-9
Sebastopol: births 1886-1898; marriages 1910; deaths 1893-1908	FO 393/3, 15-16
Theodosia (Feodosiya): births 1904-1906; deaths 1907-1918	FO 339/17-18
Vladivostok: births 1911-1927; marriages 1916-1923; deaths 1908-1924	FO 510/1-10

Singapore

births 1922	RG 36

Somalia (Somaliland)

births 1905-1920	RG 36
(partly indexed by RG 43/18)	

Spain

	(see Yeo)
deaths 1831-1920	RG 35/20-44
Aguilas: births 1875-1911; deaths 1874-1911	FO 920/1-2
Bilbao: deaths 1855-1870	FO 729/1
Cartagena: births 1847-1887; marriages 1858-1904; deaths 1855-1871	FO 920/3-6
Garrucha: births 1876-1890; deaths 1883-1905	FO 920/7-8
Pormàn: births 1907; deaths 1911	FO 920/9-10

Sudan

	(see Yeo)
births 1916-1950; marriages 1907-1950; deaths 1917-1946	RG 36
(partly indexed by RG 43/18)	

Surinam (Dutch Guiana)

Paramaribo: births 1897-1966; marriages 1922-1929; deaths 1889-1965	FO 907/1-32

Sweden

	(see Yeo)
deaths (1831-1920)	RG 35/20-44
Gothenburg: marriages 1845-1891	RG 33/153
Gothenburg: baptisms 1881-1890	FO 818/15

RG 32 - RG 36 are largely indexed by RG 43

Sweden continued

Hudiksvall: deaths 1884	FO 730/1
Oskarshamn: deaths 1887	FO 731/1
Stockholm: births, marriages and deaths 1920-1938	FO 748

Switzerland (see Yeo)

marriages 1816-1833	FO 194/1
deaths 1831-1920	RG 35/20-44
Geneva: births 1850-1934; marriages 1850-1933; deaths 1850-1923	FO 778/13-22
Lausanne: births 1886-1948; marriages 1887-1947; deaths 1887-1948	FO 910/1-20
Montreux: births 1902-1939; marriages 1927-1933; deaths 1903-1941	FO 911/1-3

Syria (see Yeo)

Aleppo: baptisms and burials 1756-1800 (at Chancery Lane)	SP 110/70
Damascus: births, marriages and deaths 1932-1938	FO 684

Tahiti

Papeete: births 1818-1941; marriages 1845-1941; deaths 1845-1936	FO 687/22-23

Taiwan (Formosa)

births, marriages and deaths 1866	FO 681/57
deaths 1873-1901	FO 721/1
(see also **China** FO 681/1)	

Tristan da Cunha

marriages 1871-1951; deaths 1892-1949	PRO 30/65
(at Kew: registers of births and baptisms, 1867-1955, were returned to Tristan da Cunha in 1982)	

Tunisia

Bizerta: deaths 1898-1931	FO 870/1
Djerba: deaths 1925	FO 871/1
Gabes: deaths 1925	FO 872/1
Goletta: births 1885-1888	FO 878/1-2
Monastir: deaths 1905-1908	FO 873/1
Sfax: deaths 1896-1931	FO 874/1
Susa (Sousse): deaths 1894-1931	FO 875/1

Turkey (see Yeo)

deaths 1831-1920	RG 35/20-44
Adana: marriages 1913, 1942 and 1946	FO 609/1-3

RG 32 - RG 36 are largely indexed by RG 43

Turkey continued

Adrianople (Edirne): births 1888-1912; marriages 1887-1914	FO 783/3-7
Ankara and Konieh: births 1895-1909	FO 732/1
Constantinople (Istanbul): marriages 1885-1958	RG 33/154
Constantinople (Istanbul): marriages 1895-1924	FO 441/1-35
Dardanelles: births 1900-1914	FO 733/1
Smyrna (Izmir): baptisms, marriages and burials 1833-1849	RG 33/155

Uganda (see Yeo)

marriages 1904-1910 RG 36
    (partly indexed by RG 43/18)

United States of America (see Yeo)

Aberdeen, Washington State: births 1916; deaths 1914	FO 700/22-23
Boston, Massachusetts: births 1871-1932; deaths 1902-1930	FO 706/1-3
Cincinnati, Ohio: births 1929, 1943-1948, 1951-1958; deaths 1947, 1950-1955	FO 700/31-35
Cleveland, Ohio: births 1914-1930, 1944-1969; deaths 1948-1969	FO 700/36-43
Dallas, Texas: births 1951-1954; deaths 1951	FO 700/24-25
Detroit, Michigan: births 1910-1969; marriages1936-1937; deaths1931-1945, 1949-1968	FO 700/44-53
El Paso, Texas: births 1916-1930; deaths 1914-1926	FO 700/26-27
Galveston, Texas: births 1838-1918; deaths 1850-1927	FO 701/23-24
Hawaii see **Hawaii**	
Kansas City, Missouri: births 1904-1922, 1944-1966; marriages 1958-1961; deaths 1920-1926, 1943-1949, 1952-1965	FO 700/54-60
Omaha, Nebraska: births 1906	FO 700/61
Pensacola, Florida: births 1880-1901; deaths 1879-1905	FO 885/1-2
Pittsburgh, Pennsylvania: births 1954-1956	FO 700/63
Portland, Oregon: births 1880-1926; deaths 1929	FO 707/1-2
Providence, Rhode Island: births 1902-1930; deaths 1920 (date of registration)	FO 700/8-9
St Paul, Minnesota: births 1943-1966; deaths 1944	FO 700/71-74
Tacoma, Washington State: births 1896-1921; deaths 1892-1907	FO 700/20-21

RG 32 - RG 36 are largely indexed by RG 43

Venezuela (see Yeo)
      marriages 1836-1838 RG 33/155

West Indies

    Antigua: baptisms and burials 1733-1734,   CO 152/21,
    1738-1745; marriages 1745   25
        (at Kew)

    Barbados: baptisms and burials 1678-1679   RG 33/156

    Cuba: baptisms 1847-1848; marriages 1842-1849   RG 33/155

    Curaçao: births 1897-1966; marriages 1922-1929;   FO 907/1-32
    deaths 1889-1965

    Danish (US) Virgin Islands:-
     St Croix: deaths 1849-1870   RG 35/4
     St John: deaths 1849-1872   RG 35/4
     St Thomas: deaths 1849-1870   RG 35/4-7

    Dominican Republic: births 1868-1932;   FO 683/2-6
    marriages 1921-1928: burials 1849-1910;
    deaths 1874-1889

    Guadeloupe: deaths 1836-1871   RG 35/16

    Haiti: births 1833-1850; marriages 1833-1893;   FO 866/14,
    deaths 1833-1850   21-22

    Haiti: births 1870-1907   FO 376/1-2

    Haiti: deaths 1836-1871   RG 35/16

    Martinique: deaths 1836-1871   RG 35/16

    Montserrat: baptisms and burials 1721-1729;   CO 152/18,
    marriages 1721-1729   25
        (at Kew)

    Nevis: baptisms and burials 1726-1727,   CO 152/16,
    1733-1734,1740-1745   21, 25
        (at Kew)

    St Kitts: baptisms and burials 1721-1730,   CO 152/18,
    1733-1734, 1738-1745; marriages 1733-1734,   21, 25
    1738-1745
        (at Kew)

Zanzibar

    births 1916-1918; marriages 1917-1919;   RG 36
    deaths 1916-1919

RG 32 - RG 36 are largely indexed by RG 43

5. Family history before the parish registers

5.1 Problems

The parish registers, which started in 1538, were the first record applicable to everyone, rich and poor alike. Before the institution of parish registers, births, marriages and deaths were simply not registered: personal information has to be sought in, or deduced from, other types of record. Many series of records of use to genealogists start well before 1538, and continue long after, but in general they contain information about the wealthier members of society: most people were very sparsely documented. Documentation about people's lives does exist, but only incidentally to the main purpose of the record: for example, many of the types of document suggested below are discussed more fully in the chapter dealing with land ownership (**41**).

Medieval records are generally much more difficult to use than those from the sixteenth century and later. In addition to the problems presented by handwriting and by letter-forms different from those of the present day alphabet, most medieval documents are in Latin, often highly abbreviated. In addition, as many of the surviving records derive from the Exchequer and the law courts, they require some knowledge of accounting and legal procedures to be fully understood. However, many records have been published, or have detailed lists and indexes, and it is advisable to start with these.

An invaluable book for tackling the problems presented by the language, palaeography (handwriting) and diplomatic (the form of documents) of medieval records is *Latin for Local History*, by E Gooder. The inexpensive *Borthwick Wallets*, by A Rycraft, contain photocopies and transcriptions of various types of records, and are very useful for those wishing to learn how to read the documents properly: they are available from the Borthwick Institute (address in **48.6**).

5.2 Possibilities

Possible sources for genealogical information fall into two kinds: those where information is arranged or has been indexed by name, and those where the arrangement is by place.

Wills are one of the most useful of the sources accessible by name, often giving considerable family detail. The PRO has those of wealthier people, proved in the Prerogative Court of Canterbury, from 1383 (PROB 11): wills proved in other courts are kept elsewhere (see **6**). Inquisitions post mortem are another fruitful source: these were enquiries conducted by a local jury to establish what lands a deceased person had held directly from the crown, and who was the next heir (see **41.6** for a fuller discussion, and **41.10** for references). There are a number of calendars in print, and many of the inquisitions have been published by local record societies.

Documents issued from, or inspected in, Chancery were recorded officially on parchment rolls, most of which have been calendared and indexed for the medieval period. Although largely concerned with people of sufficient status to have direct dealings with central government, the enrolments do contain many references to other people as well. The most important are the Patent Rolls (C 66), the Close Rolls (C 54), the Charter Rolls (C 53) and the Fine Rolls (C 60): details of the calendars are given in **5.3**. Deeds are another useful source: most of the PRO's extensive holdings of medieval deeds have been calendared and indexed. (See **41.4** for a fuller discussion, and for references).

To use the other types of records, those arranged topographically, you need to have some idea of the locality in which your ancestors lived. If you have this, then it is possible to trace fairly humble people. By using manor court rolls and other manorial records such as rentals and surveys, which recorded land transactions within the manor and other local affairs, the inheritance of a peasant tenement can be traced back through several generations. Many manorial documents are held outside the PRO: to find those of a particular manor, consult the Manorial Documents Register at the National Register of Archives. The PRO does hold a considerable number of manorial documents, mostly from those manors which formed part of the crown lands: see **41.2** and **41.5** for references.

The feet of fines are the records of fictitious law suits entered into to evade conveyancing restrictions, and they run from 1190 to 1833: see **41.3** for references. Many of these have been printed by local record societies. Taxation records can also be useful in tracing rich and poor, although the very poor were usually exempt (see **43**).

There are many pedigrees on the Early Plea and Essoin Rolls (KB 26), the *Coram Rege* Rolls (KB 27) and the *De Banco* Rolls (CP 40): see the book by Wrottesley. You may also find useful the copious extracts, mainly from the *De Banco* Rolls and similar legal records, made by General Plantagenet-Harrison in the late nineteenth century, which are available at Chancery Lane. There are several volumes, all hand-written with indexes, which are on the whole reliable. His main interests were in Yorkshire, and in all pedigrees, but you should be cautious in trusting to the accuracy of the latter.

5.3 Family history before the parish registers: bibliography and sources

[An * means this work can be seen at Chancery Lane: a # means it can be seen at Kew.]

Published works

Calendar of Charter Rolls, 1226-1516 (London, 1903-1927) *
Calendar of Close Rolls, 1227-1509 (London, 1892-1963) *
Calendar of Fine Rolls, 1272-1509 (London, 1911-1963) *
Calendar of Patent Rolls, 1216-1509, 1547-1582 (London, 1891-1986) *
A J Camp, *My Ancestor came with the Conqueror* (Society of Genealogists, 1988) *
E A Gooder, *Latin for Local History* (London, 2nd edn 1978) *
Letters and Papers of Henry VIII (London, 1864-1932) (For patent rolls, 1509-1547.)

A Macfarlane, *A Guide to English Historical Records* (Cambridge, 1983) *

J Morris, *A Latin Glossary for Family and Local Historians* (FFHS, 1989) *

Public Record Office, *Genealogy before the Parish Registers* (Information Leaflet) *#

A Rycraft, *Borthwick Wallet: English Medieval Handwriting* (York, 1973)

A Rycraft, *Borthwick Wallet: Sixteenth and Seventeenth Century Handwriting: Series 1* (York, 1973)

A Rycraft, *Borthwick Wallet: Sixteenth and Seventeenth Century Handwriting: Series 2* (York, 1972)

A Rycraft, *Borthwick Wallet: Sixteenth and Seventeenth Century Wills, Inventories and other Probate Documents* (York, 1972)

G Wrottesley, *Pedigrees from the Plea Rolls, 1200-1500* (London, c.1906) *

Unpublished finding aids

Plantagenet-Harrison notes from legal records *

Records

Chancery (at Chancery Lane)
C 53 Charter Rolls. 1199-1517
C 54 Close Rolls. 1204-1903
C 55 Supplementary Close Rolls. 1242-1434
C 60 Fine Rolls. 1199-1648
C 66 Patent Rolls. 1201-1962

Court of Common Pleas (at Chancery Lane)
CP 40 Court of Common Pleas: *De Banco* Rolls. 1272-1875

Court of King's Bench (at Chancery Lane)
KB 26 Early Plea and Essoin Rolls. 1193-1272
KB 27 *Coram Rege* Rolls. 1273-1702

6. Wills and other probate records

6.1 After 1858

Wills proved from 12 January 1858 to the present day may be read (for a small fee) at the Principal Registry of the Family Division, Somerset House, The Strand, London WC2A 1LA, between 10.00am and 4.30pm, Monday to Friday. The same applies to letters of administration, which may be granted if no will was made or could be found. Copies of wills and probate and administration grants are obtainable either in person or by post, provided you know the date of death. Applications should be addressed to the Record Keeper, Correspondence Department. A handling charge is payable in addition to the copying charge.

6.2 Before 1858

Before 1858 wills came under the jurisdiction of the ecclesiastical courts. In order to identify the court where the will was proved or administration granted you may need to acquaint yourself with the basic organisation of English and Welsh ecclesiastical administration. (However, for the period from 1796 the relevant court can often be ascertained from the indexes to the death duty registers: see **6.8**). If the deceased held property in one archdeaconry the will would be proved in the archdeacon's court; if in more than one archdeaconry but within one diocese, in the diocesan court; but if the deceased held personal property worth over £5 in two distinct dioceses or jurisdictions, then the estate was subject to the provincial court, that is to say the Prerogative Court of Canterbury (PCC) or the Prerogative Court of York. There were, however, a number of exceptions to this basic structure. For instance, deans and cathedral chapters held courts for the areas subject to their peculiar jurisdictions, and some manorial courts had the right to grant probate.

The PRO holds only records of the Prerogative Court of Canterbury, 1383-1858. Those of the Prerogative Court of York are held at the Borthwick Institute of Historical Research, St Anthony's Hall, Peasholme Green, York YO1 2PW. The surviving records of other courts with probate jurisdictions are deposited in local record offices. The most recent guide to their locations is J S W Gibson, *A Simplified Guide to Probate Jurisdictions.*

Although the PCC records relate mainly to the testamentary affairs of the wealthier sections of society in the province of Canterbury, the great prestige of the court attracted business to it that strictly speaking belonged to lower courts, and the declining value of money meant that in the eighteenth and nineteenth centuries more and more deceased persons' estates came within its jurisdiction. Furthermore property held in all parts of England belonging to persons dying overseas (including impecunious seamen) was subject to the PCC.

Between 1653 and 1660 all probate jurisdiction was administered by a single court of civil commission and its records are in unbroken series with those of the PCC itself.

6.3 PCC wills and grants of administration as sources

Wills can be a most valuable source for genealogists, but the evidence they yield needs to be interpreted with caution. Firstly, the terminology of family relationships may be used imprecisely. Thus the terms *father, brother* and *son* may be used to refer to in-laws as well as natural relatives. The term *cousin* can be used indiscriminately to refer to all types of kin. Secondly, the will might make no mention of real estate. Certain types of real estate, depending upon the terms of tenure, could be devised by will after 1540; from 1660 the only exception to this is land held by copyhold, which was not devisable by will until 1815. Nevertheless, if an eldest son was to inherit as his father's heir-at-law no mention might be made of him or his inheritance in his father's will. Similarly, married daughters might be omitted if they had had property settled upon them at the time of their marriages. Conversely, however, you should not assume that all legatees would be still alive at the time probate was granted, or that the testator necessarily left sufficient means to cover all of his or her bequests. In some instances information about a testator's marital status, occupation, or place of residence, not given in the will or in the probate clause appended to the registered copy of the will (PROB 11), may be found in the probate act book (PROB 8).

If the deceased died intestate, letters of administration might be granted by the court. Grants of administration were registered in the administration act books (PROB 6). The act book ordinarily records only the marital status and place of residence of the intestate, the name of the administrator and his or her relationship to the intestate, and the date of the grant. From 1796, and in many cases before that date, a valuation of the deceased's personal estate is given in the margin. The court was required to grant administration to the deceased's next of kin, and the entry in the administration act book may therefore include the names of relatives who had ignored summonses to appear before the court, or who had renounced their claims to administer the estate. However, you should be wary of assuming that a known relative closer in blood than the person to whom administration was granted had died by the time the grant was made, merely because the known relative is not mentioned in the administration act book.

In some instances a grant was made limited to a particular part of the deceased's estate, or to which special conditions were attached. Such grants are entered in full (PROB 6, PROB 7) and may give detailed information about the relationship of the administrator to the deceased. These grants can be of great genealogical value.

From 1529 administrators were required to enter into a bond with the court to ensure that they fulfilled their responsibilities. Bonds generally give the names, marital status, occupations and places of residence of the administrator and his or her sureties. However, the rate of survival before 1714 is poor and at present only a few sixteenth century bonds (PROB 51) and those for the period 1714-1744 (PROB 46) are available to searchers.

The date of death of an intestate, or of a testator whose executors were sworn outside London, can often be found in the warrant for the grant of administration or commission to swear executors (PROB 14).

6.4 Indexes and finding aids to PCC wills and grants of administration

For the period to 1700 indexes to testators whose wills were granted probate by the PCC have been published, compiled either from the registers of wills and the probate act books or from the probate act books alone. For 1701 there is a card index of wills and administrations. For the periods 1702-1749 and 1801-1852 searchers need to use the calendars in the class PROB 12, although at the time of writing a microfiche index to PROB 12 for the period 1701-1749 is being compiled by the Friends of the Public Record Office. These calendars are annual lists of testators and intestates arranged in separate sections and sorted by initial letter only. They are incomplete and sometimes inaccurate. For the period 1853-1858 there are calendars giving all the names in two fully alphabetised sequences (PROB 12). For the period 1750-1800 the Society of Genealogists is in the process of publishing an index to testators compiled from calendars in the class PROB 13 (which share the same defects as those in PROB 12). For a fee the Society of Genealogists will search the unpublished parts of their index.

The texts of almost all wills proved were entered in registers (PROB 11). The indexes and calendars supply the quire references to the relevant part of the register. The searcher then needs to find the piece number of the register and the relevant microfilm number from the lists available at Chancery Lane. It is necessary to give a week's notice to examine an original will (PROB 10). Generally there is no advantage in doing this unless it is wished to examine a signature or seal. Original wills survive in almost complete sequence from 1620; before that date an original will may in fact be a facsimile copy made by the court.

For the period to 1660 indexes to intestates, compiled from administration act books have been published. For 1661-1662, 1665-1700, and 1702-1858 genealogists seaching for grants of administration should use PROB 12. Typescript indexes to 1663-1664 have been compiled, and a card index to 1701 is available.

Details of published and unpublished finding aids and indexes to testators and intestates are given in **6.9**.

6.5 Inventories and accounts

Inventories, listing the deceased's personal property, and accounts, recording executors' and administrators' receipts and expenditure, may provide the most illuminating evidence about the deceased's social status, wealth and business activities, but they are not generally of strict genealogical value, unless they contain pertinent lists of creditors, or, in the case of accounts, payments for the maintenance of dependants. The rate of survival for these documents is very poor before 1666, and erratic for the later seventeenth century and early eighteenth century. After the mid eighteenth century, they were only exhibited if the estate was subject to litigation, if the administrator or executor renounced his or her responsibilities, or if the beneficiaries of the estate were minors (PROB 2 - PROB 5, PROB 28, PROB 31, PROB 32, PROB 37).

6.6 Litigation

If an estate was subject to litigation before a grant of probate or administration was issued, this may be indicated in the probate or administration act books (PROB 6 - PROB 9) or in the calendars (PROB 12), by a marginal abbreviation of the terms *by decree* and *by sentence*. Sentences, the court's final judgement in certain types of cause, were registered in PROB 11 until the end of the eighteenth century. They rarely contain data of genealogical value, but they will furnish the name of the cause, and this is often essential information because before the mid eighteenth century causes were often cited or indexed by the name of the promoter of the cause, and not by the name of the testator or intestate. The stages through which a cause passed are recorded in the acts of court (PROB 29, PROB 30). These records are concerned with procedure and you may find other classes of litigation records more fruitful: allegations in PROB 18, answers in PROB 25, depositions in PROB 24 and PROB 26, cause papers in PROB 28 and PROB 37, and exhibits in PROB 31 and PROB 36. There is a card index to PROB 18 arranged in two parts, by name of cause and by name of testator or intestate. In many cases the use of this index may be sufficient to inform a searcher as to whether or not there was a testamentary cause attached to an estate.

The PCC was only concerned with the validity of wills presented for probate or the claims of persons seeking letters of administration. Cases concerned with the inheritance and devisal of real estate were heard in Chancery (see **47.3**), which also attracted cases concerned with the validity of wills on account of its greater powers.

Appeals from the Prerogative Court of Canterbury, and other church courts, in testamentary causes, went to the High Court of Delegates, which called the proceedings of the lower courts before it (DEL 1 and DEL 2, both indexed by DEL 11/7, and DEL 7). Wills and affidavits brought into court, 1636-1857, are in DEL 10. The muniment books (DEL 9) contain transcripts of documents and exhibits in testamentary appeals, 1652-1859. Both are indexed in DEL 11/6 and DEL 11/7. After 1834, appeals lay to the Judicial Committee of the Privy Council until 1858: see PCAP 1 and PCAP 3.

After 1858, testamentary causes were no longer heard by ecclesiastical courts, but by the new Court of Probate (later part of the Probate, Divorce and Admiralty Division of the High Court), with appeal to the House of Lords. A sample of case files and papers relating to contentious probates of wills, 1858-1960, is in J 121.

6.7 Other probate records in the PRO

Other wills are found throughout the public records. Among the papers of the Bona Vacantia division of the Treasury Solicitor's Office (TS 17) there are records relating to intestates' estates which escheated to the crown when there was no next of kin. Wills were deposited in the Navy Pay Office by naval ratings, Royal Marine other ranks and some warrant officers, 1786-1909 (ADM 48, indexed by ADM 142: see also **19.25**). There are also some Royal Marine wills in ADM 96. Wills of some army officers, 1755-1881, may be found in WO 42: wills and copies of wills may be found, very occasionally, among deceased soldiers' effects in the casualty returns, 1809-1910 (WO 25/1359-2410 and 3251-3471).

The probate records of the British Consular Court at Smyrna, Turkey, 1820-1929, and of the Shanghai Supreme Court, 1857-1941, are in FO 626 and FO 917 respectively. Other wills of some Britons in China, 1837-1951, are in FO 678/2729-2931.

6.8 Death duty registers

From 1796 duty was payable on many estates over a certain value. The records of the Estate Duty Office are held by the PRO to 1903, after which date no registers survive.

They are an invaluable source for the genealogist, becoming progressively more complete as the scope of estate duty was extended throughout the nineteenth century. By finding someone in the indexes (IR 27), the court in which their will was proved may be discovered. Date of death is often stated in the register (IR 26) and relationships may be more precisely stated than in the will itself.

The death duty returns record the actual estate left by the deceased, and, unlike the will, not what he or she would have wished to bequeath. In addition, because further information was added to the registers for many years after probate, the annotations can give details on the whereabouts of the legatees up to a later date.

Details about modern indexes to some pieces in IR 26 are given below.

6.9 Wills and other probate records: bibliography and sources

[An * means this work can be seen at Chancery Lane: a # means it can be seen at Kew.]

Guides

A J Camp, *Wills and their whereabouts* (London, 4th edn 1974)*
J Cox, 'Note on the Death Duty Registers', *Genealogists' Magazine*, vol. XX, pp.261-263
J Cox, *Wills, Inventories and Death Duties* (Public Record Office, 1988) *
J S W Gibson, *Wills and where to find them* (London, 1974) *
J S W Gibson, *A Simplified Guide to Probate Jurisdictions: Where to look for wills* (FFHS, 3rd edn 1985) *
E McLaughlin, *Wills pre-1858* (FFHS, 1987)
E McLaughlin, *Wills from 1858* (FFHS, 1985)
M Overton, *A Bibliography of British Probate Inventories* (Newcastle, 1983)
Public Record Office, *Probate Records* (Information Leaflet) *#
Public Record Office, *Death Duty Registers* (Information Leaflet) *#

Published and unpublished indexes and finding aids

Wills, probate acts and sentences
Prerogative Court of Canterbury Wills, 1383-1629, 6 vols (British Record Society, Index Library, 1893-1912): 1383-1558, vols X, XI; 1558-83, vol. XVIII; 1584-1604, vol. XXV; 1605-19, vol. XLIII; 1620-29, vol. XLIV.*
Abstract of Probates and Sentences in the Prerogative Court of Canterbury, 1620-24, ed. J Matthews and G F Matthews (London, 1911)*
Sentences and Complete Index Nominum (Probate and Sentences, 1630-39), ed. J Matthews and G F Matthews (London, 1907)*
Abstracts of Probate Acts in the Prerogative Court of Canterbury, 1630-55, ed. J Matthews and G F Matthews, 7 vols (London, 1903-14)*
PCC Sentences: a rough list transcribed from the original calendars for the period 1643-52 (manuscript list)*

Prerogative Court of Canterbury Wills 1653-60, 2 vols (British Record Society, Index Library, 1925-1936): 1653-56, vol. LIV; 1657-60, vol. LXII. *

Prerogative Court of Canterbury: Wills, Sentences and Probate Acts, 1661-1670, ed. J H Morrison (London, 1935) *

Prerogative Court of Canterbury Wills, 1671-1700, 4 vols (British Record Society, Index Library, 1942-1960): 1671-75, vol. LXVII; 1676-85, vol. LXXI; 1686-93, vol. LXXVII; 1694-1700, vol. LXXX. *

An Index to the Wills proved in the Prerogative Court of Canterbury, 1750-1800, vol. I, A-Bh (1976); vol. II, Bi-Ce (1977); vol. III, Ch-G (1984); vol. IV, H-M (1988); ed. A J Camp (Society of Genealogists, continuing) *

Wills in Chancery Masters' Exhibits, C103-C115 (card index) *

Administrations

Administrations in the Prerogative Court of Canterbury 1559-80, ed. R M Glencross, 2 vols (Exeter, 1912-1917): vol. I, 1559-1571; vol. II, 1572-80 *

B Lloyd, 'Preliminary Addenda and Corrigenda to Mr R M Glencross's Letters of Administration....1559-1580' (typescript, 1979) *

Administrations in the Prerogative Court of Canterbury, 1581-1619, 3 vols (British Record Society, Index Library, 1954-1968): 1581-1595, vol. LXXVI; 1596-1608, vol. LXXXI; 1609-1619, vol. LXXXIII *

Prerogative Court of Canterbury: Letters of Administration, 1620-30, ed. J H Morrison (London, 1935) *

Administrations in the Prerogative Court of Canterbury 1631-1660, 5 vols (British Record Society, Index Library, 1944-1986): 1631-1648, vol. C; 1649-1654, vol. LXVIII; 1655-1660, vols LXXII, LXXIV, LXXV *

Index to PROB 6/38-PROB 6/39, Prerogative Court of Canterbury Administrations, 1663-1664 (typescript) *

Wills and administrations

Index to wills and administrations, 1701, card index *

Calendar of Wills and Administrations, 1702-1852 (PROB 12/72-PROB 12/271) *

Calendar of the Grants of Probate and Letters of Administration made in the Prerogative Court of Canterbury, 1853-57, 1858, 16 vols. (London, n.d.) * (Appears on shelf as PROB 12/272-288)

P W Coldham, *American Wills and Administrations in the Prerogative Court of Canterbury, 1610-1857* (Baltimore, 1989) *

A List of Wills, Administrations etc. in the Public Record Office, London, England, 12-19th century (Baltimore, 1968) (A list of probate records in non PROB classes compiled c. 1932.) *

'Wills and Administrations in the Court of Delegates', in *The Genealogist,* new series 11 [1903], pp.165-171, 224-227; 12 [1903], pp.97-101. (Probate records in DEL 9.)

Typescript list of wills and related records in E 211 *

Card index to IR 26/287-IR 26/321, and typescript index to IR 26/322-IR 26/343 and IR 26/398-IR 26/399, wills proved and administrations granted in the consistory courts of Bangor, Bath and Wells, Bristol, Canterbury, Carlisle, Chester, Chichester, Durham, Ely, Exeter, and Oxford, and lesser courts within those dioceses in the period 1796-1811. *

Inventories, accounts and records relating to testamentary causes
Details of finding aids and indexes can be found below.

Records

Admiralty (at Kew)
ADM 48 Seamen's Wills. 1786-1909
ADM 96 Royal Marines Pay Office Records.1688-1862
ADM 142 Registers of Seamen's Wills. 1786-1909

High Court of Delegates (at Chancery Lane)
DEL 1 Processes. 1609-1834
DEL 2 Cause Papers. c.1600-1834
DEL 7 Case Books. 1796-1834
DEL 9 Muniment Books. 1652-1859
DEL 10 Wills, Affidavits, etc. 1636-1857
DEL 11 Miscellaneous Lists, Indexes, etc. 1707-1868

Foreign Office (at Kew)
FO 626 Embassy and Consular Archives. Turkey, Smyrna Consular Court. 1820-1929
FO 678 Embassy and Consular Archives. China: Various, Consulates Deeds, etc. 1837-1959
FO 917 Embassy and Consular Archives. China, Shanghai Supreme Court, Probate Records. 1857-1941

Inland Revenue (at Chancery Lane)
IR 26 Estate Duty Office, Death Duty Registers. 1796-1903
IR 27 Indexes to Death Duty Registers. 1796-1903. (Seen on microfilm.)

Supreme Court of Judicature (at Chancery Lane)
J 121 Contentious Probate Case Files and Papers. 1858-1960

Judicial Committee of the Privy Council (at Chancery Lane)
PCAP 1 Processes. 1834-1875. (Last date of 1858 for testamentary cases.)
PCAP 3 Case Books. 1834-1875. (Last date of 1858 for testamentary cases.)

Prerogative Court of Canterbury (at Chancery Lane)
PROB 2 Inventories Series I. 1417-1660. (The list is accompanied by an index of personal names.)
PROB 3 Inventories Series II. 1702, 1718-1782. (The list is accompanied by an index of personal names. List and Index Society 85-86.)
PROB 4 Parchment Inventories post 1660. 1661-1720. (There are card indexes to personal and place names. List and Index Society 221 covers pieces 1-6416 only and has no index.)
PROB 5 Paper Inventories. 1661-1732. (The list is accompanied by an index of personal names in pieces 1-6088, and another for pieces 6106-6180. List and Index Society 149 covers pieces 1-6105, and contains the index to 1-6088.)

PROB 6 Act Books: Administrations. 1559-1858 (Seen on microfilm.)
PROB 7 Act Books: Limited Administrations. 1810-1858
PROB 8 Act Books: Probates. 1526-1828
PROB 9 Act Books: Limited Probates. 1781-1858
PROB 10 Original Wills. 1484-1858
PROB 11 Registered Copy Wills. 1384-1858. (Seen on microfilm.)
PROB 12 Register Books. 1383-1858
PROB 13 Manuscript Calendars. 1384-1800
PROB 14 Warrants. 1666-1858
PROB 15 Duplicate Calendars and Register Books. 1655-1858
PROB 18 Allegations. 1661-1858. (There are card indexes to names of causes and names of testators and intestates.)
PROB 19 Proxies. 1674-1718
PROB 20 Supplementary Wills Series I. 1623-1838. (The list is indexed by personal name.)
PROB 22 Supplementary Wills Series III. 1827-1857. (The list is indexed by personal name.)
PROB 24 Depositions. 1657-1809
PROB 25 Answers. 1664-1854
PROB 26 Depositions Bound by Suit. 1826-1858. (The list is indexed by cause and name of testator or intestate.)
PROB 28 Cause Papers. 1642-1722. (The list is indexed by cause and by name of testator or intestate. List and Index Society 161.)
PROB 29 Acts of Court Book. 1536-1819
PROB 30 Acts of Court. 1740-1858
PROB 31 Exhibits, Main Class. 1722-1858. (There is a typescript index of wills in this class, and there are also card indexes of personal names and place names to the inventories and some of the other exhibits.)
PROB 32 Filed Exhibits with Inventories. 1662-1720. (The list is indexed by personal name. List and Index Society 204.)
PROB 33 Indexes to Exhibits. 1683-1858. (The original index to exhibits in PROB 31 and PROB 37.)
PROB 36 Exhibits pre-1722. 1653-1721. (There are card indexes to names of causes and names of testators and intestates.)
PROB 37 Cause Papers, Later Series. 1783-1858. (The list is indexed by testators and intestates. List and Index Society 184.)
PROB 38 Orders of Court Books. 1817-1857
PROB 46 Administration Bonds. 1714-1744
PROB 51 16th Century Administration Bonds. 1530-1600
PROB 52 Commissions for Wills. 1796-1857

Treasury Solicitor (at Chancery Lane)
TS 17 Bona Vacantia Division, Administration of Estates Case Papers.1698-1964

War Office (at Kew)
WO 25/1359-2410, 3251-3471: casualty returns, with a very few wills, 1809-1910
WO 42 Certificates of Birth, etc. 1755-1908. (Includes officers' wills: an index is available at Kew.)

7. Welsh genealogy

7.1 Welsh genealogy: records elsewhere

Much Welsh material, formerly held in the WALE classes at the PRO (including the records of the courts of great sessions, roughly equivalent to the English assizes), has been transferred to the National Library of Wales. The National Library also holds many parish registers and transcripts as well as wills, tithe records and personal and estate records. *Parish Registers of Wales* is a useful guide to the whereabouts of original parish registers and copies in Welsh record offices and libraries and in the library of the Society of Genealogists. For births, marriages and deaths from 1837, go to St Catherine's House (see **3.12**).

Most of the Welsh record offices produce their own genealogical leaflets, as does the Welsh Tourist Board. The high incidence of common names and the use of patronymics make Welsh genealogy difficult. You may be able to obtain help from the Honourable Society of Cymmrodorion.

One famous source which used to be in the PRO, the Golden Grove Book of Pedigrees (an early eighteenth century genealogical collection) is now in the care of the Dyfed Archives Service, Carmarthen Office, County Hall, Carmarthen SA31 1JP.

7.2 Welsh genealogy: records in the PRO

Most of the records discussed in this book should be as helpful in tracing the history of Welsh families as they are for English families. There are some specific records which, because they relate solely to Wales, or because they are arranged topographically, may be particularly helpful.

The nonconformist registers of births, marriages and deaths in RG 4 and RG 8 are a very fruitful source for Wales, 1700-1858, because of its strong nonconformist tradition: the lists are arranged by county (see **3** for more details). Census returns are also topographically arranged (see **2**). There are registers of ex-soldiers and sailors living in Wales who were in receipt of a Chelsea or Greenwich out-pension, 1842-1863 (WO 22/114-117). Some of the entries relate to widows and children.

The assize records for the Chester and North Wales circuit and the South Wales circuit, c.1831 onwards (ASSI 57-ASSI 67, ASSI 71-ASSI 77), effectively continue the records of the courts of great sessions, which are now in the National Library of Wales.

Among the earlier records that stayed in the PRO are the records of some of the marcher lordships and of the principality. Because of the history of its conquest by the Normans and Plantagenets, medieval Wales was composed of the principality (basically Anglesey, Caernarvon, Merioneth, Cardigan and Carmarthen), run by the crown, and several quasi-independent marcher lordships, some of which had fallen into the crown's possession. In the 1530s and 1540s Wales was divided into shires and given a form of local government based on the English model. The marcher lordships were not actually abolished, and some of them continued to provide local courts.

The PRO has an unsurpassed collection of records from the marcher lordship of Ruthin or Dyffryn Clwyd, stretching from the thirteenth to the nineteenth centuries, including court rolls with lists of tenants, views of frankpledge, lists of freeholders and inhabitants, and proceedings in the lordship court, which handled debt cases until the 1820s. The court rolls are in SC 2; the other records are in WALE 15.

There are also records from some other marcher lordships; most of these records are court rolls and surveys, and they are not as extensive as those of Ruthin. Records of marcher lordships held by the Duchy of Lancaster (Kidwelly, Ogmore, Monmouth, Brecon, Caldicot, Iscennen, etc) are in DL 28-DL 30, DL 41-DL 42 and SC 2). Records of marcher lordships which had fallen into crown hands are in SC 2, SC 6, SC 11, SC 12, LR 2, LR 9, LR 11 and LR 13. For more details, see **7.3** and the *Current Guide*, Part 1, section 353.

7.3 Welsh genealogy: bibliography and sources

[An * means this work can be seen at Chancery Lane: a # means it can be seen at Kew.]

Published works

C J Williams and J Watts-Williams, *Cofrestri Plwyf Cymru, Parish Registers of Wales* (National Library of Wales and Welsh County Archivists Group, 1986) *

G Hamilton Edwards, *In search of Welsh Ancestry* (Chichester, 1986) *

T J Morgan and P Morgan *Welsh Surnames* (Cardiff, 1985) *

B Rawlins, *The Parish Churches and Nonconformist Chapels of Wales: their records and where to find them* (Salt Lake City, 1987)

Guide to Genealogical Sources at the National Library of Wales (National Library of Wales leaflet).

Records

Assizes (at Chancery Lane)

ASSI 57 Chester and North Wales Circuit: Civil Minute Books. 1843-1934

ASSI 58 Chester and North Wales Circuit: Certificates of Judgement. 1914-1926

ASSI 59 Chester and North Wales Circuit: Pleadings. 1840-1927

ASSI 60 Chester and North Wales Circuit: Returns of Assize Business. 1867-1912

ASSI 61 Chester and North Wales Circuit: Crown Minute Books. 1831-1938

ASSI 62 Chester and North Wales Circuit: Crown Books. 1835-1883

ASSI 63 Chester and North Wales Circuit: Miscellaneous Books. 1694-1942

ASSI 64 Chester and North Wales Circuit: Indictments. 1831-1945

ASSI 65 Chester and North Wales Circuit: Depositions. 1831-1944

ASSI 66 Chester and North Wales Circuit: Coroners' Inquisitions. 1788-1891

ASSI 67 Chester and North Wales Circuit: Miscellanea. 1820-1890

ASSI 71 South Wales Circuit: Indictments. 1834-1945

ASSI 72 South Wales Circuit: Depositions. 1835-1944
ASSI 73 South Wales Circuit: Miscellanea. 1839-1937
ASSI 74 South Wales Circuit: Judgement Books. 1841-1842
ASSI 75 South Wales Circuit: Minute Books (Civil Court). 1846-1943
ASSI 76 South Wales Circuit: Minute Books (Crown Court). 1844-1942
ASSI 77 South Wales Circuit: Miscellaneous Books. 1837-1884

Palatinate of Chester (at Chancery Lane)
CHES classes (see *Guide to the Contents of the PRO*, vol. I) All 38 classes may
    contain information on inhabitants of Chester, Flint and parts of North Wales.

Duchy of Lancaster (at Chancery Lane)
DL 28 Duchy of Lancaster: Various Accounts. Edward I to Victoria
DL 29 Duchy of Lancaster: Ministers' Accounts. Edward I to 1851
DL 30 Duchy of Lancaster: Court Rolls. Edward I to 1925
DL 41 Duchy of Lancaster: Miscellanea. Henry III to Victoria
DL 42 Duchy of Lancaster: Miscellaneous Books. John to 1894

Auditors of Land Revenue (at Chancery Lane)
LR 2 Miscellaneous Books. Henry V to 1841
LR 9 Land Revenue Auditors' Memoranda. Edward I to 1834
LR 11 Land Revenue Estreats of Court Rolls. Edward I to George III
LR 12 Land Revenue Receivers' Accounts Series III. Henry VII to 1832

General Register Office (at Chancery Lane)
RG 4 General Register Office: Registers of Births, Marriages and Deaths, surren-
    dered to the Non-Parochial Registers Commissions of 1837 and 1857. 1567-
    1858
RG 8 General Register Office: Registers of Births, Marriages and Deaths, surren-
    dered to the Non-Parochial Registers Commission of 1857, and other registers
    and church records. 1646-1970.

Special Collections (at Chancery Lane)
SC 2 Court Rolls. c.1200-c.1900
SC 6 Ministers' and Receivers' Accounts. Henry III to 1691
SC 11 Rental and Surveys (Rolls). Henry III to William IV
SC 12 Rental and Surveys (Portfolios). Henry III to William IV

Principality of Wales (at Chancery Lane)
WALE 15 Ruthin Records. 1343-1808
WALE 20 Caernarvon Plea Rolls. 1386-1533
WALE 29 Ancient Deeds Series F. Edward I to Elizabeth I
WALE 30 Ancient Deeds Series FF. c.1507-1633
WALE 31 Modern Welsh Deeds. James II to 19th century

War Office (at Kew)
WO 22/114-117: Chelsea and Greenwich pensions, payable in West Wales and East
    Wales, 1842-1862

89.2 Bing etc.

Dolphin

YOU CAN'T BUY A BETTER SHOWER

THE BEST SHOWER MONEY CAN BUY

SENSORFLOW

- 100% SAFE FOR CHILDREN
- 28 DIFFERENT SETTINGS
- SAVE TIME AND MONEY ON TAKING A BATH. IT'S 10 TIMES BETTER VALUE
- TOTAL CONTROL OF WATER TEMPERATURES AT THE TOUCH OF A BUTTON
- FABULOUS RANGE OF CABINETS
- LOW PRESSURE PROBLEM? NO PROBLEM!
- TOTAL SERVICE FROM SURVEY TO GUARANTEE.

8. Scottish genealogy

8.1. Scottish genealogy: records in Scotland

Civil registration of births, marriages and deaths began in Scotland on 1 January 1855. The records, along with many parish registers (c.1700-1855), minor foreign registers from 1855, and the decennial census returns for 1841-1891, are held by the Registrar General in Edinburgh at New Register House, Edinburgh EH1 3YT.

Wills, judicial records, deeds etc., are in the Scottish Record Office: see Sinclair's guide to genealogical research in the Scottish Record Office. The Scottish Genealogy Society, the Scots Ancestry Research Society and the Association of Scottish Genealogists and Record Agents are available to undertake paid research. For information about clans, contact the Scottish Tartan Society.

8.2 Scottish genealogy: records in the PRO

The PRO has the wills of Scots possessed of property in the form of goods, money and investments in England (see **6**), and also the records of Scottish churches in England (see **3.4** and **3.8**). The Apprenticeship Books include details of Scottish apprentices (see **27**) and Scotsmen are well represented in the records of the Merchant Navy (see **25**), the Metropolitan Police (see **23.1**), and of course, the armed forces.

The records of the Army are particularly fruitful, because of the territorial base of so many regiments and militia regiments (see **18**). For ex-soldiers and ex-sailors living in Scotland and in receipt of a Chelsea or Greenwich pension, there are registers arranged by district pay office (e.g. Ayr, Paisley) for 1842-1862 (WO 22/118-140). Some of the entries relate to widows and children. For Scottish emigrants to North America see **14.7**.

8.3 Scottish genealogy: bibliography and sources

[An * means this work can be seen at Chancery Lane: a # means it can be seen at Kew.]

Published works

J P S Ferguson, *Scottish Family Histories* (Edinburgh, 1986)
* G Hamilton Edwards, *In search of Scottish Ancestry* (Chichester, 1986)
D Moody, *Scottish Family History* (London, 1988)
* *Scotland, A Genealogical Research Guide* (Salt Lake City, 1987)
C Sinclair, *Guide to Ancestry Research in the Scottish Record Office* (London, 1990)
D J Steel, ed., *Sources for Scottish Genealogy and Family History* (London, 1970) *

Records

War Office (at Kew)
WO 22/118-140: Chelsea and Greenwich pensions payable in Scotland, 1842-1862

9. Irish genealogy

9.1 Irish genealogy: records in Ireland

So many Irish records have been lost or destroyed that it is well worth making a preliminary approach to the Irish Genealogical Research Society for help: the address is given at **48.2**.

The civil registration of births, marriages and deaths in Ireland began on 1 January 1864. The records for the whole of Ireland until 1921, for the republic of Ireland from 1921 to date, and of non-Roman Catholic marriages from 1 April 1845 are in the custody of the Registrar General in Dublin. Surviving Church of Ireland parish registers are still with the incumbents concerned or in the Irish Public Record Office. The National Library in Kildare Street, Dublin, holds microfilm copies of Roman Catholic parish registers, few of which pre-date 1820.

Census returns for all of Ireland are held in the Public Record Office in Dublin. Unfortunately, the survival of Irish census returns is slight before 1901. Returns for 1901 and 1911 are fairly complete and are open; D F Begley's book, *Irish Genealogy*, lists what other returns still exist county by county.

Virtually all Irish probate records prior to 1904 were destroyed in 1922: Vicars's index to them is now the only clue to what was there. For records of land holding from 1708, try the Registry of Deeds in Dublin.

The records of births, marriages and deaths in Northern Ireland since 1 January 1922 are with the Registrar General in Belfast. Many Presbyterian registers are still with the congregations, while others are held by the Presbyterian Historical Society in Belfast, which specialises in the history of Presbyterianism and its ministers.

The Public Record Office of Northern Ireland has copies and extracts of many Ulster wills, and for a fee, the Ulster Historical Foundation (at the same address), will undertake genealogical searches. The Ulster Genealogical and Historical Guild publishes a newsletter and a regular list of research in progress.

9.2 Irish genealogy: records in the PRO

Some of the records discussed more fully elsewhere in this book may be helpful in tracing Irish family history. The wills of Irish people who died with goods in England may have been proved by the Prerogative Court of Canterbury before 1858 (see **6**). The records of the Irish Tontines of 1773, 1775 and 1777 (discussed in **44**) cover 1773-1871, and list many people, with addresses. The records of the Royal Irish Constabulary are full and informative: see **23.2**.

Of course, many Irishmen served in the Army and the Navy, and their records should be explored as described in **18** and **19**: see, for example, the muster rolls of the Irish militia, 1793-1876, in WO 13. Before the Union with the United Kingdom in 1801, Ireland had a separate Army with its own organisation and establishment. From 1801, Ireland remained a separate command, and the Irish regiments retained their Irish identity, but the Army was merged with the British Army. Records relating to the Army in Ireland, 1775-1923, are in WO 35.

The Royal Kilmainham Hospital, founded in 1679, acted as a permanent hospital for disabled soldiers (in-pensioners) and also distributed money to out-pensioners: there are registers of in- and out-pensioners in the admission books, 1704-1922 (WO 118), and discharge documents, 1783-1822 (WO 119). Other Irish soldiers and sailors had their pensions paid by the Royal Chelsea Hospital or by Greenwich Hospital. Records of these pensions, 1842-1862 and 1882-1883, are in WO 22/141-205 and 209-225, arranged by district: they are useful for tracing changes of residence and dates of death.

The only separate naval records for Irishmen are of nominations to serve in the Irish Coastguard, 1821-1849 (ADM 175/99-100).

For Irish Revenue Police, 1830-1857, who tried to prevent illicit distilling, try CUST 111: see also **24.4**.

For records in the PRO relating to Irish history, and only incidentally to Irish genealogy, see A Prochaska's book, *Irish History from 1700: A Guide to Sources in the Public Record Office*.

9.3 Irish genealogy: bibliography and sources

[An * means this work can be seen at Chancery Lane: a # means it can be seen at Kew.]

Published works

D Begley, *Handbook on Irish Genealogy* (Dublin, 1976)
D Begley, ed. *Irish Genealogy; a Record Finder* (Dublin, 1982)
B de Breffny, *Bibliography of Irish Family History and Genealogy* (Cork and Dublin, 1974)
E MacLysaght, *Bibliography of Irish Family History* (2nd edn 1982)
W Nolan, *Tracing the Past. Sources for Local Studies in the Republic of Ireland* (Dublin, 1982)
A Prochaska, *Irish History from 1700: A Guide to Sources in the Public Record Office* (British Records Association and Institute of Historical Research, 1986)*
A Vicars ed., *Index to the Prerogative Wills of Ireland, 1536-1810*, (Dublin, 1897) *

Records

Admiralty (at Kew)
ADM 175/99-100: nominations for appointment to serve in the Irish Coastguard, 1821-1849

Board of Customs and Excise (at Kew)
CUST 110 Board of Excise: Irish Board and Establishment. 1824-1833
CUST 111 Irish Revenue Police. 1830-1857

National Debt Office (at Kew)
NDO 3 Irish Tontines. 1773-1871

War Office (at Kew)
WO 13 Militia and Volunteers Muster Books and Pay Lists. 1780-1878
WO 2/141-203 and 209-225: Chelsea and Greenwich pensions payable in Ireland,
    1842-1862 and 1882-1883
WO 35 Ireland. 1775-1923. Some pieces closed for 50 or 75 years.
WO 118 Royal Hospital Kilmainham Admission Books. 1704-1922
WO 119 Royal Hospital Kilmainham Discharge Documents of Pensioners. 1783-
    1822

10. Isle of Man genealogy

10.1 Manx genealogy

The civil registration of marriages on the Isle of Man began in 1849, and of births and deaths in 1878.The *IGI* (see **3.3**) is complete for Manx baptisms and marriages.The records are held by the island's General Registry, and searches of them will be made by that office for a fee. You can also obtain information about wills from the Registry, but all other records are kept in the Manx Museum Library.

In the PRO there are lists of charitable Manx bequests (HO 99). The censuses also cover the Isle of Man (see **2**). Of course, islanders may well turn up in any of the armed services and other records as described in this book: topographically arranged records, such as the payments of pensions to ex-soldiers and sailors on the Isle of Man, 1852-1862 in WO 22/207, are particularly useful.

10.2 Manx genealogy: bibliography and sources

Published works

J Narasinham, *The Manx Family Tree: A Beginners' Guide to Records in the Isle of Man* (Isle of Man, 1986)

Records

Home Office (at Kew)
HO 99 Channel Islands, etc., Entry Books. 1760-1921

War Office (at Kew)
WO 22/207: Chelsea and Greenwich pensions payable to ex-soldiers and sailors in the Isle of Man, 1852-1862

11. Channel Islands genealogy

11.1 Jersey

Records of baptism, marriage and burial before 1842 are held by the parish clergy, who may issue extracts from the registers in their custody. The civil registration of births, marriages and deaths in Jersey began in 1842. Registers of births, non-Anglican marriages and deaths are held by the Registrars of the island's twelve parishes. The registers of marriages in the Anglican church are still in the custody of the parish priests. Duplicate registers of all births, marriages and deaths are held by the Superintendent Registrar and he, like the Parochial Registrars and the clergy, can undertake searches and issue certified extracts from those registers in his custody. The Superintendent Registrar is unable to undertake genealogical research of a general nature. In such cases the enquirer is advised to contact either the Société Jersiaise or the Channel Islands Family History Society, one of whose members may be prepared to assist in the search.

Some records of births, marriages and deaths in Jersey are in the PRO, among the foreign registers in RG 32, indexed by RG 43.

The Association Oath roll for Jersey (C 213/462) appears by its length to contain the signatures, or marks and names, of all the island's men in 1696. The censuses also cover Jersey (see **2**).

Details of ex-soldiers and sailors in receipt of a Chelsea or Greenwich pension, or their widows and orphans, living in Jersey, 1842-1862, may be found in WO 22/205-206. Many of the other records described in this book will also include islanders.

11.2 Guernsey, Alderney and Sark

Pre-civil registration records are held by the rectors of the ten Guernsey parishes, and by the vicars of Alderney and Sark.

Civil registration of births, deaths and non-Anglican marriages in Guernsey began in 1840; in Alderney in 1850; and in Sark, of deaths in 1915, marriages in 1919 and births in 1925. From 1919 all marriages and from 1925 all births and deaths in Guernsey, Alderney and Sark have been registered centrally in Guernsey by Her Majesty's Greffier in his capacity as Registrar-General of Births, Deaths and Marriages. Enquiries relating to Alderney should be addressed to the Clerk of the Court; and to Sark to the Registrar.

Some records of births, marriages and deaths in Guernsey, Alderney and Sark are in the PRO, among the foreign registers in RG 32, indexed by RG 43.

Deeds, judicial records and wills may be consulted by searchers in person at the Greffe, Guernsey; all are indexed. Permission to consult wills of personalty from 1664 should be obtained from the Registrar of the Ecclesiastical Court.

Microfilm copies of the 1841-1881 census returns for Guernsey, Alderney and Sark are also held at the Greffe (see also **2**).

Pedigrees of leading island families are held at the Priaulx Library, St Peter Port, Guernsey.

Details of ex-soldiers and sailors in receipt of a Chelsea or Greenwich pension, or their widows and orphans, living in the Channel Islands, 1842-1852, may be found in WO 22/205.

11.3 Channel Islands genealogy: bibliography and sources

Published works

L R Burnes, 'Genealogical Research in the Channel Islands', *Genealogists' Magazine,* vol. XIX, pp. 169-172
J Conway Davies,'The Records of the Royal Courts', La Société Guernesiaise, *Transactions*, vol. XVI, pp. 404-414
David W Le Poidevin, *How to Trace your Ancestors in Guernsey* (Taunton, 1978)
List of Records in the Greffe, Guernsey (List and Index Society, 1969-1978). Additional lists may be consulted in typescript at the Greffe.

Records

Chancery (at Chancery Lane)
C 213/462: Association Oath roll for Jersey, 1696

Home Office (at Kew)
HO 99 Channel Islands etc., Entry Books. 1760-1921

General Register Office (at Chancery Lane)
RG 32 Miscellaneous Foreign Returns. 1831-1958
RG 43 Miscellaneous Foreign Returns of Births, Marriages and Deaths: Indexes

War Office (at Kew)
WO 22/205: Chelsea and Greenwich pensions payable in the Channel Islands, 1842-1852
WO 22/206: Chelsea and Greenwich pensions payable in Jersey, 1852-1862

12. Immigrants to Britain

12.1 Immigration records

A system of registration of aliens (i.e. foreigners) entering the country was first set up by the Aliens Act of 1793, and was modified by subsequent statutes. Declarations signed by the aliens were certified into the Aliens Office, which became part of the Home Office in 1836. The early certificates appear to have been destroyed by the Home Office, but there are two survivals. Aliens arriving in English ports, 1810-1811, may be traced in FO 83/21-22. Additionally, an index of destroyed certificates, 1826-1849, survives in HO 5/25-32.

Home Office certificates of aliens arriving in England and Scotland between 1836 and 1852 are available, giving nationality, profession, date of arrival, last country visited and sometimes other information as well (HO 2): they are arranged by year, under the ports of arrival. Lists of alien passengers, 1836-1869, were sent into the Home Office by the masters of ships (HO 3): they are bound up in date order, and there is no name index.

For immigrants arriving by sea between 1878 and 1960, from places outside Europe and the Mediterranean area, the Inward Passenger Lists (BT 26) can be a useful source of information. They give name, age, occupation and address in the United Kingdom, and the date of entry, but no indication of the intended length of stay. Unfortunately, there are no name indexes and, as BT 26 is a very large class, it is vital to know at least an approximate date of arrival, or the port of entry, or the name of the ship. After 1906 the Registers of Passenger Lists (BT 32) give, under each port, the names of the ships and their dates of arrival. The Passenger Lists after 1960 have not been preserved: there are none for arrivals by air.

12.2 Refugees

Many early refugees came to England to escape religious persecution of Protestants and Jews on the continent (see section **32.4** and **35**). Others came for political reasons. Many of the exiles from the Palatinate, shipped from Holland to England *en route* to the Americas in 1709, chose to stay in England instead: for more details see **14.4**.

The PRO has records of annuities and pensions paid to some refugees for services to the crown. These include, for example, pensions to American loyalists, 1780-1855, allowances to Polish refugees, 1828-1856 (PMG 53, and T 1/409), and allowances to Spaniards, 1855-1909 (PMG 53, and T 1/4285). The influx of French émigrés between 1789 and 1814 produced much government documentation (HO 69, PC 1, FO 95 and WO 1). In particular, the records of the Treasury's French Refugee Relief Committee, 1792-1828, contain lists of names of those receiving pensions (T 50, T 93).

For Belgian refugees, 1914-1919, there is a considerable amount of material entered on the 'history cards' in MH 8/39-93. Each card relates to a whole family, unless the refugee was single with no known relatives. The details given are names, ages, relationships, wife's maiden name, allowances and the address for payment.

For the Second World War, there are the personal files relating to internees, 1940-1949 (HO 24): some of these are closed for 50 years. For Poles who fought in Polish units attached to allied armies, try the records of the Polish Resettlement Corps, set up in 1946 to ease their transition to civilian life in Britain and abroad (WO 315).

Other records relating to Polish resettlement are in AST 18. Many of these records are in Polish, and some are closed for 75 years.

12.3 Denization and naturalisation

Foreigners resident in England, wishing to regularise their position, could apply for denization (which granted them most of a free subject's rights and the protection of the king's laws) or naturalisation (which granted them all). However, most foreign settlers did not bother to go through these legal formalities, and so do not appear in these records.

An alien was made a denizen by letters patent from the crown: as a denizen, he could purchase land, but could not inherit it. Any children born after the parents' denization appear to have been subjects: those born before could only be denizens. Denizens had the additional burden of paying a higher rate of tax, and were ineligible for government posts. Letters patent of denization were enrolled on the Patent Rolls (C 66) and the Supplementary Patent Rolls (C 67). Denizations before 1509 can be traced through the indexes to the *Calendar of Patent Rolls:* in the early volumes individual names are not given in the index, and it is necessary to look under 'Denizations' or *'Indigenae'*. For the period 1509 to 1800, indexes to denizations have been published by the Huguenot Society. A copy of these, together with a typescript index to denizations between 1801 and 1873, is attached to the list of HO 1, available at both Kew and Chancery Lane.

Naturalisation was more expensive than denization: it originally required a private act of Parliament, as well as swearing of the oaths of allegiance and supremacy. It made the foreigner into the king's subject, able to inherit land, and affected the children born before naturalisation as well. Indexes to naturalisation by private act of Parliament up to 1900 are attached to the HO 1 list, available at both Kew and Chancery Lane. Between 1708 and 1711, all foreign Protestants who took the oaths of allegiance and supremacy in open court were deemed to have been naturalised (KB 24, E 169/86; see **15.1**). The information from these oath rolls has been published by the Huguenot Society. Between 1740 and 1773, foreign Protestants in the Americas were naturalised by the same process: see **14.4**.

In 1844, naturalisation procedure was simplified, and the Home Office began granting certificates of naturalisation. Copies of naturalisation certificates issued between 1844 and 1871 are available in HO 1 (they were also enrolled on the Close Rolls, C 54, until 1873): those issued between 1870 and 1949 are in HO 334. Related correspondence on individual naturalisations may exist in HO 1 for 1844 to 1871, in HO 45 for 1872 to 1878, and in HO 144 from 1879 to 1919. The Home Office will consider applications from descendants to see closed correspondence after 1920. There is a joint index to these classes (HO 1, HO 45, HO 144 and HO 334), attached to the HO 1 list. This gives name, country of origin, date of the certificate, place of residence (e.g. Liverpool), and the reference to the copy of the certificate and to any related papers. This index goes up to 1935: between 1936 and 1962, annual returns of aliens were presented to Parliament, and were printed as parliamentary papers. These are available in the Reference Room at Kew.

Enquiries about recent naturalisations should be sent to the Home Office: see **48.7** for the address.

12.4 Immigrants to Britain: bibliography and sources

[An * means this work can be seen at Chancery Lane: a # means it can be seen at Kew.]

Published works

Calendar of Close Rolls, 1227-1509 (London, 1892-1963) *

Calendar of Patent Rolls, 1216-1509, 1547-1582 (London, 1894-1986) *

Calendar of State Papers, Domestic Series, 1547-1704 (London, 1856-1972) *

Calendar of Treasury Papers, 1557-1728 (London, 1868-1889) *#

Home Office Certificates of Naturalisation, Index, 1844-1935 (London, 1908-1937)*#

R E G Kirk, *Returns of Aliens in London, 1523-1603* (Huguenot Society, vol. X, London, 1900-1908)

W Page, *Denization and Naturalisation of Aliens in England, 1509-1603* (Huguenot Society, vol. VIII, Lymington, 1893)

Public Record Office, *Immigrants: Documents in the PRO* (Information Leaflet) *#

Registers of Churches, of Huguenots in London and elsewhere (Huguenot Society, London, 1887-1956)

Rotuli Parliamentorum, Edward I to Henry VII (London, 1783, Index, London, 1832)*

W A Shaw, *Letters of Denization and Acts of Naturalisation for Aliens in England, 1603-1800* (Huguenot Society, Lymington, 1911, Manchester, 1923 and London, 1932) *#

Unpublished finding aids

Index to Denizations, 1801-1873, and to Acts of Naturalisation, 1801-1935, attached to HO 1 list *#

Indexes to 'Foreign' Churches *

Index of Memorials for Denizations and Naturalisations, 1835-1844 *

B Lloyd, List and Registers of Dutch Chapel Royal, 1689-1825 *

Records

National Assistance Board (at Kew)
AST 18 Polish Resettlement. 1946-1968. (Some pieces closed for 75 years.)

Board of Trade (at Kew)
BT 26 Passenger Lists, Inwards. 1878-1960
BT 32 Registers of Passenger Lists. 1906-1951

Chancery (at Chancery Lane)
C 54 Close Rolls. 1204-1903. (For enrolments of naturalisation certificates, 1844-1873.)

C 65 Parliament Rolls. 1327-1986
C 66 Patent Rolls. 1201-1962
C 67 Supplementary Patent Rolls. 1275-1749

Colonial Office (at Kew)
CO 388 Board of Trade, Original Correspondence. 1654-1792

Exchequer (at Chancery Lane)
E 169 Oaths of Allegiance, etc. 1709-1868
E 179 Subsidy Rolls. Henry VIII to William and Mary. (For lists of foreigners in
    London, 1423-1581.)
E 196 Sacrament Certificates. 1700-1827

Foreign Office (at Kew)
FO 83/21-22: aliens arriving in English ports, 1810-1811
FO 95 Miscellanea. 1639-1950

Home Office (at Kew)
HO 1 Denizations and Naturalisations. 1789-1871
HO 2 Aliens Act 1836, Certificates of Aliens. 1836-1852. (Index to this class is in HO
    5/25-32.)
HO 3 Aliens Act 1836, Returns and Papers. 1836-1869
HO 5 Aliens Entry Books. 1794-1921
HO 45 Registered Papers. 1839-1971
HO 69 Bouillon Papers. 1779-1809
HO 144 Registered Papers, Supplementary. 1868-1947. (Some closed for up to 100
    years: all papers up to 1919 are open.)
HO 214 Internees: Personal Files. 1940-1949. Some closed for 50 years.
HO 334 Duplicate Certificates of Naturalistion. 1870-1949

Court of King's Bench (at Chancery Lane)
KB 24 Swearing or Oath Books. 1673-1944. (Published in Huguenot Society vol.
    XXVII.)

Ministry of Health (at Kew)
MH 8 War Refugees Committee. 1914-1919

Privy Council Office (at Chancery Lane)
PC 1 Papers. 1481-1946

Paymaster General's Office (at Kew)
PMG 53 Allowances to Polish Refugees and Distressed Spaniards. 1855-1909

State Paper Office (at Chancery Lane)
SP 10 State Papers, Domestic, Edward VI
SP 11 State Papers, Domestic, Mary I
SP 12 State Papers, Domestic, Elizabeth I
SP 44 Entry Books. 1661-1828 (For denizations, 1681-1688, see SP 44/67.)

SP 84 State Papers, Foreign, Holland. c.1560-1780

Treasury (at Kew)
T 50 Documents relating to Refugees. 1780-1856
T 93 French Refugees' Relief Comittee. 1792-1828

War Office (at Kew)
WO 1 In-Letters. 1732-1868
WO 315 Army Records Centre (Polish Section): Polish Records, 1939-1950. 1932-
    1953. (Some pieces closed for 75 years.)

13. British nationals abroad

13.1 Licences to pass beyond the seas

For the late sixteenth and early seventeenth century, there are registers of people
going overseas, in E 157. The earliest dates from 1572-1578. There are lists of
soldiers taking the oath of allegiance before going to the wars in the Low Countries,
1613-1624, and licences to go abroad, mostly to Holland, 1624-1632. The registers
of passengers to New England, Barbados and other colonies, 1634-1639, and 1677,
have been printed by J C Hotten.

13.2 Passports

Before the First World War, it was rare for someone travelling abroad to apply for a
passport: most holders of passports were merchants or diplomats. Records of
passports are disappointing for the genealogist, as they contain little information.

Entry books of passes issued by the Secretaries of State, 1697-1784, are in SP 44/386-
411, at Chancery Lane: another entry book, 1748-1794, is in FO 366/544, at Kew.
There is no index.

There are registers of passports issued, 1795-1948 in FO 610: for March to May 1915,
the register is in FO 613/2. The entries are chronological, and show merely the date,
the number of the passport issued, and the name of the applicant. There are indexes
for 1851-1862 and 1874-1916, but they give no more information (FO 611).

A very miscellaneous collection of over 2,000 British and foreign passports, 1802-
1961, is in FO 655; they are listed haphazardly, giving date and place of issue. A small
selection of case papers, 1916-1983, is in FO 737.

For more detail, it may be worth checking in the correspondence of the Passport
Office, 1815-1905 (FO 612/21-71). Records of British passports issued in foreign
countries and British colonies may sometimes be found in consular and colonial
records; see the published guides to Foreign Office and Colonial Office records for

more information. These may also be useful for general records of Britons abroad.

For births, marriages and deaths of Britons abroad, see **4**. For wills proved in British probate courts in Turkey and China, see **6.7**.

13.3 The British in India

The PRO is not the place to trace Britons in India. Most of the records of the British in India, including the registration of baptisms, marriages and burials, and also wills, are preserved at the India Office Library and Records. The National Army Museum also has useful material (see **18.26**), and there is a good selection of printed material in the library of the Society of Genealogists. The British Association for Cemeteries in South Asia is also worth contacting: the address is given at **48.3**.

13.4 British nationals abroad: bibliography and sources

[An * means this work can be seen at Chancery Lane: a # means it can be seen at Kew.]

Published works

I A Baxter, *Brief Guide to Biographical Sources in the India Office Library* (London, 1979)
British Library, *India Office Records, Sources for Family History Research* (London, 1988)
I V Fitzhugh, 'East India Company Ancestry', *Genealogists' Magazine*, vol. XXI, pp. 150-154
J C Hotten, *Original Lists of Persons Emigrating to America, 1600-1700* (London, 1874) *
M Moir, *A General Guide to the India Office Records* (London, 1988)
Public Record Office, *The Records of the Colonial and Dominions Office* (London, 1964) *#
Public Record Office, *The Records of the Foreign Office 1782-1939* (London, 1969) *#
Public Record Office, *Passport Records* (Information Leaflet) *#

Records

Exchequer (at Chancery Lane)
E 157 Licences to pass beyond the seas. 1572-1677

Foreign Office (at Kew)
FO 366/544: entry books of passes, 1748-1794
FO 610 Passport Office: Passport Registers. 1795-1948
FO 611 Passport Office: Index to Names. 1851-1916
FO 612/1-71: Passport Office correspondence, 1815-1905
FO 613/2: passport register, March-May 1915
FO 655 Passports. 1802-1961
FO 737 Passport Office Case Papers. 1916-1983

14. Voluntary emigrants

14.1. Emigrants: general sources

For records of births, marriages and deaths of Britons abroad, see **4**.

If you are trying to trace ancestors back *into* the United Kingdom, there is little likelihood of finding a family before the central registration of births, marriages and deaths (1837 in England and Wales, 1855 in Scotland) *unless* their place of origin is known. It is essential to do some preliminary research among published means of reference and in the archives of the emigrant's place of destination before starting the search in the Public Record Office. For more information on possible sources, see the sections on specific destinations, below.

The PRO has many records relating to emigration but, because of the nature and limited scope of many of them, there can be no certainty of finding information on any particular individual. The PRO information leaflet, *Emigrants: documents in the Public Record Office*, is full of suggestions of possible sources. Involuntary emigrants are easier to trace: see **40**, on the transportation of convicts. For emigrants to specific places, read the relevant sections below, as well as this one.

Much of the more easily accessible information about emigrants to America and Australia has been published over the years: the most useful items are listed in the bibliographies at **14.7** and **40.5**.

The records of the Colonial Office include much material relating to emigrants. Emigration Original Correspondence, 1817-1896 (CO 384) contains many letters from settlers or people intending to settle in North America, Australia, the West Indies and other places: there are separate registers for North America for 1850-1863 (CO 327) and 1864-1868 (CO 328). The Emigration Entry Books, 1814-1871 (CO 385) and the Land and Emigration Commission Papers, 1833-1894 (CO 386) give names of emigrants.

Another possibility, for all colonies, is to trawl the registers of Colonial Office correspondence, which are arranged geographically: some are kept in the Reference Room, Kew. However, many of the documents referred to in the registers have not survived.

The Treasury handled a considerable volume of colonial business: the best way to find relevant information is to use the published calendars, where they exist, which give references back to the records. Similarly, the best way to discover material in the Privy Council records relating to emigrants is to use the printed *Acts of the Privy Council of England, Colonial Series 1613-1783*.

Many poor emigrants were provided with assistance for the passage by their parish, under the provisions of the 1834 Poor Law Amendment Act. The records of the administration of this assistance (MH 12) can include lists of emigrants, giving their occupation and destination: however, they are arranged by county and Poor Law Union, not by name, and can be very difficult to find. Other records relating to parish-organised emigration will be found locally: see the article by Burchall.

Outwards Passenger Lists, 1890-1960 (BT 27) are lists of passengers leaving the United Kingdom by sea for destinations outside Europe and the Mediterranean area. They give the name, age, occupation and some sort of address of the passengers, but they are arranged by year and port of departure, and there are no name indexes. The Registers of Passenger Lists, 1906-1951 (BT 32) list the ships leaving each port, which can be a useful way of finding the right record in BT 27.

A long search in the following sample of records may be successful. The Admiralty records include, for instance, medical journals from emigrant ships (ADM 101), and registers of troops (ADM 108, MT 23) shipped to various parts of the world. The Audit Office accounts have references to pensions paid to colonists (AO 1 - AO 3), and the Patent Rolls (C 66) contain entries relating to grants of offices and lands in America and elsewhere.

One potentially useful source for tracing people in receipt of a pension payable by the War Office (usually ex-soldiers and sailors, but also members of the East India Services) may be the registers of pension payments, 1842-1883, in WO 22, which are arranged by place of payment. There are separate registers for places like Canada, New South Wales and New Zealand, but also composite registers for miscellaneous colonies and for 'consuls' - who presumably had the responsibility for administering payments in foreign countries rather than colonies. The pensions were sometimes to widows or dependent children.

The awards of pensions to soldiers in British regiments stationed abroad, and in native or colonial regiments, 1817-1903, may be traced in WO 23/147-160. These registers are arranged by the date of the board which granted admission to pension, but entries relating to a particular place (e.g. Canada, West Indies, the Cape) are fairly easy to find. These registers can provide a birthplace and details of service. Many of the entries relate to British soldiers who left the army while their regiment was abroad, and who appear to have settled there.

14.2 Emigrants to North America and the West Indies: material elsewhere

If you are tracing an ancestor back into Britain from North America, try to do some research locally before coming to the Public Record Office. In particular, try to get some idea of the port and date of entry into the new country, and the county or smaller area in the United Kingdom that your ancestor came from.

Records of immigration to the USA are held in the National Archives in Washington, along with service records, land records and census returns. Proper censuses began in the USA in 1790, and are available on microfilm. Registers of births, marriages and deaths are held by the individual state archives. The Public Archives of Canada has census returns on microfilm going back to the earliest French-Canadian census of 1666 and 1667. The French-Canadian records at Quebec are particularly full.

Photocopies, microfilms and transcripts of much of the PRO's North American material can be consulted at the Library of Congress, some state libraries, and the Public Archives of Canada. The Genealogical Society of Utah has microfilm copies of the 1841-1881 census returns for England and Wales, and a huge index containing a great deal of information from British sources.

There are several genealogical societies in North America, which it may prove useful to contact. The main national ones are the National Genealogical Society, for the USA, and the Family History Association of Canada. There is also the International Society for British Genealogy and Family History, based in North America.

14.3 Emigrants to North America and the West Indies: British emigrants

The PRO has a lot of material relating to early emigration to the West Indian and American colonies. Much of this has been printed in some form. Most of it is administrative in character, but it can include useful genealogical material. Main published sources include the records of the Privy Council (PC 1, PC 2 and PC 5), printed as *Acts of the Privy Council of England, Colonial Series*. Various useful classes of Treasury papers have been described and indexed in the *Calendar of Treasury Papers, 1557 to 1728* and the *Calendar of Treasury Books and Papers, 1729 to 1745*.

The major early collection of papers relating to the West Indies and the American colonies (CO 1) has been described and indexed in the *Calendar of State Papers, Colonial, America and West Indies*, which includes references to the many other succeeding classes as well.

For unfree emigrants, see **40**.

Registers of passengers bound for New England, Barbados, Maryland, Virginia and other colonies survive for 1634-1639, and for 1677 (E 157): the information in them, together with similar information (from CO 1) has been printed in Hotten. There is a considerable amount of information on the inhabitants of Barbados, 1678-1680, including lists of property owners, their wives, children, servants and slaves, some parish registers, and lists of the militia (CO 1/44 no. 47 i-xxxvii, CO 29/9 pp.1-3): there is a descriptive list of the various records (with no names) in the *Calendar of State Papers, Colonial America and West Indies, 1677-1680*, no. 1236 i-xxxvii, which should be consulted first. The white inhabitants of Barbados were listed in a census in 1715 (CO 28/16).

A useful, though unfortunately short-lived, register (T 47/9-12) was kept of emigrants going from England, Wales, and Scotland to the New World between 1773 and 1776.

The information for England and Wales has been summarised in a card index, available at Kew, which gives name, age, occupation, reason for leaving the country, last place of residence, date of departure, and destination.

Some information on colonists is contained in the correspondence and papers of the Colonial Office, which cover the West Indies as well as the continent of America, and start in 1574: see the printed calendars listed in **14.7**. The Chancery Town Depositions (C 24) contain interesting information about life in early colonial America, including much genealogical data, but they are not well listed: see the article by Currer-Briggs for reference to an index.

Details on tracts of land in West and East New Jersey, Pennsylvania, New England and elsewhere are in the records of the West New Jersey Society (TS 12), a company formed in 1691 for the division of the land. There are many names in the correspondence, minute books, share transfers, deeds and claims.

In 1696, the mayor, recorder and commonalty of New York City swore the oath of association in support of William III: the resulting oath roll contains the signatures and marks of much of the male population of the city (C 213/470: see **15.1**).

Records relating to slave owners in the West Indies, 1812-1846, are among Treasury, Audit Office and National Debt Office papers (T 71, AO 14, NDO 4).

During and after the American War of Independence, many people suffered losses on account of their loyalty to the British crown. They were entitled to claim compensation under the Treaty of Peace in 1783 and a new Treaty of Amity between Great Britain and the United States of America in 1794. The Treasury records contain the reports of commissioners investigating individual claims, and some compensation and pension lists, 1780-1835 (T 50, T 79). Commissioners were also appointed in 1802, and their papers contain lists of claimants of pensions, and papers supporting their claims (AO 12, AO 13). The Declared Accounts of the Audit Office (AO 1) contain the accounts of payments and pensions made. Similar claims for compensation to loyalists were made when East Florida was ceded to Spain in 1783, and they are now among the Treasury records (T 77).

Americans who died with goods in the United Kingdom had their wills proved in the Prerogative Court of Canterbury (see **6**). They have been indexed by P W Coldham (1600-1858).

For nineteenth century and later emigrants, see **14.1**.

The muster rolls for Canadian militia and volunteers, 1837-1843, may be worth checking (WO 13/3673-3717): earlier records are in Canada. For ex-soldiers and sailors (or their widows and orphans) in receipt of a Chelsea or Greenwich pension, who had settled in Canada, the registers of payment of the pension may be useful. There are separate volumes for Canada, 1845-1862 (WO 22/239-242) and for Nova Scotia, 1858-1880 (WO 22/294-296). The composite volumes for several colonies, 1845-1875, may also be useful (WO 22/248-257).

14.4 Emigrants to North America and the West Indies: foreign emigrants

Emigrants from other countries to the American colonies can sometimes be traced through records in the PRO. Lists of the names of Palatine subjects, who emigrated to America by way of Holland and England in 1709, occur in several classes: the easiest way to discover them is to use the published works by Knittle, MacWethy and the *New York Genealogical and Biographical Review*. (See also **12.2**).

Between 1740 and 1772, foreign Protestants living in the Americas could become naturalised British citizens by the act 13 George II, c.7: this required seven years' residence, the swearing of oaths of allegiance (making an affirmation for Quakers), and taking the sacrament according to the Anglican rite (the last requirement was waived for Quakers and Jews). Every year lists of those naturalised (now in CO 5) had to be sent to the Commissioners for Trade and Plantations in London, where they were copied into entry books (CO 324/55-56). These provisions covered the West Indies as well as the American continent, but in fact only Jamaica (1740-1750), Maryland (1743-1753), Massachusetts (1743), New York (1740-1770), Pennsylvania (1740-1772), South Carolina (1741-1748), and Virginia (1743-1746) returned the lists to London. Over 7,000 foreign Protestants took advantage of this act: their names have been printed by M S Giuseppi in the Huguenot Society volume XXIV.

Another method of naturalisation, used by hundreds rather than thousands, was by the expensive process of obtaining an act of the colonial assembly (CO 5). To trace one of these naturalisations it will usually be necessary to have a good idea of the date and also the colony of residence.

14.5 Emigrants to Australia and New Zealand

For general records relating to emigrants, see section **14.1**. There are few records relating to voluntary emigrants to Australia and New Zealand until the Passenger Lists (BT 27) begin in 1890. For Australia, there is far more extensive documentation of the transportation of convicts (see **40**). However, to some extent the records of convict transportation also cover free emigrants: in some cases, a convict's family would accompany him as voluntary emigrants, and can be traced through some of the same records.

Censuses of convicts were conducted at intervals between 1788 and 1859 in New South Wales and Tasmania (HO 10): although primarily concerned with the unfree population, they do contain the names of those members of the convicts' families who 'came free' or who were 'born in the colony'. The fullest is that of 1828: see the edition by Sainty and Johnson, *New South Wales: Census ... November 1828*.

New South Wales Original Correspondence (CO 201) starts in 1784, and contains lists of settlers (and convicts),1801-1821. The correspondence of 1823 to 1833 has also been indexed. The papers of the Land and Emigration Commission (CO 386) also contain correspondence and entry books of the South Australian Commission.

New Zealand was not used as a penal colony. Details of emigrants may be found in the New Zealand Company records, which contain registers of cabin passengers emigrating, 1839-1850, applications for free passage, 1839-1850, lists of German emigrants, and lists of maintained emigrants (CO 208).

Between 1846 and 1851, Army pensioners were encouraged to settle in New South Wales and New Zealand, although many of them failed as settlers. References to the settlement of ex-soldiers in Australia and New Zealand will be found in the PRO's *Alphabetical Guide to Certain War Office and Other Military Records*, under *Australia and New Zealand* and there are lists of ex-soldier emigrants, 1830-1848, to Australia (WO 43/542) and New Zealand (WO 43/543).

Pensions from the Army and Navy were payable at district offices: records survive for offices in New South Wales, 1849-1880 (WO 22/272-275); in South Australia, Queensland, Tasmania and Victoria, 1876-1880 (WO 22/227, 297, 298 and 300); and in New Zealand, 1845-1854 and 1875-1880 (WO 22/276-293).

Microfilms of many PRO documents are available in Australia at the National Library in Canberra, and at the Mitchell Library in Sydney.

14.6 Emigrants to South Africa

Registers of payments to Army and Navy pensioners (including some widows and orphans) at the Cape of Good Hope and elsewhere in South Africa, 1849-1858 and 1876-1880, are in WO 22/243-244. The muster rolls of the Cape Levies, 1851-1853, may prove useful (WO 13/3718-3725).

Military records as a whole may be worth exploring for troops in South Africa (see **18**). For example, there are records of claims by civilians for compensation for property requisitioned during the Boer War, which are indexed (WO 148).

The Genealogical Society of South Africa will give advice: see also Lombard's article.

14.7 Emigrants: bibliography and sources

[An * means this work can be seen at Chancery Lane: a # means it can be seen at Kew.]

Published works

General
Acts of the Privy Council of England, Colonial Series, 1613-1783 (London, 1908-1912) *#
Calendar of State Papers, Colonial, America and West Indies, 1574-1738 (London, 1860-1969) *#
Calendar of Treasury Books, 1660-1718 (London, 1904-1962) *#

Calendar of Treasury Papers, 1557-1728 (London, 1868-1889) *#
Calendar of Treasury Books and Papers, 1729-1745 (London, 1898-1903) *#
W P Filby ed., *Passenger and Immigration Lists Bibliography 1538-1900* (Michigan,1981)
J S W Gibson, 'Assisted Pauper Emigration, 1834-1837', *Genealogists' Magazine*, vol. XX, pp. 374-375
Journals of the Board of Trade and Plantations, 1704-1782 (London, 1920-1938)
Public Record Office, *Alphabetical Guide to Certain War Office and other Military Records preserved in the Public Record Office*, Lists and Indexes, vol. LIII (London, 1931) *#
Public Record Office, *Emigrants: documents in the Public Record Office* (Information Leaflet) *#
Public Record Office, *List of Colonial Office Records*, Lists and Indexes, vol. XXXVI (London, 1911) *#
Public Record Office, *List of Records of the Treasury, Paymaster General's Office, Exchequer and Audit Department and Board of Trade, prior to 1837*, Lists and Indexes vol. XLVI (London, 1922) *#
Public Record Office, *List of State Papers, Domestic, 1547-1792, and Home Office Records, 1782-1837*, Lists and Indexes vol. XLIII (London, 1914) *#
Public Record Office, *The Records of the Foreign Office, 1782-1939* (London, 1969) *#
R B Pugh, *The Records of the Colonial and Dominions Office* (London, 1964) *#

North America and West Indies

C M Andrews, *Guide to the Materials for American History to 1783 in the Public Record Office of Great Britain* (Washington, 1912 and 1914) *
C E Banks and E E Brownell, *Topographical Dictionary of 2885 English Emigrants to New England, 1620-1650* (New York, 1963, 1976) *
C Boyer ed., *Ships' Passenger Lists: The South* (1538-1825); *National and New England* (1600-1825); *New York and New Jersey* (1600-1825) (Newhall, California, 1980)
M J Burchall, 'Parish-Organised Emigration to America', *Genealogists' Magazine*, vol. XVIII, pp. 336-342
P W Coldham, *American Loyalist Claims*, (Washington, 1980) (Indexes AO 13/1-35, 37, which contain claims for compensation from American loyalists who escaped to Canada, 1774-1793.) #
P W Coldham, *Bonded Passengers to America, 1615-1775* (Baltimore, 1983) *#
P W Coldham, *The Complete Book of Emigrants in Bondage, 1614-1775* (Baltimore, 1987) *
P W Coldham, *Emigrants from England to the American Colonies, 1773-1776* (Baltimore, 1988)
P W Coldham, *English Adventurers and Emigrants, 1609-1660 Abstracts of Examinations in the High Court of Admiralty, with Reference to Colonial America* (Baltimore, 1984) *
P W Coldham, *English Estates of American Colonists: American Wills and Administrations in the Prerogative Court of Canterbury, 1610-1699 and 1700-1799* (Baltimore, 1980) *

P W Coldham, *English Estates of American Settlers: American Wills and Administrations in the Prerogative Court of Canterbury, 1800-1858* (Baltimore, 1981) *

P W Coldham, *Lord Mayor's Court of London, Depositions relating to America, 1641-1736*, National Genealogical Society (Washington, 1980)

N Currer-Briggs, 'American Colonial Gleanings from Town Depositions', *Genealogists' Magazine*, vol. XVIII, pp. 288-294

R H Ellis, 'Records of the American Loyalists' Claims in the Public Record Office', *Genealogists' Magazine*, vol. XII, pp. 375-378, 407-410, 433-435

P W Filby, *American and British Genealogy and Heraldry* (Chicago, 2nd edn 1975)

P W Filby and M K Meyer ed, *Passenger and Immigration Lists Index*, 6 volumes (Michigan, 1981-1985.) (Lists 500,000 names of immigrants to USA and Canada from printed arrival lists.) *

M S Giuseppi, *Naturalizations of Foreign Protestants in the American and West Indian colonies*, Huguenot Society, vol. XXIV, 1921 *

J C Hotten, *Original Lists of Persons emigrating to America, 1600-1700* (London, 1874) *

C B Jewson, *Transcript of Three Registers of Passengers from Great Yarmouth to Holland and New England, 1637-1639*, Norfolk Record Society, vol. XXV (1954)

J and M Kaminkow, *A list of Emigrants from England to America, 1718-1759* (Baltimore, 1964) *

W A Knittle, *Early Eighteenth Century Palatine Emigration* (Philadelphia, 1937)

A H Lancour, *A Bibliography of Ships' Passenger Lists, 1538-1825* (New York, 1963)

G E McCracken, 'State and Federal Sources for American Genealogy', *Genealogists' Magazine*, vol XIX, pp.138-140

L D MacWethy, *The Book of Names especially relating to the Early Palatines and the First Settlers in the Mohawk Valley* (New York, 1932)

B Merriman, 'Genealogy in Canada', *Genealogists' Magazine*, vol. XIX, pp. 306-311

National Archives and Record Service, *A Guide to Genealogical Research in the National Archives* (Washington, 1982)

New York Genealogical and Biographical Records, vols. XL and LXI (New York, 1909 and 1910) (for Palatine emigrants)

C J Stanford, 'Genealogical Sources in Barbados', *Genealogists' Magazine*, vol. XVII, pp. 489-498

M Tepper ed., *New World Immigrants*, (Baltimore, 1980) (a consolidation of passenger lists)

D Whyte, *A Dictionary of Scottish Emigrants to the USA* (Baltimore, 1972)

Australia and New Zealand

P Burns and H Richardson, *Fatal Success: A History of the New Zealand Company* (Auckland, 1989)

Y Fitzmaurice, *Army Deserters from HM Service* (Forest Hill, Victoria, 1988 continuing) #

M Gillen, *The Founders of Australia, A Biographical Dictionary of the First Fleet* (Sydney, 1988) *

D T Hawkings, *Bound for Australia* (Guildford, 1987) *

L Marshall and V Mossong, 'Genealogical Research in New Zealand', *Genealogists'
Magazine,* vol. XX, pp. 45-49.

J Melton, *Ship's Deserters 1852-1900* (Sydney, 1986)

M R Sainty and K A Johnson ed., *New South Wales: Census...November 1828...*
(Sydney, 1980) #

N Vine Hall, *Tracing your Family History in Australia - A Guide to Sources* (London,
1985)

H Woolcock, *Rights of Passage: Emigration to Australia in the 19th Century*
(London, 1986)

South Africa

R J Lombard, 'Genealogical Research in South Africa', *Genealogists' Magazine,* vol.
XIX, pp. 274-276

E Mosse Jones, *Rolls of the British Settlers in South Africa* (Capetown, 1971)

P Philip, *British Residents at the Cape 1795-1819* (Capetown, 1981)

Records

Admiralty (at Kew)
ADM 101 Medical Journals. 1785-1880
ADM 108 Transport Department Records. 1773-1868

Exchequer and Audit Office (at Kew)
AO 1 Declared Accounts. 1536-1828
AO 2 Declared and Passed Accounts. 1803-1848
AO 3 Accounts, Various. 1539-1886
AO 12 American Loyalists' Claims, Series I. 1776-1831
AO 13 American Loyalists' Claims, Series II. 1780-1835
AO 14 Claims, Various. 1795-1846

Board of Trade (at Kew)
BT 27 Passenger Lists, Outwards. 1890-1960
BT 32 Registers of Passengers Lists. 1906-1951

Chancery (at Chancery Lane)
C 24 Town Depositions. 1524-1853
C 66 Patent Rolls. 1201-1962
C 213 Association Oath Rolls. 1696-1697

Colonial Office (at Kew)
CO 1 Colonial Papers, General. 1574-1757
CO 5 America, Original Correspondence. 1606-1822
CO 28 Barbados, Original Correspondence. 1681-1951
CO 29 Barbados, Entry Books. 1627-1872
CO 201 New South Wales, Original Correspondence. 1784-1903
CO 202 New South Wales, Entry Books. 1786-1873
CO 208 New Zealand Company, Original Correspondence, etc. 1837-1861

CO 323 Colonies, General, Original Correspondence. 1689-1952
CO 324 Colonies, General, Entry Books. 1622-1872
CO 327 British North America Emigration Registers. 1850-1863
CO 328 British North American General Registers. 1850-1868
CO 381 Colonies General, Entry Books. 1740, 1740-1872
CO 384 Emigration, Original Correspondence. 1817-1896
CO 385 Emigration, Entry Books. 1814-1871
CO 386 Land and Emigration Commission. 1833-1894

Exchequer (at Chancery Lane)
E 157 Licenses to Pass Beyond the Seas. Elizabeth I to 1677

Home Office (at Kew)
HO 10 Settlers and Convicts, New South Wales and Tasmania. 1787-1859

Ministry of Health (at Kew)
MH 12 Poor Law Union Papers. 1833-1909

Ministry of Transport (at Kew)
MT 23 Admiralty Transport Department, Correspondence and Papers. 1795-1917

National Debt Office (at Kew)
NDO 4 West Indies Slave Compensation. 1835-1842

Privy Council Office (at Chancery Lane)
PC 1 Papers. 1481-1946
PC 2 Registers. 1540-1978
PC 5 Plantation Books. 1678-1806

Treasury (at Kew)
T 47 Registers, Various. (Includes registers of emigrants, 1773-1776, T 47/9-12: card index available.)
T 50 Documents Relating to Refugees. 1780-1856
T 71 Slave Registration and Compensation. 1812-1846
T 77 East Florida Claims Commission. 1740-1789
T 79 American Loyalist Claims Commission. 1777-1841
T 99 Minute Books, Supplementary, 1690-1691. 1830-1832

Treasury Solicitor's Office (at Chancery Lane)
TS 12 West New Jersey Society. 1658-1921

War Office (at Kew)
WO 1 In-Letters. 1732-1869. (For emigration of Army pensioners, 1846-1851.)
WO 13 Militia and Volunteers Muster Books and Pay Lists. 1780-1878
WO 22 Royal Hospital Chelsea Pension Returns. 1842-1883
WO 23 Royal Hospital Chelsea, Chelsea Registers etc. 1702-1917
WO 43 Secretary of War: Correspondence: Selected 'Very Old Series' and 'Old Series Papers'. 1809-1857. (For emigration of Army pensioners: index available.)
WO 148 South African War Claims. 1900-1905

15. Oaths of allegiance

15.1 Oath rolls

Between the sixteenth and nineteenth centuries, people were required on various occasions to swear oaths in support of the crown and the Anglican church. Some of these oaths were sworn by those taking up or holding official positions and by lawyers on being admitted to the courts, others were sworn by aliens in the process of becoming naturalised British subjects, and others still were taken by people to signify their loyalty to the crown in times of political upheaval.

Anyone taking up any civil or military office was required by the Corporation Act of 1661 and the Test Act of 1673 to take the oaths of allegiance and supremacy, and to deliver a certificate into court stating that they had received the sacrament of the Lord's Supper according to the rites of the Church of England. The Sacrament Certificates, signed by the minister and churchwardens of the parish, survive from 1672 to 1828, but are not always easy to use (C 224, E 196, KB 22). The oath rolls are found in different places, depending on the occupation of the person taking the oath. Oath rolls, including classes devoted to the oaths of lawyers (see **28**), survive in the records of Chancery (C 193/9, C 184, C 214, C 215), Common Pleas (CP 10), Exchequer (E 169, E 200, E 3), and King's Bench (KB 24, KB 113). Oath rolls of attorneys in the courts of Chester and Durham also exist (CHES 36/3, DURH 3/217).

Between 1708 and 1711, all foreign Protestants who took the oaths of allegiance and supremacy in court, and who produced a sacrament certificate, were deemed to have been naturalised (KB 24, E 169/86: see **12.3**). The rolls in the PRO have been indexed by the Huguenot Society, in their volumes XXVII and XXV: other rolls, of oaths taken before the Quarter Sessions, may survive in county record offices. See **14.4** for oaths of allegiance on naturalisation, in North America and the West Indies.

The Association Oath Rolls (C 213 and C 214) contain the signatures or marks and names of people subscribing to the 'Solemn Association' of 1696, in support of William III after an attempt had been made to assassinate him. The oath of association was taken by everyone in a position of any authority - all members of Parliament, all military, naval and civil office-holders of the crown, the clergy and the gentry, freemen of the city companies, and others besides. In some places, such as Jersey, almost every adult male appears to have subscribed. The list is partly by occupation and partly by place: the rolls were partially indexed by Bernau.

15.2 Oaths of allegiance: bibliography and sources

[An * means this work can be seen at Chancery Lane: a # means it can be seen at Kew.]

Published works

C R Webb, 'The Association Oath Rolls of 1695', *Genealogists' Magazine*, vol. XXI, pp.120-123.

W A Shaw ed., *Letters of Denization and Acts of Naturalisation for Aliens in England and Ireland 1701-1800*, (Huguenot Society, vol. XXVII, Manchester 1923) *
A Supplement to Dr W Shaw's Letters of Denization and Acts of Naturalisation, (Huguenot Society, vol. XXXV, Frome 1932) *

Unpublished finding aids

Bernau Index, Society of Genealogists

Records

Chancery (at Chancery Lane)
C 184 Crown Office: Oath Rolls. 1701-1858
C 193/9: officers sworn by the Clerk of the Crown, 1639-1701
C 213 Association Oath Rolls. 1696-1697
C 214 Various Oath Rolls. Charles II to Victoria

C 215 Enrolments of Oaths. Charles II to Anne
C 224 Petty Bag Office: Sacrament Certificates. 1673-1778

Palatinate of Chester (at Chancery Lane)
CHES 36/3: attorneys' oath rolls, 1729-1800

Court of Common Pleas (at Chancery Lane)
CP 10 Common Pleas: Attorneys' Oath Rolls. 1779-1847

Palatinate of Durham (at Chancery Lane)
DURH 3/217: attorneys' oath rolls, 1730-1841

Exchequer (at Chancery Lane)
E 3 Exchequer of Pleas: Attorneys' Oath Rolls. 1830-1872
E 169 Exchequer: Oaths of Allegiance etc. 1709-1868
E 196 Exchequer: Sacrament Certificates. 1700-1827
E 200 Exchequer: Solicitors and Commissioner for Oaths Oath Rolls. 1730-1841

Court of King's Bench (at Chancery Lane)
KB 22 King's Bench: Sacrament Certificates. 1676-1828
KB 24 King's Bench: Swearing or Oath Rolls. 1673-1944
KB 113 King's Bench: Plea Side: Attorneys' Oath Rolls. 1750-1874

16. Electoral registration

16.1 Poll books and electoral registers

Poll books are locally compiled lists of men who were entitled to vote, and sometimes of votes cast, dating from the seventeenth to the nineteenth century. There are large collections in the British Library, the Guildhall Library and the library of the Society of Genealogists. County record offices and local libraries have collections relating to their own areas.

After the 1832 Reform Act an annual register of persons entitled to vote was kept. A selection of registers is available at Chancery Lane: see the list in **16.2.** Most come from the early 1870s, but there are some for Norfolk from 1832-1833.

16.2 Electoral registration: bibliography and sources

[An * means this work can be seen at Chancery Lane: a # means it can be seen at Kew.]

Published Works

J S W Gibson and C Rogers, *Electoral Registers since 1832 and Burgers Rolls* (FFHS, 1989) *
J S W Gibson and C Rogers, *Poll Books c.1696-1872* (FFHS, 1989)

Electoral registers in the PRO (at Chancery Lane)

England
Bedfordshire 1874
Berkshire 1874; Wallingford 1874
Bristol City 1874
Buckinghamshire 1874; Aylesbury 1874; Buckingham 1874
Cambridgeshire 1872; Isle of Ely 1874
Cheshire East 1874; Mid 1874; West 1874
Cumberland East 1874; West 1874; Carlisle City 1875; Cockermouth 1874; Whitehaven 1875
Cornwall 1872-1875; East 1874; West 1874; Bodmin 1874; Helston 1874; Launceston 1874; Liskeard 1872, 1873; St Ives 1875
Derbyshire East 1868-69, 1870; North 1870; South 1870
Devon 1875; East 1874; North 1874; South 1874; Barnstaple 1874
Dorset 1872, 1874; Poole 1870; Shaftesbury 1872; Wareham 1871
Durham North 1874; South 1874; Hartlepool 1874; Stockton 1875
Essex East 1875; South 1875; West 1875; Colchester 1874
Gloucestershire 1872, 1874; Cirencester 1872; Stroud 1873; Tewkesbury 1874
Hampshire 1874; North 1874; South 1874; Andover 1874; Petersfield 1874
Herefordshire 1874
Hertfordshire 1875
Huntingdonshire 1874; Huntingdon 1874
Kent East 1874; Mid 1874; West 1874; Canterbury 1873
Lancashire North 1874; North East 1874; South East 1874; South West 1874; Oldham 1873
Leicestershire South 1874
Lincolnshire Mid Lincs, Kesteven 1874; Mid Lincs, Lindsey 1874; North Lincs, Lindsey 1874; South Lincs, Kesteven 1874; Grantham 1874
Middlesex 1874

Monmouthshire 1874

Norfolk East 1832-33; North 1874; South 1874; West 1832-33, 1874

Northamptonshire North 1874; South 1874; Peterborough 1874

Northumberland North 1874; South 1874; Berwick-upon-Tweed 1875

Nottinghamshire North 1874; South 1874; East Retford 1872, 1874; Newark 1873

Oxfordshire 1874; New Woodstock 1873-74

Rutland 1874

Shropshire North 1874; South 1874; Shrewsbury 1874; Wenlock 1874

Somerset East 1874

Staffordshire East 1874; North 1874; West 1874; Newcastle-under-Lyme 1873; Stafford 1874; Stoke-on-Trent 1871-72; Tamworth 1871-72; Walsall 1874; Wednesbury 1874; Wolverhampton 1874

Suffolk East 1873, 1874, 1875; West 1874; Eye 1875

Surrey East 1872; Mid 1872; West 1872; Guildford 1873

Sussex 1871, 1873; East 1874; West 1874; Chichester 1874; Horsham 1872; Midhurst 1871; New Shoreham 1871; Rye 1874

Warwickshire North 1873, 1875; South 1874; Coventry City 1874

Westmorland 1872

Wiltshire 1872, 1874, 1875; South 1874; Calne 1874; Chippenham 1871; Cricklade 1873; Malmesbury 1871; Westbury 1874; Wilton 1874

Worcestershire East 1874; West 1874

Yorkshire East Riding 1874; North Riding 1874; West Riding, North 1874; West Riding, South 1874; Dewsbury 1874; Huddersfield 1875; Leeds 1874; Wakefield 1874; York City 1873

Wales

Anglesey 1873, 1874, 1875; Beaumaris 1870, 1874

Brecon 1871

Cardigan 1871-72, 1874; Aberystwyth, Cardigan and Lampeter 1871; Adpar 1871; Lampeter-Pontstephen 1871

Carmarthen 1872; Carmarthen Borough 1871

Caernarvon 1873, 1874, 1875; Caernarvon Borough 1873

Denbigh 1874, 1875

Flint 1874; Flint Borough 1875

Glamorgan 1873, 1874, 1875; Loughor and Neath 1874

Merioneth 1874

Montgomery 1872, 1874; Montgomery Borough 1874

Pembroke 1871-72; Pembroke Borough 1875

Radnor 1875; New Radnor 1873

17. Changes of name

17.1 Change of name by deed poll

Until the nineteenth century many people used an alias without going through any legal formality. From the late nineteenth century, deeds poll of change of name were sometimes (although by no means always) enrolled, and these enrolments may be seen at the PRO, Chancery Lane (C 54, J 18). Since 1914, all enrolled deeds poll have been published in the *London Gazette* (available at Kew), but for a change of name in the last three years, apply to Room 81, Royal Courts of Justice (address in **48.7**). For deeds poll that were not enrolled, look in the local and national press, and if all else fails your family solicitor may be able to help. It should be noted that a deed poll of change of name has no legal validity, and that anyone executing such a deed may have continued to use a previous (or indeed another) name.

17.2 Changes of name: bibliography and sources

[An * means this work can be seen at Chancery Lane: a # means it can be seen at Kew.]

Published works

J F Josling, *Change of Name, Oyez Practice Notes I* (London, 1980)
London Gazette (London, 1665 to date) #
W P W Phillimore and E A Fry, *An Index to Change of Names, 1760-1901* (London, 1905)
Public Record Office, *Change of Name* (Information Leaflet) *#

Unpublished finding aids

Indexes to deed poll enrolments *

Records

Chancery (at Chancery Lane)
C 54 Close Rolls. 6 John - 1903

Supreme Court of Judicature (at Chancery Lane)
J 18 Enrolment Books. 1903-1981

London Gazette (at Kew)
ZJ 1 *London Gazettes*. 1665-1986. This class is open immediately.

18. The Army

18.1 Army records: introduction

Many of the service records of British Army soldiers discharged before 1913 are in the PRO: service records for soldiers discharged after 1913 have not yet been transferred to the PRO (see **18.31**). There is very little before 1660, and, for other ranks, not much more before about 1730. However, from the mid-eighteenth century onwards, a considerable amount can be discovered about Army ancestors. This book can only indicate the most generally useful records: for more information on general sources see *Records of Officers and Soldiers who have served in the British Army*, a brief guide published by the PRO (soon to be superseded by a revised and extended version to be called *Military Records for Genealogists*). However, there are also so many records of specific interest that time spent browsing in Part 2 of the *Current Guide* and through the class lists may well prove to be a good investment.

This would also give some indication of the wide range of War Office records which are not discussed here: that is, those that relate to warfare and Army administration, and not to individuals. However, these records too can be of great interest in discovering more about a soldier's life. If you do wish to trace records relating to a particular campaign or action, or to do with the general administration of the Army, you will find the *Alphabetical Guide to certain War Office and other Military Records preserved in the Public Record Office* to be a very useful descriptive index. The range of Army activity and interests, up to the Boer War, disclosed by this book is quite remarkable. Most entries are to subjects or places (e.g. Lunatic Soldiers:- Asylums for, at Chatham and Yarmouth, cessation of, and suggestions for future treatment, 1841-1854; or Bermuda:- As health resort for soldiers, 1790) but some relate to particularly eminent soldiers (e.g. Moore, Sir John, Lieutenant-General:- Monument to, at Coruna, its neglected state, etc., 1809-1816). In addition, it contains a similar index for regiments (including colonial, foreign and militia regiments, and volunteer corps), which likewise includes entries of interest for family and social history (e.g. Lancashire, The East, Regiment:- Serjeant T Hurford's legacy for clothing poor children of Regt., 1840).

There are many other places to look for information about soldier ancestors, outside the official War Office records in the PRO. The most obvious are the Imperial War Museum, the National Army Museum and the various regimental museums: these specialise in the life of the Army, and you should be able to discover how your ancestor lived as a soldier. Most regiments have their own museums, some of which have archival collections; a search may be productive. The Royal Military Police became a separate organisation from the middle of the nineteenth century, and enquiries should be sent direct to them (address at **48.7**). The National Army Museum and the Army Museum Ogilby Trust also have collections. See the *Guide to Military Museums* by Wise, available at Kew. If private papers exist, they may be traceable through the National Register of Archives.

18.2 Army registers of births, marriages and deaths at St Catherine's House

The history of Army registration of births, marriages and deaths is not quite clear. Most of the records are in the General Register Office, St Catherine's House, and cannot be inspected; upon payment, information relating to birth, marriage and death is extracted and written into a modern-form certificate: see also **4.2** and **18.4**. A few Army registers or records of births, marriages and deaths are in the PRO (see **18.3**); others may still be in the custody of the regiment.

The General Register Office has registers of Army births and marriages from 1761 to

1987, and of deaths from 1796 to 1987. There are several series, some of them over-lapping, with an uncertain amount of duplication and omission. The regimental registers of births/baptisms and marriages run from 1761 to 1924, covering events in Britain (from 1761) and abroad (from c.1790). There is an index to the births (giving name, place, year and regiment), but not to the marriages. To find out details of a marriage, you have to know the husband's regiment and a rough date. At St Catherine's House there is a list of the marriage registers, arranged by regiment: if your regiment is there, with entries for the right period, ask at the enquiry desk in St Catherine's House to be put in touch with the Overseas Section, which may conduct a search for you.

Overlapping with the regimental registers are the Army chaplains' returns of births, baptisms, marriages, deaths and burials, 1796-1880. These all relate to events abroad, and they are indexed. Unfortunately, the indexes do not give the regiment, simply name, place and date range. From 1881 they appear to be continued by the Army returns, 1881-1955, of births, marriages and deaths overseas. From 1920, entries relating to the Royal Air Force are included.

From 1956-1965, there are indexes to combined service department registers of births and marriages overseas: after 1965, separate service registers were abandoned, and entries were made in the general series of overseas registers.

Records for the Ionian Islands appear to have been kept separately. At St Catherine's House there are registers, 1818-1864, of births, marriages and deaths: the index is to a military register, a civil register, and a chaplain's register. It gives names only. Other registers from the Ionian Islands are in the PRO, at Chancery Lane: the register for Zante gives baptisms, marriages, deaths and burials 1849-1859 (RG 33/82).

18.3 Army registers of births, marriages and deaths at the PRO

The Public Record Office has a small number of regimental registers of births, baptisms, marriages and burials, of the kind kept at St Catherine's House. Some of these are annotated with information on discharge: others have the baptismal entries of the children entered on the same page as the marriage certificate of the parents.

The PRO has registers for:

3rd King's Own Yorkshire Light Infantry, formerly the 1st West Yorkshire Militia: baptisms and marriages, 1865-1904 (WO 68/499)
Rifle Brigade, 6th battalion, formerly the 114th Westmeath Militia: baptisms and marriages, 1834-1904 (WO 68/439)
Royal Horse Artillery: baptisms and marriages, 1817-1827, 1859-1883 (WO 69/63-73, 551-582)
Somerset Light Infantry, 3rd and 4th battalions, formerly the Somerset Militia: baptisms and marriages, 1836-1887, 1892-1903 (WO 68/441)
West Norfolk Regiment: baptisms and marriages, 1863-1908 (WO 68/497)
West Yorkshire Rifles, 3rd battalion, formerly the 2nd West Yorkshire Militia: baptisms and marriages, 1832-1877 (WO 68/499)

In addition, there are Army registers of baptisms for Dover castle, 1865-1916 and 1929-1940; Shorncliffe and Hythe, 1878-1939; Buttervant, 1917-1922; and Fermoy, 1920-1921 (WO 156). This class also includes burial registers for the Canterbury garrison, 1808-1811, 1859-1884 and 1957-1958, and baptisms and banns of marriage for Army personnel in Palestine, 1939-1947.

The baptism, marriage and burial registers of the Royal Chelsea Hospital, for 1691-1856, are at Chancery Lane (RG 4/4330-4332, and 4387).

See **18.13** and **18.23** for other references to families.

18.4 Army war dead

Each regiment made regular returns of its casualties, where the usual round of one or two deaths from sickness is suddenly broken by long lists of men killed in action: see **18.18**, for more details. Nominal rolls of the dead were kept for many of the campaigns fought during the second half of the nineteenth century:

China	1857-1858	WO 32/8221, 8224, 8227
	1860	WO 32/8230, 8233, 8234
New Zealand	1860	WO 32/8255
	1863-1864	WO 32/8263-8268, 8271, 8276-8280
South Africa	1878-1881	WO 25/3474, 7770, 7706-7708, 7727, 7819
Egypt	1882,1884	WO 25/3473
Sudan	1884-1885	WO 25/3473, 6123, 6125-6126, 8382
Burma	1888	WO 25/3473
Sierra Leone	1898	WO 32/7630-7631
South Africa	1899-1902	WO 108/89-91, 338
China	1915	WO 32/4996B

Some of these have been published: F and A Cook's *The Casualty Roll for the Crimea*, and the *South Africa Field Force Casualty List, 1899-1902*, are available at Kew, as are microfilm copies of *Soldiers who died in the Great War*, arranged by regiment, and *Officers who died in the Great War* (the First World War).

At St Catherine's House are indexed death registers for the Army war dead for the Boer War, 1899-1902, the First World War, 1914-1921, and the Second World War, 1939-1948: see **4.2**. At the PRO, Chancery Lane, there are French and Belgian certificates of deaths for British soldiers who died in hospitals or elsewhere outside the immediate war zone, 1914-1920, arranged by first letter of surname (RG 35/45-69). For the Second World War, there are retrospective registers of deaths from enemy action in the Far East 1941-1945 (RG 33/11 and 132, indexed in RG 43/14).

18.5 Soldiering before the Restoration

Before the Civil War (1642-1649) there was no regular standing army in Britain. Although some records of soldiers do exist before 1660, it is extremely unlikely that they will provide any useful genealogical material on individuals. From medieval times, able-bodied men aged between 16 and 60 were liable to perform military service within their counties, and occasionally outside them, in times of need. From the 1540s, the records of musters of this militia were returned to the secretaries of state, and many of these, with some earlier ones from 1522 onwards, are scattered among various classes in the PRO, Chancery Lane: see Gibson and Dell's *Tudor and Stuart Muster Rolls*, available at Chancery Lane, for a county-organised analysis and directory. Some muster books, however, were retained by the deputy lieutenants of the counties, and these are now in private collections or county record offices.

From the sixteenth century, regiments were raised to meet special requirements and were usually known by the names of colonels who commanded them: there was no central administration. Such few references as there are to individual soldiers should be sought among the State Papers Domestic, State Papers Foreign, and the Exchequer and Audit Office Accounts (AO 1 - AO 3): the regimental index in the *Alphabetical Guide* (see **18.1**) is a good place to start. Other places to look are Exchequer Issues (E 403) and Exchequer Accounts (E 101) for the payment of military wages, the State Papers for widows' pensions, the licences to pass beyond the seas (E 157) for oaths of allegiance taken by soldiers going to the Low Countries, 1613-1624, and the Commonwealth Exchequer Papers for the Army during the Interregnum (SP 28). All officers serving in the Civil War and Commonwealth period are listed in E Peacock's book *The Army List of Roundheads and Cavaliers*. Warrants for commissions of the seventeenth century can be found in the State Paper Entry Books (SP 44).

18.6 The Army after 1660: organisation

After the Civil War, a standing army became a permanent feature of government . Its administration was the responsibility of the secretary-at-war, with the help of an established bureaucracy which developed into the War Office. As a result, the records of the Army after 1660 are much fuller.

Some understanding of the organisation of the Army is necessary for the proper use of military records. The basic unit of the Army was the regiment, under the command of a colonel. The regiments were of various types; cavalry, infantry, artillery and engineers. A regiment usually consisted of two (or, later, more) battalions, each with about ten companies (troops in the cavalry) of about a hundred men each. One of these battalions would be based at the regimental depot, to recruit and train soldiers for the active battalions. Whenever a new regiment was needed a colonel was given a 'beating order' to enlist, and recruitment headquarters were established, usually in local inns. Garrisons were established for the quartering of troops throughout the country, and in times of war when the garrison troops were needed elsewhere, special battalions of veterans would be raised to take their place.

The Army was manned by commissioned officers (from the wealthier classes: commissions were generally bought), and other ranks (often drawn from the poorest classes, including criminals and paupers). From 1780 to 1914 there was voluntary enlistment, normally for life. Few stayed the course for life: some bought themselves out; some were wounded, incapacitated and discharged; many were discharged at the end of various wars. Boys, in law if not in practice, had to be eighteen before they could enlist: younger boys often enlisted as drummers.

18.7 Militia regiments, volunteers and the Territorial Army

The eighteenth and nineteenth century militia was a county-based part-time force, additional to the standing army: it was not the same as the earlier militia (see **18.5**). Most militia records will be found in local record offices, although the PRO does have some major sources.

By the 1757 Militia Act, militia regiments were re-established in all counties of England and Wales, after a period of dormancy. A form of conscription was used: each year, the parish was supposed to draw up lists of adult males, and to hold a ballot to choose those who had to serve in the militia. The militia lists (of all men) and the militia enrolment lists (of men chosen to serve) should in theory provide complete and annual censuses of all men aged between 18 and 45 from 1758 to 1831. The surviving lists, held locally, can be very informative, giving details about individual men and their family circumstances. However, the coverage of the country, for various reasons, is not complete. For more information see the article by Medlycott or the book by Gibson and Medlycott. Records of the militia once formed are also usually in county record offices. Other locally-held sources are the poor law records, which can include orders for the maintenance of the children of militia men.

There are some major records relating to the militia in the Public Record Office. Muster rolls of regiments of militia, 1780-1876, supplementary militia, 1798-1816, and local militia, 1808-1816, are in WO 13, together with those of other volunteer forces such as the fencibles, the yeomanry and the volunteers. In most cases, these muster rolls do not indicate place of origin.

More useful for family history are the Militia Attestation Papers, 1806-1915 (WO 96), which were filled in at recruitment, and, in most cases, were annotated to the date of discharge to form a record of service. They include the date and place of birth. Most date from the mid nineteenth century. Despite the covering dates, attestation papers are arranged in the order of precedence of the regular army unit to which the militia regiments were attached after the reorganisation of the Army in 1881. The class list of WO 96 gives the name of the regular unit as at 1881, not the earlier militia unit. The way round this problem is to consult the *Army List* of 1882 or after, and to find out from there which militia regiments were attached to which regiment.

The Militia Records, 1759-1925 (WO 68), include records of some militia regiments in Great Britain and Ireland, and consist of enrolment books, description books, pay lists, returns of officers' services, casualty books, regimental histories etc., and also registers of marriages, births and baptisms (see **18.3**). The Military Correspondence, 1782-1840 (HO 50), and the Military Entry books, 1758-1855 (HO 51) contain much material on the militia.

A few militia soldiers qualified for pensions as a result of service in the French Revolutionary and Napoleonic wars, and their discharge certificates among the ordinary Soldiers' Documents (WO 97) give their place of birth and age on enlistment: see **18.17**. Other details of militia pensioners, admitted to pension between 1821 and 1829, may be found in a peculiar register drawn up in 1858, and arranged first by year of admission, and then by age on admission (WO 23/25). There are also lists of militia men, wives and children who were eligible for pensions among the Subsidiary Documents to the Receivers' Accounts (E 182), but there are no indexes.

In 1908 the militia was restyled the Special Reserve, and it retained this title until after the First World War, when it became the militia once again before disappearing. The volunteer units of infantry, yeomanry (cavalry) and artillery, etc., were formed into the Territorial Force in 1908, which was renamed the Territorial Army in 1920. Most of the records are held locally: the muster rolls of some London and Middlesex Volunteer and Territorial regiments (1860-1912) are in the PRO (WO 70).

18.8 Commissioned officers: *Army Lists* and printed sources

The broad outline of an officer's career should be fairly easy to discover, using the *Army Lists*. Details of officers granted commissions before 1727 can most easily be traced in C Dalton's *English Army Lists and Commission Registers, 1661-1714*, in his *Irish Army Lists, 1661-85,* and in his *George I's Army, 1714-1727*, all available in the Reference Room at Kew. Manuscript lists of Army officers were kept from 1702-1752 (WO 64); there is an index in the Reference Room. The first official *Army List* was published in 1740; since 1754 they have been published regularly. There are complete record sets, with manuscript amendments, of the annual lists (1754-1879) and the quarterly lists (1879-1900) in WO 65 and WO 66: incomplete sets are on open access in the Reference Room at Kew. Large reference libraries may also have a set.

The *Army List* was arranged by regiment, with a name index from 1766 (engineer and artillery officers were included in the index only from 1803). From 1879 it included a gradation list of officers - i.e. a list in order of seniority, giving dates of birth and promotions, and, from April 1881, details of service. For later *Army Lists*, see *Records of Officers and Soldiers*.

Hart's Army List was an unofficial list, produced between 1839 and 1915; it is particularly useful because it contains details of war service from 1839, which the official lists did not do until 1881. A set covering 1840-1882 is available at Kew: a full set, and Hart's own papers, which can include additional biographical information for 1838-1875, are in WO 211.

For Royal Artillery officers, check the *List of Officers of the Royal Regiment of Artillery, 1716 - June 1914*: for Royal Engineer officers, consult the *Roll of Officers of the Corps of Royal Engineers from 1660 to 1898*. These are both in the Reference Room, Kew.

The *Royal Military Kalendar* has details of officers of field rank (major) upwards. It was compiled in 1820, of officers then alive, so that the service covered goes back well into the eighteenth century. Ask for this at the Reference Desk, Kew.

There are also various works on militia officers, who were not included in the *Army Lists* until the mid nineteenth century: ask at the Reference Desk, Kew, for more information. Brief biographies of eminent soldiers may be found in the *Dictionary of National Biography*, and the *British Biographical Archive*.

18.9 Commissioned officers: commissions

There were four sorts of commissioned officer:

> *general officers*, who co-ordinated the efforts of the whole army:- field marshal, general, lieutenant-general, major-general.
> *regimental officers*:- colonel (in command of a regiment), lieutenant-colonel, major.
> *company officers*:- captain (in command of a company) and his subalterns, lieutenant, cornet (cavalry), ensign (infantry). In 1871 cornets and ensigns became second lieutenants.
> *others*:- paymaster, adjutant, quartermaster, surgeon and chaplain.

There were also many other ranks, such as brigadier-general, colonel-commandant, brigade-major, etc. Officers were graded by seniority, which ruled promotion within the regiment: if an officer was promoted out of sequence, he was given brevet rank, e.g., as a brevet-major. Some officers held two ranks at the same time, the regimental rank, which was higher, and was usually a special appointment, and the army rank, which was the actual rank of his commission.

Officers held their rank by virtue of a royal commission. There is a small collection of original commissions, 1780-1874, in WO 43/1059. Until 1871, entry commissions could be bought: as they were expensive, entry was usually restricted to the well-off. Promotion too could be bought, although it was also awarded for merit. Warrants for the issue of commissions for cavalry and infantry officers, 1679-1782, are in SP 44, continued after 1782 by HO 51. Commission books were kept by the War Office, 1660-1873 (WO 25/1-88) and others. Applications for, and resignations of, commissions between 1793 and 1870 contain some personal details such as birth certificates and statements of service (in WO 31). Correspondence about the purchase and sale of commissions, 1701-1858, is in WO 4/513-520 (with internal indexes).For more information on commissions, see **18.8** and *Records of Officers and Soldiers*.

Royal Artillery and Royal Engineer officers were the responsibility of the Board of Ordnance until 1855, when they were transferred to the War Office: before 1855, there are separate records for them. Their original warrants and patents of appointment, 1670-1855, are in WO 54/939-945: other commission records too are available.

18.10 Commissioned officers: regimental service records

Service records were kept by the regiments only, until the early nineteenth century, when the War Office began to taken an interest. There are two indexes available at Kew, to both the Regimental and War Office series (WO 76 and WO 25), one an index to regiments, and the other to names.

Regimental records of officers' services start in 1755: however, most of the records date from the nineteenth century. There are a very few from after the First World War. Almost all are in WO 76, but the records of the Gloucester Regiment, 1792-1866, are in WO 67/24-27, and those of the Royal Garrison Regiment, 1901-1905, are in WO 19. There are also some oddments in WO 25. Artillery officers' services, 1727-1751, are in WO 54/684: for 1771-1870, they are in WO 76. Returns of engineer officers, 1786-1850, are in WO 54/248-259, with service records, 1796-1922, in WO 25/3913-3919. Not all regiments are represented, and the records of some were lost. The information kept by the regiments varies a great deal, but it usually gives the ranks held, service details, and some personal particulars. There is an incomplete card index to regimental service records in the Reference Room, Kew. There are many regimental publications of officers' services.

Not all officers were regimental officers. For staff officers, there is a staff pay index, 1792-1830 (WO 25/695-699), lists of staff at various dates between 1802 and 1870, some with addresses (WO 25/700-702) and general returns of staff in British and foreign stations, 1782-1854 (WO 25/703-743). There are general returns of the service of commissariat officers, who were not military officers, for 1798-1842 (WO 61/1-2), followed by a register of Commissariat and Transport staff, 1843-1889 (WO 61/5-6). Senior staff of the War Office are included in the *Army Lists*.

18.11 Commissioned officers: War Office returns of service

War Office records of officers' service started with five returns of service made by the officers themselves. The first series, made in 1809-1810, is arranged alphabetically, and gives details of military service only (WO 25/744-748). The second, compiled from returns made in 1828 by officers retired or on half pay (and therefore referring to service completed some years before), also gives age at commission, date of marriage and date of children's birth: it is arranged alphabetically (WO 25/749-779). Similar information was collected from serving officers in 1829, but this third series is arranged by regiment (WO 25/780-805). The fourth series was a repeat of the second, but made in 1847 (WO 25/808-823). The fifth series, of returns made mainly between 1870 and 1872, is arranged by year of return and then by regiment; it also gives personal details (WO 25/824-870).

There is an incomplete card index to these service records in the Reference Room, Kew.

18.12 Commissioned officers: pension records

Before 1871 there was no general entitlement to a retirement pension; an officer would either move off the active list onto half pay, or would sell that valuable piece of property, his commission. The system of half pay to officers still holding a commission, but not on active service, was set up in 1641 to provide a retainer for the officers of disbanded regiments. It eventually expanded to become almost a kind of retirement pay, albeit one that was open to a lot of abuses. Half pay officers are included in the *Army List*, but sometimes do not appear in the index. Records of half pay do not contain much genealogical information. The most useful are probably the ledgers of payment, 1737-1921, in PMG 4. These give dates of death or of sale of the commission (which ended entitlement to half pay): from 1837 they also give addresses. Later ledgers give date of birth as well. From 1737 to 1841, the ledgers are arranged by regiment and are unindexed: from 1841 they are in one alphabetical sequence of names.

When the system of purchasing commissions was finally abolished, the current holders of commissions were eligible for compensation on their retirement. Registers were drawn up of all officers holding a commission on 1 November 1871, with the dates and estimated value of their commission, and with later annotations to show the date of retirement and the sum granted in compensation. These registers, which are in WO 74, do not give personal details.

Pensions were available for wounded officers from 1812. Registers of such pensioners, 1812-1892, are in WO 23/83-92; correspondence on such claims, 1812-1855, can be found in WO 4/469-493. Further correspondence, 1809-1857, can be found in WO 43: there is a card index in the Reference Room, Kew. Actual records of payments are in PMG 9 (including First World War payments) and PMG 12.

18.13 Commissioned officers: families

Provision of an authentic baptismal certificate was mandatory for those in government service: membership of the established church implied loyalty to the crown. As a result there are many baptismal certificates for Army officers in the War Office records. There are two main caches, for 1777-1868 in WO 32/8903-8920 (code 21A) and for 1755-1908 in WO 42. The latter also contains certificates of marriage, birth of children, death and burial (see below). Indexes to both are available in the Reference Room, Kew.

Reports by officers of their marriage, 1830-1882, are in WO 25/3239-3245; some of the marriages date from the early years of the century. The various military registers of births, marriages and deaths (see **18.2** and **18.3**) include references to officers' families, if they had followed the drum.

Other than this, more information is only likely to be found in military records if the officer died leaving his family in want. From 1708 there was provision for the payment of pensions to the widows of officers killed on active service; from 1720, pensions were also paid to the children and dependent relatives (usually indigent mothers over 50) in similar cases, out of the Compassionate Fund and the Royal Bounty. These pensions were not an automatic right, and applicants had to prove their need. Application papers for widows' pensions and dependents' allowances, 1755-1908, which can include proofs of birth, marriage, death, and wills, etc., are in WO 42: other such papers, of uncertain date (1760-1818?) are in WO 25/3089-3197, arranged alphabetically, with abstracts of applications, 1808-1825, in WO 25/3073-3089. There is an index in the Reference Room, Kew.

There are lists of widows receiving pensions, 1713-1829 (WO 24/804-883), and 1815-1892 (WO 23/88-92). Registers of payments, 1735-1811, are in WO 25/3020-3058, with indexes to pensions for 1748-1811 (WO 25/3120-3123). Similar registers for 1815-1895 are in WO 23/105-123. Ledgers of payments of widows' pensions, 1808-1920, are in PMG 11, but they give little information. Correspondence relating to widows' pensions, 1764-1816, is in WO 4/1023-1030: the volumes are internally indexed, and contain details on many widows. Selected correspondence on widows' pensions is also in WO 43: there is a card index in the Reference Room, Kew.

There are registers of compassionate allowances awarded to dependents, 1773-1812 (WO 25/3124-3125). Registers of those placed on the Compassionate List, 1858-1894 are in WO 23/114-119, with a summary for 1805-1895 in WO 23/120-123. There are also about 2,000 'compassionate papers' for 1812-1813 (WO 25/3110-3114), which are affidavits by the widows and children, in receipt of a compassionate pension, that they received no other government income. They are in rough alphabetical order, and give details of the officer, often the age of the children, and sometimes the name of the guardian, as well as some indication of county or country of residence (they were sworn before local justices). Correspondence relating to the Compassionate Fund, 1803-1860, is in WO 4/521-590. There are ledgers of payments, for 1779-1812 (WO 24/771-803), and for 1812-1915 (PMG 10), but they give little information. Ledgers of pension payments for the widows of foreign officers, 1822-1885, are in PMG 6 and PMG 7. For pensions and compassionate allowances to the widows and dependents of commissariat officers, 1814-1834, see WO 61/96-98.

Registers of pensions to the widows of Royal Artillery and Royal Engineer officers, 1833-1837, are in WO 54/195-196, with ledgers of payments, 1836-1875, in PMG 12. There is also a series of indexed registers of letters of attorney, 1699-1857, relating to Ordnance officers, civilian staff and creditors who expected to receive payments of any kind from the Ordnance Office (WO 54/494-510): many of these letters were made in favour of the wife or other close relative, or were letters granted by the probate courts to the widow as executrix.

Similar registers of powers of attorney for Army officers in general are in PMG 14 and PMG 51. There are entry books of powers of attorney apparently arranged by date, for 1759-1816 (PMG 14/104-125). For 1811-1814, there are alphabetical entry books (PMG 14/126-137). Registers of letters of attorney, 1756-1827, are in PMG 14/142-167: they include separate volumes of letters of attorney granted by widows, 1802-1821 (PMG 165-167). There is a single register of letters of attorney, 1755-1783, at WO 30/1. Later registers, 1836-1899, are in PMG 51.

18.14 Commissioned officers: chaplains

Until the end of the eighteenth century, chaplains were employed on a regimental basis, but after 1796 one chaplain served three or four regiments. The first Presbyterian chaplains were appointed in 1827; Catholic chaplains in 1836; Wesleyans in 1881, and Jewish chaplains in 1892. As chaplains were commissioned officers, they will be found in the *Army List* (see **18.8**). Certificates of service, 1817-1843, are in WO 25/256-258. Records of payment, 1805-1842, are in WO 25/233-251. The registers of retired pay, 1806-1837 (WO 25/252-253), give details of chaplains who saw service in the eighteenth century. Letters from chaplains, 1808-1836, are in the Chaplain General's Letter Books (in WO 7). See also **31.2**.

18.15 Other ranks: introduction

In the Army, the 'other ranks' were the privates (infantry) and troopers (cavalry), trumpeters and drummers, supervised by corporals and sergeants who were non-commissioned officers promoted from the ranks: specialist regiments and corps used different names. The basic information kept on each soldier reappears in different permutations in different types of document. This basic personal information comprises name, age, place of birth, trade on enlistment, place of enlistment, physical description and date of death or discharge. Some records contain information on wife, children or other next of kin.

Almost all service records were kept by the individual regiments, not by any central authority. As a result, if you are searching for an individual soldier, you really do need to know the regiment in which he served unless you are prepared for a lengthy and speculative search. This subject is discussed more fully in **18.16**. However, there are two series of Army-wide returns of service of non-commissioned officers and men. One contains statements of periods of service and of liability to serve abroad, as on 24 June 1806 (WO 25/871-1120). The other contains returns of the service of non-commissioned officers and men not known to be dead or totally disqualified for service, who had been discharged between 1783 and 1810 (WO 25/1121-1131). However, both series are still arranged by regiment, and only then alphabetically.

The main everyday service records of men in active service kept by the Army were the regimental muster book and the regimental pay list (see **18.20**). These provide a fairly complete guide to a soldier's Army career from enlistment, through movements with the regiment throughout the world, to discharge. However, because there are so many muster books and pay lists, and because they each cover such a short space of time, it can be a very lengthy task to search through them. It is worth investigating other records first, particularly the service records of soldiers retired to pension (see **18.17**), where the personal information is consolidated and is far more easily found, even if you are not sure that your ancestor received a pension. If you find that he was discharged without a pension before 1883, you may have to use the muster books and pay lists (but see **18.16** first). If your soldier died in service, you may find out quite a lot of information if you know the regiment, by using the casualty returns (see **18.18**): if these prove no use, try the muster books.

18.16 Other ranks: how to find the regiment

As most records before 1873 are arranged by regiment, you really do need to know which regiment your ancestor served in before beginning to search the main sources of information. After 1873, the alphabetically arranged soldiers' documents in WO 97 are the first place to look (see **18.17**). You may already have details of the regiment, from family knowledge or previous research. However, if you do not, there are still some possible ways to find out the regiment, other than through the identification of uniforms from old photographs (see the article by Barnes on this subject).

The regimental registers of births, 1761-1924, at St Catherine's House are indexed: the index gives the regiment and place of birth of children born to the wives of serving soldiers, if they were attached to the regiment. If you have some knowledge of offspring or areas of service, this can be an easy way to narrow the field. To actually identify the correct child, parent and regiment, you may have to buy more than one certificate (see **4.2** and **18.2**).

If you know the county or country in which your ancestor was living between 1842 and 1862 for England and Scotland, or between 1842 and 1882 for Ireland and abroad, you may be able to find the regiment fairly easily. Between these dates there are records of payment of pensions, arranged by the district pay offices, which name the regiment served in (WO 22, and PMG 8 for payments in Hanover).

Another possibility, if the soldier died in service, would be to check the records of dead soldiers' effects, 1810-1822, 1830-1844 and 1862-1881, mentioned in **18.18**. These are arranged by initial letter of surname and give the regiment, which opens up the regimental records to you. However, if the soldier died owing money to the Army, instead of *vice versa*, you are unlikely to find a reference to him here.

If you have any information on place of service, you may be able to identify the regiment from Kitzmiller's *Guide to British Army units and their whereabouts*. There is a similar guide by L Maws for the various batteries of the Royal Artillery. Both of these can be seen at the Reference Desk, Kew.

There are other possibilities as well, although using the following suggestions may be a lengthy process. Depending on the known information, an area of records to be searched can be limited. If a rough date of discharge is known, it may be possible to trace the regiment in which a soldier served by using various registers of discharges. These are not complete but, especially before the records in WO 97 are arranged purely alphabetically (see **18.17**), they are a useful potential source of information. A number of these pieces contain information on soldiers whose discharge document would not, in any case, be contained in WO 97. These discharges were:

1817-1829	by purchase	WO 25/3845-3847
1830-1838	by own request	WO 25/3848-3849
1830-1856	with modified pension	WO 25/3850
1838-1855	free or free deferred pension	WO 25/3851-3858
1856-1861	free permanent pension	WO 25/3859-3861
1861-1870	free permanent pension, modified/ deferred pension, or purchase	WO 25/3863-3868
1852-1870	first period, incorrigible, ignominy, penal servitude, or 21 years with militia	WO 25/3869-3878

(continued)

(continued)

1856-1857	regiment under reduction	WO 25/3879-3882
1866-1870	Limited Service Act	WO 25/3883-3893
1863-1878	on return from India	WO 12/13077-13105
1871-1884	general register	WO 121/223-238
1882-1883	Gosport discharge depot musters	WO 16/2284
1883-1888	Gosport discharge depot musters (index in Reference Room, Kew)	WO 16/2888-2916
1884-1887	without pension (gives address to which discharged)	WO 121/239-257

18.17 Other ranks: service records

As yet, the PRO has no service records after 1913 (see **18.31**). In general, there is no record of the whole of the soldier's service unless he was discharged to a pension.

Pension records, by their very nature, refer to service often begun many years before the date of the pension award. Do remember this when looking at the covering dates given below - they do not refer to the dates of service. A soldier may have been discharged to a pension for disability, or for long service of 21 years: after 1883, soldiers discharged after completing one of the new limited engagements or who had bought their discharge were also eligible for consideration. In all these cases, there should be a cumulative record of the soldier's service in the class of Royal Hospital Chelsea Soldiers' Documents, 1760-1913 (WO 97). This class, WO 97, is generally the first place to look in tracing a soldier ancestor.

In using the Soldiers' Documents (WO 97) between 1760 and 1872, you do need to know the regiment, as the documents are arranged by regiment. However, from 1873 they were kept in four alphabetical sequences of surname (cavalry, artillery, infantry and corps), which reduces the searching: after 1883 they were kept in one alphabetical sequence. The Soldiers' Documents give age, birthplace, trade or occupation on enlistment, a record of service including any decorations, the reason for discharge to pension, and, in some cases, place of residence after discharge and date of death. From 1883, they also contain details of next of kin, marriage and children.

There are other, similar, records for Chelsea, which may be worth checking if there is nothing in WO 97. The main class to check is WO 121, Discharge Documents of Pensioners. For the period 1787-1813 this class contains the documents which one would expect to find in WO 97. They are not duplicates of WO 97. In fact, they even include the papers of soldiers who were refused a pension. The records are arranged by date of the meetings of the admission board, and then by regimental seniority: they include approximately 20,000 certificates (WO 121/1-136).

Other possible sources are the Chelsea Regimental Registers, c.1715-1857 (WO 120): these are chronological lists of discharges to pension by each regiment (see **18.22**). There is a partial index for 1806-1838, available on request at the Reference Desk, Kew. Also worth checking are the records of deferred pensions, 1838-1896 (WO 131); and the Discharge Documents of Pensioners, Foreigners' Regiments,

1816-1817 (WO 122). See also **18.22**, for records relating to the actual payment of the pension to your soldier, which can provide information on his life after leaving the Army. If you suspect that your soldier was on the Irish establishment, check the Kilmainham Discharge Documents of Pensioners, 1783-1822 (WO 119). These are arranged by discharge number, but there are indexes to these numbers in WO 118.

For more information on pensions and the Chelsea and Kilmainham Hospitals, see **18.22**.

18.18 Other ranks: casualty returns and registers of effects

If you know the regiment of your soldier, and have been unable to find his discharge documents, try the casualty returns, 1797-1910, which can provide quite a lot of personal information.

The main collection of monthly and quarterly regimental casualty returns covers 1809-c.1875, with a few entries and annotations in the indexes continuing up to 1910 (WO 25/1359-2410, 3251-3260, indexed in WO 25/2411-2755, 3261-3471). Despite their title, the casualty returns refer to absences, desertions and discharges as well as to the dead and wounded. The information given is name, rank, place of birth, trade at enlistment, the date, place and nature of the casualty, any debts or credits, and the next of kin or legatee. Wills, inventories of effects, letters from relatives, and accounts are included very infrequently. There is also a series of entry books of casualties, 1797-1817, from the Muster Master General's Office (WO 25/1196-1358).

If you do not know the regiment, try the records relating to payments to next of kin of dead soldiers: there are gaps in these records but they are arranged alphabetically and are easy to use. These are the registers of authorities to deal with the effects (possessions) of dead soldiers, 1810-1822 (WO 25/2966-2971); an index of effects, 1830 (WO 25/2974); a register of effects and credits, 1830-1844 (WO 25/2975); and record books of effects, 1862-1881 (WO 25/3476-3490, indexed by WO 25/3491-3501). The registers for 1810-1822 are very informative: they give name, regiment, period of death, amount of effects and credits, date of order to agent, agent's name, person applying (usually next of kin) and his or her address. Later records are not so informative, but still give regiment, which can be very useful.

18.19 Other ranks: deserters

Information on deserters was forwarded to the Army authorities by the casualty returns, 1809-1910 (see **18.18** for more details). There are registers of deserters, 1811-1852, in WO 25/2906-2934. Until 1827 they are kept in three series, for cavalry, infantry and militia (the latter up to 1820 only). After 1827 they are arranged by regiment. These registers give descriptions, dates and place of enlistment and desertion, and outcome. There are registers of captured deserters, 1813-1845, in WO 25/2935-2951, with indexes up to 1833 in WO 25/2952-2954. Deserters who surrendered themselves under proclamation, 1803-1815, are in WO 25/2955. On capture, some deserters were sentenced to imprisonment on the *Savoy* hulk: there are unindexed registers for the hulk, 1799-1823 (WO 25/2956-2961).

For 1828 to 1845, the police newspapers *Hue and Cry* and the *Police Gazette* carried details of deserters, giving name, parish and county of birth, regiment, date and place of desertion, a physical description and other relevant information. For deserters in Australia (HO 75), consult Fitzmaurice's book, available at the Reference Desk, Kew.

18.20 Other ranks: muster books, pay lists, description books and numbers

The basic regimental service records were the muster books, pay lists and description books: these were used for the day-to-day administration of the regiment. The main series of muster books and pay lists is in WO 12, which covers 1732-1878: other series are of the artillery, 1710-1878 (WO 10), the engineers, 1816-1878 (WO 11), the militia and volunteers, 1780-1878 (WO 13), the troops at the Scutari depot involved in the Crimean War, 1854-1856 (WO 14), and the British, German and Swiss legions, 1854-1856 (WO 15). For the years 1877 to 1898, WO 10 - WO 12 are continued by WO 16, but coverage is incomplete and the information given is very limited.

In general, each muster book and pay list occupies one volume per year, and you may therefore have to search through several volumes. The first entry for the recruit in the muster generally gives his age, place of enlistment and trade, but does not give birthplace. If the soldier died in service, or was discharged, you should find an entry to that effect in one of the quarterly lists of men becoming non-effective: however, these lists are not always present. Where one does exist, it should give the birthplace of the man discharged or dead, his trade and his date of enlistment.

From about 1868 to about 1883, the musters also contain marriage rolls, which sometimes give information about children as well as wives, if they occupied married quarters.

There are two main series of description books. The regimental description and succession books are in WO 25/266-688: covering dates are 1778-1878, but not all the regiments' books start so early or go on so late, and only a small percentage of all soldiers are included. Some are arranged alphabetically, others by date of enlistment. The books give a description of each soldier, his age, place of birth and trade and successive service details. The depot description books, 1768-1908 in WO 67, give the same information, gathered as recruits were assembled at the regimental depot.

These description books in WO 25 are not books containing details of every man in the regiment who served between the covering dates. They began to be compiled in approximately 1825, or slightly earlier, after an investigation into the fraudulent claims of service. Regiments had to write down the services of every man in the regiment who was still serving at that time, and to list them in chronological order of enlistment (or alphabetically). Consequently, the further back one goes, the fewer the men from that period. Most books would appear to have between 1,000 and 1,500 names (some have a lot more), but considering that regimental strength was 1,000 and the regiments had been through twenty-two years of war and wastage, this is a small percentage of the total number. Depot rolls or description books (WO 67) are usually much fuller. Men were usually allotted a number, but this number does not appear on any forms until the 1830s. Depot rolls, however, do not list soldiers who enlisted where the regiment was stationed. Neither do they list soldiers who transferred from one regiment straight into another.

Incidentally, regimental numbering began as a direct result of this commission of enquiry. Each man, as he joined, was allotted a consecutive number. This would not be carried throughout his career: if he transferred into another regiment, he would be allotted a new number. It is possible to estimate when a soldier enlisted in a particular regiment if a point of reference is known, i.e. if a muster provides details of a man with a regimental number close to that of the ancestor. It is then possible to guess a year of discharge (add 21!). In 1917, the system changed and the first series of Army numbers came in. This was very short-lived and the second series (superseding the first) came in in 1922. This allotted 'blocks' of numbers to particular regiments, and a man on first enlistment would be given a number in the relevant block which he would retain even on transfer to another regiment. This numbering system ran out in c.1941 and another began.

18.21 Other ranks: Artillery and Engineer (Sapper and Miner) service records

Because the Royal Artillery, the Royal Engineers, and the Royal Corps of Sappers and Miners were the responsibility of the Ordnance Office (and not of the War Office) until 1855, they have a different set of records. Until 1772, the Royal Engineers were officers only, using casual labour for the physical work: after this a Corps of Royal Military Artificers, composed of other ranks only, was raised. In 1811, it became the Royal Corps of Sappers and Miners, with both officers and other ranks. This was amalgamated with the Royal Engineers after the abolition of the Ordnance Office in 1856.

However, many documents relating to Sappers and Miners are described in the lists as relating to Royal Engineers. Entry books of discharges, casualties, and transfers of Artillery and Engineer (Sapper and Miner) soldiers, 1740-1859 are in WO 54/317-337. Service records of the Royal Artillery, 1791-1855, and for the Royal Horse Artillery, 1803-1863, are in WO 69. These include attestation papers, and show name, age, description, place of birth, trade, and dates of service, of promotion, of marriage, of discharge and of death. They are arranged under the unit in which the soldier last served: to find this, use the indexes and posting books (WO 69/779-782 and WO 69/801-839). This class also contains records of births and marriages (see **18.3**). Laws's guide to the location of Artillery batteries may be useful if you know only the area of service: it can be seen at the Reference Desk, Kew.

There is a miscellaneous collection of records of service for soldiers in the Artillery, Sappers and Miners, etc., and for civilian subordinates of the Board of Ordnance, arranged alphabetically in the Ordnance Office In-Letters (WO 44/695-700). There is an incomplete series of registers recording the deaths of soldiers in the Artillery, 1821-1873, in WO 69/583-597. Papers relating to Artillery and Engineer (Sapper and Miner) deaths and personal effects, 1824-1859, are in WO 25/2972-2973 and 2976-2978. Admission registers to pension for Royal Artillery disability and long service pensioners, 1833-1913, are in WO 116/125-185. Registers of Artillery and Sapper and Miner pensioners, compiled in 1834 but dating back to the Napoleonic wars, are in WO 23/141-145; they include descriptions.

Musters and pay lists for the Royal Artillery, 1708-1878, are in WO 10; for the Royal Sappers and Miners, and the Engineers, 1816-1878, they are in WO 11. Musters for both Artillery and Engineers, 1878-1898, are in WO 16.

18.22 Other ranks: pension records

The main system of Army pensions to other ranks was operated by the Royal Hospital Chelsea (London, founded 1681) and, for soldiers in the Irish establishment, the Royal Hospital, Kilmainham (near Dublin, founded 1679). Before (and after) the founding of these Royal Hospitals, disabled ex-soldiers were often granted places as almsmen in royal church foundations:petitions for such places, often giving details of service and wounds, for 1660 to 1751, are in SO 5/31.

Chelsea and Kilmainham supported both in-pensioners, who lived in the hospitals, and a much larger number of out-pensioners. Kilmainham operated a system of out-pensioners from 1698 to 1822, when its out-pensioners were transferred, as out-pensioners, to Chelsea. The last Kilmainham in-pensioners were transferred to Chelsea as in-pensioners, or to out-pension, in 1929. The service records of those soldiers who were discharged to pension have been described in **18.17**. However, both hospitals have other records which can be very useful, particularly for the period before the discharge documents start (i.e. 1756 for Chelsea and 1783 for Kilmainham), and for the ex-soldier's life after leaving the Army.

Admission registers for Kilmainham in- and out-pensions, 1704-1922, are in WO 118. Chelsea has two series, one for long service pensions, 1823-1920 (WO 116), and one for disability pensions, 1715-1913 (WO 118). These admission registers, which are arranged by date of discharge/admission to pension, generally give a brief description of the pensioner, age, place of birth, particulars of service and the reason of discharge. Royal Artillery disability and long service pensioners, 1833-1913, have separate admission registers (WO 116/125-185).

The Chelsea Regimental Registers (WO 120, seen on microfilm) give regimental lists of discharges to pension. They give a brief description, age, place of birth, particulars of service and reason of discharge, for the period c. 1715-1843. For 1843 to 1857, they give only the date of award, rate of pension and the district pay office where the pension was paid. From about 1812 the dates of death have been added, the last dating from 1877. There is a partial index, covering 1806-1838, available at Kew.

For 1842 to 1883, out-pensions were paid through district pension offices, including many abroad. These records are arranged by place of the pension office, which can be very useful if you know only the area or country in which the man, or his dependents, resided, and not his regiment (WO 22, and PMG 8 for payments made in Hanover). There are separate registers of men admitted to pension from colonial regiments, 1817-1903, who did not have to appear in person. In many of these cases, details of service and birthplace are given (WO 23/147-160). Some of these entries relate to men from the British Army who retired while their regiment was overseas, and who were given permission to receive their pension there.

There are many other records from Chelsea Hospital, which can be very useful. In particular, the Chelsea registers etc., 1702-1917 (WO 23), contain a vast amount of information, such as an alphabetical list of in-pensioners in 1837, muster rolls of the hospital, 1702-1789 and 1865; pension claims from soldiers in colonial regiments, 1836-1903; East India Company Army pensioners, 1814-1875; and the Chelsea registers, 1805-1895, of pensioners by regiment (as in WO 120), pensions for the Victoria Cross, wounds or other merit, and bounty.

A new class, PIN 71, contains the personal files on over 5,000 disabled soldiers and naval ratings who served before 1914 and received disability pensions; the information contained includes medical records, accounts of how injuries were incurred, and the men's own account of the incident, and conduct sheets. These conduct sheets give place of birth, age, names of parents and siblings, religion, physical attributes, marital and parental status. The class is alphabetically arranged.

18.23 Other ranks: families

Information on other ranks' families may be found in the regimental registers at St Catherine's House (see **4.2** and **18.2**). There are sometimes references to next-of-kin in the casualty returns and registers of effects (**18.18**). From 1868-1883 marriage rolls, containing information of those wives and children who were on the regimental books, may be found with the muster books (**18.20**). A new class, PIN 71, contains over 1,000 personal files on the widows of Army other ranks and naval ratings whose service was before 1914. This is only a selection of such files, but it is alphabetically arranged, and the information contained is extensive.

18.24 Other ranks: schools for orphans and other children

The Royal Military Asylum was founded at Chelsea in 1801, as a boarding school for children of serving or dead soldiers. It was renamed the Duke of York's Military School in 1892, and was moved to Dover in 1909. Girls were admitted to the female branch until 1840: this was abolished in 1846.

At first, many of the children were not orphans, but most later entrants appear to have lost at least their father and quite frequently both parents. Children appear to have been admitted between the ages of 2 and 10, and were discharged in their mid-teens. Most of the girls not claimed by their parents were apprenticed, often as servants: the boys went into the Army, or were apprenticed if they were not fit for military service.

The admission and discharge registers, 1803-1923, are very informative: unfortunately they are arranged by date of admission (WO 143/17-26): one of the boys' registers, for 1804-1820, is in letter order. The information for the girls is the fuller: number, name, age, date of admission, from what regiment, rank of father (P, T, S etc., for private, trooper, sergeant), parents' names and if living, parochial settlement (on discharge ?), when dismissed, and how disposed of (e.g. died, retained by parents while on pass, apprenticed). The boys' admission register gives the same information except that it does not give the parents' names. The discharge registers give more information on apprenticeship, regiment or other fate.

The Royal Hibernian Military School was founded in Dublin in 1769, for the children of soldiers on the Irish establishment: in 1924 it merged with the Duke of York's Military School. Unfortunately, most of its records were destroyed by enemy bombing in 1940: what survives is a boys' index book (WO 143/27), drawn up in 1863 with retrospective entries from c.1835, and with annotations up to c.1919. This gives name, class, references to petitions and registers now lost, corps, and remarks (e.g. volunteered 16th Foot 5 August 59).

18.25 Army medical services

The easiest way to start looking for officers is to consult *Commissioned Officers in the Medical Services of the British Army,* by Peterkin, Johnston and Drew, which is available in the Reference Room at Kew.

There is a series of records of service of officers of the Medical Department, 1800-1840, in WO 25/3896-3912, which includes details of the professional education of surgeons. These records are indexed. There is a certain amount of information for 1811-1818 in WO 25/259-263: for 1809-1852, there are casualty returns of medical staff (WO 25/265, 2384-2385, and 2395-2407). For the period 1825-1867, there are registers of the qualifications of candidates for commissions in the Medical Department (WO 25/3923-3944). The Royal Army Medical Corps has a medal book, 1879-1896, which may be worth a look (WO 25/3992).

Testimonials of women wishing to nurse in the Crimea, c.1851-c.1856, may be found in WO 25/264. A few women nursed at Netley Hospital and on campaign after then. The much larger Army Nursing Service was established in 1884, and renamed Queen Alexandra's Imperial Military Nursing Service (QAIMNS) in 1902. Two reserve military nursing services were also established. In 1894 Princess Christian's Nursing Reserve was set up, to be renamed Queen Alexandra's Imperial Military Nursing Service Reserve in 1908. The Territorial Force Nursing Service, established in 1908, became in 1921 the Territorial Army Nursing Service.

The PRO has no service records for the Army Nursing Service. There are records of professional qualifications and recommendations for appointment of staff nurses in QAIMNS, 1903-1926, in WO 25/3956. There are some pension records, but few nurses served long enough to qualify for a pension. Pension records for nurses appointed before 1905 are in WO 23/93-95 and 181; pensions for QAIMNS nurses, 1909-1928, are in PMG 34/1-5; and First World War disability pensions for nurses are in PMG 42/1-12. There are some service records for National Aid Society Nursing Sisters, 1869-1891 (WO 25/3955).

The Royal Red Cross medal was instituted especially for military nurses in 1883 (WO 145). Nurses were also awarded medals for service in Egypt, 1882, and South Africa, 1899-1902 (WO 100) and the First World War (WO 329); the latter has a separate name index for nurses on microfiche.

18.26 The Indian Army and the British Army in India

There was an army in India which was maintained by the East India Company until 1859. This army consisted of separate divisions of European and Indian troops, which were both officered by Europeans. After 1859 the Company's Indian troops became the Indian (Imperial) Army. The European Regiments became Regiments of the Line, and the Company's Artillery and Engineers became part of the Royal Artillery and Royal Engineers: these formed the British Army in India.

The service records of the British Army in India will be found with the other army records in the PRO: see **18.17**. There are musters of regiments in India from 1883 to 1889 (in WO 16), but there are none for the Artillery or the Engineers. When a soldier was discharged on his return home, this was recorded in the depot musters of his regiment (WO 67), in the musters of the Victoria Hospital, Netley, 1863-1878 (WO 12/13077-13105), or in the musters of the Discharge Depot, Gosport, 1875-1889 (in WO 16).

British officers after 1859 were trained at Sandhurst (cavalry and infantry) before beginning their careers in India. Their commission papers are thus at the PRO (see **18.8-18.9**), while their records of service are with the India Office Library and Records. These can be consulted up to 1947.

The service records of European officers and soldiers of the Honourable East India Company's service, and of the Indian (Imperial) Army are mainly preserved at the India Office Library and Records, but there are some records in the PRO. Lists of officers of the European Regiments, 1796-1841, are in WO 25/3215-3219. Compensation for the sale of Indian Army commissions, 1758-1897, is recorded in WO 74. Alphabetical lists of East India Company Army pensioners (other ranks) for 1814-1866 are in WO 23/21-23, and there are more detailed registers for 1849-1868 in WO 23/17-20, and for 1824-1856 in WO 25/3137.

Registers of the death of officers in all the Indian services for the Second World War are at the General Register Office, St Catherine's House (see **4.2**). The National Army Museum has Hodson's Index, a very large secondary source card index of British officers in the Indian (Imperial) Army, the Bengal Army and the East India Company Army (but not the British Army in India): many of the entries go beyond bare facts to include colourful stories of life. Civilians and government staff are included if they had seen Army service. The cards from this index relating to the Bombay Marine, the East India Company's Navy, are to be passed to the National Maritime Museum: the main deposit of Bombay Marine records is in the India Office Library and Records.

18.27 American War of Independence, 1776-1783

The muster books and pay lists of many regiments involved in this war may be found (see **18.20**), but the certificates of men discharged in North America, which give the age and place of birth, can seldom be traced. It is unlikely that you will find anything but a man's name, rank and date of discharge in the musters. There are some pay lists and account books for Hessian troops, but they provide few personal details. Muster rolls of the Hessian troops in British pay in North America are held in West Germany: there is an index available at the Reference Desk, Kew. Some Audit Office accounts (AO 3) may be useful. The Loyalist Regiment Rolls for Provincial Troops are in the Public Archives of Canada.

18.28 South African (Boer) War, 1899-1902

The service documents of British regular soldiers who served in South Africa, and were discharged before 1913 are in WO 97 (see **18.17**): the service records of soldiers discharged after 1913 were, for the most part, destroyed by enemy bombing in the Second World War. The Medal Rolls (WO 100) sometimes contain a few personal details, such as the date of discharge or death, and the home address. For the British Auxiliary Forces, some records of the City Imperial Volunteers are at the Guildhall Library: the soldiers' documents of the Imperial Yeomanry, 1899-1902, are in the PRO (WO 128, indexed by WO 129). Other forces were raised locally in South Africa, and these records are in the PRO. Enrolment forms and nominal rolls of the local armed forces, 1899-1902, are in WO 126 and WO 127.

Death registers of British soldiers who died in South Africa, 1899-1902, are at St Catherine's House: they are indexed (see **4.2**).

18.29 Military wills

If a soldier died abroad before 1858 and left assets over a certain amount (specified by statute), grants of probate or administration were issued in the Prerogative Court of Canterbury (see **6**). Military wills of small estates did not have to be proved in court, so there is no record of these unless they have survived among pension applications and casualty returns in the War Office records: see **18.13** and **18.18** for more details. For registers of powers of attorney, see **18.13**.

18.30 Military medals

There are a considerable number of records relating to the creation and award of military medals, but they generally only give the barest details about the recipient. Because medal records contain little genealogical information, they are not discussed at length here: for more information see the information leaflets *Records of Medals; Service Medal and Award Rolls: War of 1914-1918 (WO 329)*; and *First World War War: Indexes to Medal Entitlement*. If you are interested in tracing the history of a medal's creation and design, consult the records of the Royal Mint, particularly

MINT 16. This class also contains a little correspondence from a few recipients of medals.

There were three main types of military medal: for a particular campaign; for gallantry; and for long service and good conduct.

Campaign medals began with the Waterloo Medal. There was a medal for earlier service, mostly in the Peninsular War and America, 1793-1814, called the Military General Service Medal, but in fact this was not issued until 1847, and then only to men who had survived until that date: see the books by Kingsley-Foster and Challis, which are available in the Reference Room, Kew.

The Waterloo Medal Book records the corps and regiments engaged in the battle, giving the name and rank of officers and men (MINT 16/112). Wellington's despatch of 29 June 1815, listing the officers killed and wounded, was printed as a supplement to the *London Gazette* of 1 July 1815: copies can be found in ZJ 1 and also in MINT 16/111. After Waterloo, medals were awarded for most major campaigns: examples are the Indian Mutiny Medal of 1857 and the Queen's South Africa Medal of 1899. Clasps were often awarded for particular battles within a campaign, such as a Sebastopol clasp for a Crimea Medal. The medal rolls for campaign medals, 1793-1912, are in WO 100 (seen on microfilm): they are arranged by regiment. Correspondence and papers relating to some of the actual medals are in MINT 16. The campaign medals for the First World War are in WO 329.

Gallantry medals were first awarded during the Crimean War: there is a list of the many sources available, attached to the PRO information leaflet *Records of Medals*, which should be consulted.

Records of Long Service and Good Conduct Medals, for other ranks who had served 18 years, run from 1831 to 1953 (WO 102). The records of the Meritorious Service Medal, for non-commissioned officers, run from 1846 to 1919 (WO 101). The records include details of candidates for, as well as recipients of, these awards. A register of annuities paid to recipients of the meritorious or long service awards, 1846-1879, is in WO 23/84.

18.31 Records after 1913

Service records (like those in WO 97) for soldiers discharged after 1913 are not yet in the PRO. However, a large proportion of the service records of soldiers serving between 1914 and 1920 was destroyed by bombing in the Second World War. Those records that survive are held by the Ministry of Defence, CS(R)2b, Bourne Avenue, Hayes, Middlesex UB3 1RF, to whom written enquiry should be made.

In the PRO are the registers of payments of pensions to disabled officers and men (PMG 9, PMG 42) and to the widows, children and dependents of officers killed or missing in action (PMG 11, PMG 44 - PMG 47) during the First World War. At Chancery Lane, there are the death certificates issued by the French and Belgian authorities for British and Commonwealth soldiers who died in circumstances where the civilian authorities could make such a return (e.g. in hospital): these are arranged alphabetically (RG 35/45-69). The British death certificates for the First and Second World Wars are at St Catherine's House (see **4.2**). Information about burials abroad in both world wars can be obtained fron the Commonwealth War Graves Commission: see **4.5**. For other suggestions, read N Holding's books, *World War One Army Ancestry* and *More Sources of World War One Army Ancestry*.

18.32 The Army: bibliography and sources

[An * means this work can be seen at Chancery Lane: a # means it can be seen at Kew.]

Published works

Army Lists, etc., of personnel
Army List (London, annually from 1754) #
British Biographical Archive (London, 1984 continuing) #
L S Challis, *Peninsula Roll Call* (London, 1948) #
F and A Cook, *The Casualty Roll for the Crimea* (London, 1976) #
C Dalton, *English Army Lists and Commission Registers, 1661-1714* (London, 1892-1904) #
C Dalton, *Irish Army Lists, 1661-1685* (London, 1907) #
C Dalton, *George I's Army, 1714-1727* (London, 1910-1912) #
C Dalton, *Waterloo Roll* (London, 2nd edn 1904) #
Dictionary of National Biography (London, 1909 continuing) *#
E Dwelly, *Waterloo Muster Rolls: Cavalry* (Fleet, 1934) #
H G Hart, *Army List* (London, 1839-1915) #
Imperial War Museum, *Officers died in the Great War* (London, 1921) #
Imperial War Museum, *Soldiers died in the Great War* (London, 1921-1922) #
K D N Kingsley-Foster, *Military General Service Medal, 1793-1814* (London, 1947) #
List of Officers of the Royal Regiment of Artillery, 1716-June 1914 (London, 1914) #
E Peacock, *The Army List of Roundheads and Cavaliers* (London, 2nd edn 1874) #
A Peterkin, W Johnston and R Drew, *Commissioned Officers in the Medical Services of the British Army* (London, 1968) #
Roll of Officers of the Corps of Royal Engineers from 1660 to 1898 (London, 1898) #
Royal Military Kalendar (London, 1820) #
South Africa Field Force Casualty List, 1899-1902 (1972) #

General works
D Ascoli, *A Companion to the British Army, 1660-1983* (London, 1983)
D J Barnes, 'Identification and Dating: Military Uniforms', in *Family History Focus*, ed., D J Steel and L Taylor (Guildford, 1984)
A P Bruce, *An Annotated Bibliography of the British Army, 1660-1714* (London, 1975)
P Dennis, *The Terrtiorial Army 1907-1940* (Royal Historical Society, 1987)
C Firth and G Davis, *The Regimental History of Cromwell's Army* (Oxford, 1940)
Y Fitzmaurice, *Army Deserters from HM Service* (Forest Hill, Victoria, 1988) #

J Gibson and A Dell, *Tudor and Stuart Muster Rolls* (FFHS, 1989) *

J Gibson and M Medlycott, *Militia Lists and Musters, 1757-1876* (FFHS, 1989) *

G Hamilton Edwards, *In Search of Army Ancestry* (London, 1977)

N Holding, *The Location of British Army Records: a National Directory of World War One Sources* (FFHS, 2nd edn 1987)

N Holding, *More Sources of World War One Army Ancestry* (FFHS, 1986)

N Holding, *World War One Army Ancestry* (FFHS, 1982)

J M Kitzmiller, *In Search of the 'Forlorn Hope': a Comprehensive Guide to Locating British Regiments and their Records* (Salt Lake City, 1988) #

M E S Laws, *Battery Records of the Royal Artillery, 1716-1877* (Woolwich, 1952-1970) #

M Medlycott, 'Some Georgian 'Censuses': the Militia Lists and 'Defence' Lists', *Genealogists' Magazine*, vol. XXIII, pp. 55-59.

Public Record Office, *Alphabetical Guide to certain War Office and other Military Records preserved in the Public Record Office* (Lists and Indexes, vol. LIII) *#

Public Record Office, *First World War: Indexes to Medal Entitlement* (Information Leaflet) *#

Public Record Office, *Lists of War Office Records* (Lists and Indexes, vol. XXVIII and Supplementary vol. VIII) *#

Public Record Office, *Military Records for Genealogists* (forthcoming)

Public Record Office, *Nurses and the Nursing Services: Record Sources in the Public Record Office* (Information Leaflet) *#

Public Record Office, *Records of Courts Martial: Army* (Information Leaflet) *#

Public Record Office, *Records of Medals* (Information Leaflet) *#

Public Record Office, *Records of Officers and Soldiers who have served in the British Army* (London, 1985) *#

Public Record Office, *Service Medal and Award Rolls: War of 1914-1918 (WO 329)* (Information Leaflet) *#

E E Rich, 'The Population of Elizabethan England', *Economic History Review*, 2nd ser., vol. II, pp. 247-265. (Discusses the Elizabethan muster rolls.)

A Swinson ed., *A Register of the Regiments and Corps of the British Army: the Ancestry of the Regiments and Corps of the Regular Establishments of the Army* (London, 1975)

C T Watts and M J Watts, 'In Search of a Soldier Ancestor', *Genealogists' Magazine*, vol. XIX, pp. 125-128

A S White, *A Bibliography of the Regiments and Corps of the British Army* (London, 1965)

T Wise, *A Guide to Military Museums* (Doncaster, 1986) #

Unpublished finding aids

There are many indexes to Army records in the PRO, some of which have been mentioned in the text of this chapter; for more information, ask at the Reference Desk, Kew.

Hodson's Index: officers of the East India Company Army, Bengal Army and Indian (Imperial) Army (at the National Army Museum)

Records

Exchequer and Audit Office Accounts (at Kew)
AO 1 Declared Accounts (In Rolls). 1536-1828
AO 2 Declared and Passed Accounts (In Books). 1803-1848
AO 3 Various Accounts. 1539-1886

Exchequer (at Chancery Lane)
E 101 King's Remembrancer: Accounts Various. Henry II to George III
E 157 King's Remembrancer: Licences to Pass Beyond the Seas. 1572-1677
E 182 Receivers' Accounts of Land and Assessed Taxes: Documents subsidiary to.
    1689-1830
E 351 Pipe Office Declared Accounts. 1500-1817
E 403 Exchequer of Receipt: Enrolments and Registers of Issues. Henry III to 1834

Home Office (at Kew)
HO 50 Home Office: Military Correspondence. 1782-1840
HO 51 Home Office: Military Entry Books. 1758-1855
HO 75 *Hue and Cry* and *Police Gazette*. 1828-1845

Royal Mint (at Kew)
MINT 16 Medals. 1805-1948

Ministry of Pensions (at Kew)
PIN 71 Selected War Pensions Awards Files: Pre 1914. 1854-1975. (Open immediately.)

Paymaster General's Office (at Kew)
PMG 4 Army Establishment Half Pay. 1737-1921
PMG 6 Army Establishment Foreign Half Pay, Pensions etc. 1822-1885
PMG 7 Army Establishment, Hanover, Foreign Half Pay, Pensions etc. 1843-1862
PMG 8 Army Establishment, Hanover, Chelsea Out-Pensions. 1844-1877
PMG 9 Army Establishment Pensions for Wounds. 1814-1921
PMG 10 Army Establishment Compassionate List and Royal Bounty. 1812-1916
PMG 11 Army Establishment Widows' Pensions. 1810-1920
PMG 12 Ordnance Half Pay, Pensions etc. 1836-1875
PMG 14 Army Establishment Miscellaneous Books. 1720-1862
PMG 34 Army Establishment Schoolmistresses' and Nurses' Pensions. 1909-1928
PMG 42 Ministry of Pensions, Disability Retired Pay, Gratuities, etc. 1917-1920
PMG 44 Ministry of Pensions, Pensions to Relatives of Deceased Officers. 1916-
    1920
PMG 45 Ministry of Pensions Widows' Pensions. 1917-1919
PMG 46 Ministry of Pensions Children's Allowances. 1916-1920
PMG 47 Ministry of Pensions Relatives of Missing Officers. 1915-1920
PMG 51 Power of Attorney Registers. 1800-1899

General Register Office (at Chancery Lane)
RG 4/4330-4332, 4387: registers of baptisms, marriages and burials, Royal Chelsea
    Hospital, 1691-1856

RG 33 Miscellaneous Foreign Registers and Returns. 1627-1958
RG 35 Miscellaneous Foreign Deaths. 1830-1921
RG 43 Miscellaneous Returns of Births, Marriages and Deaths: Indexes

Signet Office (at Chancery Lane)
SO 5/31: includes petitions from disabled soldiers for places as almsmen, 1660-1751

Secretaries of State (at Chancery Lane)
SP 28 Commonwealth Exchequer Papers. 1642-1660
SP 44 Secretaries of State: State Papers: Entry Books. 1661-1828

War Office (at Kew)
WO 4   Secretary at War Out-letters. 1684-1861
WO 7 Department Out-Letters. 1715-1862
WO 10 Artillery Muster Books and Pay Lists. 1708-1878
WO 11 Engineers Muster Books and Pay Lists. 1816-1878
WO 12 General Muster Books and Pay Lists. 1732-1878
WO 13 Militia and Volunteers Muster Books and Pay Lists. 1780-1878
WO 14 Scutari Depot Muster Books and Pay Lists. 1854-1856
WO 15 Foreign Legions Muster Books and Pay Lists. 1854-1856
WO 16 New Series Muster Books and Pay Lists. 1877-1898
WO 19 Royal Garrison Regiment. 1901-1906
WO 22 Royal Hospital Chelsea Pension Returns. 1842-1883
WO 23 Royal Hospital Chelsea, Chelsea Registers, etc. 1702-1917
WO 24 Establishments. 1661-1959
WO 25 Various Registers. 1660-1938
WO 30/1: registers of letters of attorney, 1755-1783
WO 31 Commander in Chief, Memoranda Papers. 1793-1870
WO 32 Registered Files: General Series. 1853-1983
WO 42 Certificates of Births, etc. 1755-1908
WO 43 Secretary at War: Correspondence: Selected 'Very Old Series' and 'Old
    Series' Papers. 1809-1857
WO 44 Ordnance Office In-Letters. 1682-1873
WO 54 Ordnance Office Registers. 1594-1871
WO 61 Commissariat Department Registers. 1791-1889
WO 64 Manuscript Army Lists. 1702-1823
WO 65 Printed Annual Army Lists. 1754-1879
WO 66 Printed Quarterly Army Lists. 1879-1900
WO 67 Depot Description Books. 1768-1913
WO 68 Militia Records. 1759-1925
WO 69 Artillery Records of Services, etc. 1756-1911
WO 70 Volunteer and Territorial Records. 1860-1964
WO 74 Army Purchase Commission Papers. 1758-1908
WO 76 Records of Officers' Services. 1764-1954
WO 96 Militia Attestation Papers. 1806-1915
WO 97 Royal Chelsea Hospital Soldier's Documents. 1760-1913
WO 100 Campaign Medals and Award Rolls: General Series. 1793-1949. (Seen on
    microfilm.)

WO 101 Meritorious Service Awards. 1846-1919. (Seen on microfilm.)

WO 102 Long Service and Good Conduct Awards. 1831-1953

WO 108 South African War Papers. 1899-1905

WO 116 Royal Hospital Chelsea Admission Books, Disability and Royal Artillery. 1715-1913

WO 117 Royal Hospital Chelsea Admission Books, Length of Service. 1823-1920

WO 118 Royal Hospital Kilmainham Admission Books. 1704-1922

WO 119 Royal Hospital Kilmainham Discharge Documents of Pensioners. 1783-1822

WO 120 Royal Hospital Chelsea Regimental Registers. c.1715-1857. (Seen on microfilm.)

WO 121 Royal Hospital Chelsea Discharge Documents of Pensioners. 1783-1822

WO 122 Royal Hospital Chelsea Discharge Documents of Pensioners, Foreigners' Regiments. 1816-1817

WO 126 South African War, Local Armed Forces Enrolment Forms. 1899-1902

WO 127 South African War, Local Armed Forces Nominal Rolls. 1899-1902

WO 128 South African War, Imperial Yeomanry Soldiers' Documents. 1899-1902

WO 129 South African War, Imperial Yeomanry Registers. 1899-1902

WO 131 Royal Hospital Chelsea Documents of Soldiers Awarded Deferred Pensions. 1838-1896

WO 143 Duke of York's School and Royal Hibernian School. 1801-1980

WO 145 Royal Red Cross. 1883-1928

WO 156 Registers of Baptisms and Banns of Marriage. 1808-1958

WO 211 H G Hart Papers. 1838-1875

WO 329 Service Medal and Award Rolls: War of 1914-1918. 1917-1926

19. The Royal Navy

19.1 Naval records: introduction

There are no systematic records listing men serving in the Navy before the Restoration (1660). The various seventeenth-century SP classes can contain much information on the Navy, particularly during the Interregnum: these have been calendared, and are therefore fairly easy to use. In 1660, officers and men serving in the fleet took an oath of allegiance to Charles II (C 215/6): similarly, an oath of association to support William III was taken by the officers of the fleet in 1696 (C 213/385-389). All these early records are in the PRO at Chancery Lane.

For the period 1660-c.1890, the relevant records are in the PRO at Kew, although tracing individuals is not particularly easy until the mid-nineteenth century. The best way of investigating the possible sources is to use N A M Rodger's *Naval Records for Genealogists*. This describes the various kinds of naval officers and ratings, the extensive range of service records (identifying 32 main types and giving descriptions and references), and provides lists of discrete series of records now split between several classes or submerged in one enormous class. As a result it is quite a complex book to use, but it has a comprehensive index. The information given here is only a small selection of the immense range of records that Rodger lists, and it concentrates on the period before the late nineteenth century. For information on the later records, you should consult Rodger.

This chapter on naval records is basically in two parts: sections **19.2-19.21** concentrate on service records while sections **19.22-19.25** discuss the wider range of personal information which can be discovered in pension records.

Of course, there are other places to discover more about life in the Navy, notably the National Maritime Museum at Greenwich, which has a huge collection of naval artefacts, records etc., the Royal Naval Museum, and the museum ships, HMS *Victory* and HMS *Belfast*; the addresses are given in **48.6**.

19.2 Commissioned officers: published sources

The fighting officers of the Royal Navy held office by virtue of a royal commission: they were, in descending order of rank, admiral of the fleet, admiral, vice-admiral, rear-admiral, commodore, captain, commander, lieutenant-commander, lieutenant and sub-lieutenant. The initial promotion to the commissioned rank of lieutenant was by examination: subsequent promotions were by merit and luck as far as captain, and by seniority above that. The names of the ranks changed their meanings somewhat over time, and in particular 'captain' was often used as the title for the officer in command of a vessel, whether he was a captain or a lieutenant.

From the end of the eighteenth century, it is fairly easy to trace the outlines of a commissioned officer's career in the Royal Navy. Start with the printed *Navy Lists*, which began as *Steel's Navy List* in 1782 and were updated quarterly from 1814. These contain seniority lists of officers, from lieutenant upwards, which are keyed to disposition lists of ships of the Navy with the officers appointed to them. The *Navy Lists* are available on open shelves in the Reference Room at Kew; the wartime confidential editions of 1914-1918 and 1939-1945 have been treated as records, and are in ADM 177.

Other printed sources are also available in the Reference Room. W R O'Bryne's *Naval Biographical Dictionary* gives the services of all commissioned officers alive in 1846. Admirals' and captains' services may be described in Charnock's *Biographia Navalis* (up to 1798). Campbell's *Lives of the British Admirals* (up to 1816), Marshall's *Royal Naval Biography* (up to 1835), and in the *Dictionary of National Biography*. See also the *British Biographical Archive*, available on request at Kew. The typescript *Commissioned Sea Officers' List*, issued by the National Maritime Museum in 1954, gives a summary list of commissioned officers and their seniorities, 1660-1815.

19.3 Commissioned officers: service records to c.1890

Before the mid-nineteenth century, documents concerning commissioned officers do not include comprehensive records of service. The surveys, described in **19.9**, are the most convenient and complete records of officers' service, but they do not cover all officers and are not always to be trusted.

There are various versions of an early list of all admirals, captains and commanders, with notes of their service, death or fate: the easiest to use are probably the alphabetical lists, 1660-1685 (ADM 10/15), 1660-1688 (ADM 10/10, which continues to 1746 arranged by seniority) and 1688-1737 (ADM 7/549). The first two also include lieutenants. For 1837, there is an address book for commissioned officers, mates, masters, surgeons, pursers and chaplains (PMG 73/2).

The Officers' Full Pay Registers, kept by the Navy Pay Office, were the authoritative record of an officer's service (ADM 24). They run from 1795 onwards, with a separate register for each commissioned rank (including surgeons and chaplains) until 1830, when a general register began; both series have indexes. The information included is not very full: name, rank and successive appointments. The Registers of Officers' Half Pay (a retainer for the services of unemployed officers, also used as a kind of pension for 'retired' officers) can provide addresses and other information over a much longer period, 1693-1836 (ADM 25/1-255; in seniority order). Earlier records of half pay, 1668-1689, are in Bill Books, entered in no particular order with many other entries as well (ADM 18/44-67); later ones, 1836-1920, are either indexed or in alphabetical order (PMG 15).

These full and half pay registers were used for the issue of certificates of service, needed as a passing qualification for a commission, or to establish entitlement to a pension. The passing certificates of master's mates and midshipmen qualifying as lieutenants often include certificates of service to date, and sometimes include baptismal certificates. Bound volumes of passing certificates and supporting documents, 1691-1832, are in ADM 107/1-63; there are indexes in the Reference Room at Kew to ADM 107/12-50, and to the baptismal certificates found in ADM 107/7 and 12-63. There is an incomplete collection of original passing certificates for 1744-1819, bound up in alphabetical order for each year (ADM 6/86-116). There are also registers of the examination of prospective lieutenants, 1795-1832, which give name, age, qualifying service and remarks for each candidate (ADM 107/64-70). Registers of service of prospective candidates, 1802-1848, are in ADM 107/71-75.

The earliest service registers were compiled by binding together certificates and annotating them. The first of these, covering admirals, captains, commanders and lieutenants, was compiled between c.1845-1875; the information contained predates this by many years (ADM 196/1-6, with an index in ADM 196/7). Later service registers are much fuller, containing dates of birth, marriage and death, names of parents and wives (but almost never of children), details of pay and pension, and assessments of character and ability. These registers were kept by several different departments, and an officer's career may be entered in three or four almost identical registers: this can be useful, as there are frequent gaps in the various series. These fuller service registers, dating from the mid nineteenth century onwards, but sometimes including information from before then, are mostly in ADM 196. There are indexes on open access in the Reference Room at Kew. For an analysis of the various series, see N A M Rodger's book.

19.4 Warrant officers: introduction

The senior warrant officers were the master, purser, boatswain, gunner, carpenter and surgeon (see **19.20** for surgeons): engineers were added later. However, masters became commissioned officers in 1808, as did pursers and surgeons in 1843, and engineers in 1847. Junior warrant officers (i.e. those who did not have to keep accounts) were the armourer, chaplain, cook, master at arms, sailmaker and school-master. Rodger gives much more detail (particularly of the expansion of the warrant officers from three branches in 1867 to twenty-four in 1945, of which all but one could proceed to commissioned rank), and his book contains many references to scattered sources relating to the junior warrant officers, which are not given here.

Chaplains can be traced through succession books (see **19.10**): there is also a published work, A G Kealy's *Chaplains of the Royal Navy, 1626-1903*. More recent records of chaplains are still held by the Chaplain of the Fleet.

As with commissioned officers, genuine service records do not start until the mid-nineteenth century. Before then, there are certificates of service, required either for promotion or pension purposes. There is a set of certificates of service for pension purposes for senior warrant officers, with compilation dates of 1802-1814, which includes service dating well back in the 1700s. The records relating to pensions, benefits to widows and orphans, and the Royal Greenwich Hospital and School are worth investigation: see **19.13** and **19.22-19.24**. There is also a black book of warrant officers not to be employed for future service, 1741-1814 (ADM 11/39). For 1837, there is an address book for commissioned officers, mates, masters, surgeons, pursers and chaplains (PMG 73/2).

See also **19.10** for a description of the succession books.

19.5 Warrant officers: masters' service records to c.1890

Masters' passing certificates for qualifications in seamanship date from c.1660-1830 (ADM 106/1908-2950); they may include certificates of baptism and service. One master may have had several certificates, as promotion to a different rate of ship required a different qualification. The certificates are arranged alphabetically.

There is an unusual series of service records for masters, compiled in the 1830s and 1840s, but covering the period 1800-1850 (ADM 6/135-268). Records were kept in individual files, containing passing certificates, certificates of service and a variety of other certificates and correspondence: the files are in alphabetical order of surname. Later registers of the more usual sort cover 1848-1882 (ADM 196/74-81).

19.6 Warrant officers: pursers' service records to c.1890

Pursers, later renamed paymasters, oversaw the supply and issue of the ship's stores, and also of the seamen's pay, when it became customary to pay them regularly. There are notes on candidates for promotion for 1803-1804 (ADM 6/121), and again for

1847-1854 (ADM 11/88). Passing certificates, giving service to date, are available for 1813-1820 (ADM 6/120), for 1851-1867 (ADM 13/79-82), and for 1868-1889 (ADM 13/247-8). The main series of service registers for pursers and paymasters covers 1852-1922 (ADM 196/11-12, 82 and 85 and ADM 6/443-444); for others, going back to 1843, see ADM 196/1 and 74-9.

19.7 Warrant officers: boatswains', gunners' and carpenters' service records to c.1890

Passing certificates, often giving previous service, for boatswains are available for 1810-1813 (ADM 6/122), 1851-1855 (ADM 13/83), 1856-1859 (ADM 13/85) and 1860-1887 (ADM 13/193-4). Certificates for gunners start earlier: they are available for 1731-1748, 1760-1797, and 1803-1812 (ADM 6/123-9). There are joint service registers for boatswains, gunners and carpenters, 1848-1855, in ADM 196/74-6; other registers, for 1855-1890, are in ADM 196/29-32, with an index in ADM 196/33. Boatswains and carpenters could and did transfer between sea service and dockyard work: records relating to dockyard employees are discussed in **19.16**.

19.8 Warrant officers: engineers' service records to c.1890

There are two series of service registers for engineers. One, including ratings and boys as well as officers, covers 1837-1879 (ADM 196/71 for 1837-1839, and ADM 29/105-11 for 1839-1879; with internal indexes). The other covers 1856-1886 (ADM 196/23-25, indexed by ADM 196/26-28). Both these series include the complete careers of engineers entering the service between these years; the latter also includes the complete careers of engineers actually in service in 1856.

19.9 Naval officers: surveys, 1817-1851

The end of the Napoleonic wars in 1815 meant that the Navy shrank in operational strength from 145,000 to 19,000 men. Because there was no means of retiring officers, there were ten times as many as were required. In order to discover which officers had the best claims to be employed, the Admiralty sent out circular letters to both commissioned and warrant officers, asking them to provide dates of birth or details of service: the replies were bound up and used for reference by the Admiralty. However, the coverage is by no means complete, as it depended on the officer receiving and replying to the letter: many replies were lost, and the accuracy of some of them is doubtful.

There are returns for surveys in 1816-1818 for boatswains, gunners and carpenters (ADM 11/35-37), and by commissioned officers (ADM 9/2-17, indexed by ADM 10/2-5, and with strays at ADM 6/66). Another survey in 1822, repeated in 1831, asked for details of age from commissioned officers and masters (ADM 6/73-85; ADM 106/3517). Admirals were surveyed in 1828 (ADM 9/1, with an index at ADM 10/1 and strays at ADM 6/66). Between 1833 and 1835 masters and pursers were surveyed (ADM 11/2-3, masters; ADM 6/193-196, pursers). A survey of 1846 required commissioned officers to state age, address and previous service (ADM 9/18-61, with indexes at ADM 10/6-7): in 1851 masters were asked to provide the same information (ADM 11/7-8, indexed in ADM 10/6-7). Other surveys of masters were carried out in 1855 and 1861 (ADM 11/9), and pursers were surveyed again in 1852 and 1859 (ADM 11/42-4).

19.10 Naval officers: succession books

Succession books were a type of officers' service record arranged by ship, not by individual officer: however, most are indexed by name as well as ship, so they can provide a fairly easy way of tracing a commissioned or warrant officer from ship to ship.

In the usual form, a page was devoted to each ship, and the successive appointments to each position in the ship were listed. The earliest succession books cover commissioned and warrant officers, 1673-1688 (ADM 6/425-426), followed by admirals, captains and commanders only, 1688-1725 (ADM 7/655). There is a later series for captains, commanders and lieutenants, which covers the years 1780-1847 (ADM 11/65-72).

Masters, surgeons, surgeon's mates, sailmakers and some others appear in one series of succession books, 1733-1807, with a gap 1755-1770 (ADM 106/2896-2901). Another series is of pursers, gunners, boatswains and carpenters, as well as some dockyard officers, 1764-1831 (ADM 106/2898 and 2902-2906), with a further series of the same, 1800-1839 (ADM 76/192 and ADM 11/31-33).

Succession books, 1699-1824, of junior officers appointed by Admiralty warrant or order (i.e., midshipmen ordinary, volunteers per order, chaplains, masters at arms, schoolmasters and scholars of the Royal Naval Academy) are in ADM 6/427 and 185.

19.11 Naval officers: other sources

There are many other possible sources of information on an officer's career, such as records of candidates for promotion, black books of officers not to be employed again, confidential reports, and registers of officers unfit for service. These records are numerous and scattered: the easiest way to locate the ones relating to the particular rank that you are interested in is to consult Rodger's *Naval Records for Genealogists*.

In addition, there are, of course, the records of the ships in which the officer served. Logs kept by the captain (ADM 51, ADM 53, ADM 55), the master (ADM 52, ADM 54) and by lieutenants (at the National Maritime Museum) do not contain any personal information, but they do provide a professional record of the ship's voyages which can prove fascinating.

Surgeons, however, were required to keep a general journal on the health of all the ship's company and on possible circumstances affecting it, as the Navy had a keen interest in preserving the health of its men: as a result these logs are often the most approachable source for the history of a voyage (ADM 101: a selection only).

19.12 Naval ratings: musters and pay books

There was no centralised record of ratings' services until the introduction of continuous service in 1853. Before then, the main sources for tracing a seaman are the individual ship's muster book and pay book. To use these, you need to know the ships on which he served. If you are fortunate enough to have a seaman who was in receipt of a Chatham or Greenwich pension, for which there are indexed registers, you ought to be able to discover the ships he worked in quite easily (see **19.22-19.24**). Otherwise, you may need luck and hard work: a preliminary search in the certificates of service which were issued to some ratings (see **19.13**) might be well worth while.

Musters, or lists of the ship's company, are available at Kew from 1667 to 1878 (ADM 36-ADM 41): there are a few medieval ones in E 101, at Chancery Lane. The musters followed a standard format, described by Rodger, whose book should be consulted for the various abbreviations used, and for the meaning of the whole exercise. There were general musters, held annually, and eight-weekly monthly musters, which contain extra information on various deductions from pay, such as for treatment for venereal disease. Information on each member of the ship's company was entered into the following columns in both general and monthly musters: Number, Entry & Year, Appearance [i.e. arrival on board], Whence & Whether Prest or not, Age [added in 1764: it means age at entry to the ship, not at the time of the muster], Place & Country of Birth [added in 1764], No. and Letter of Ticket [for wages], Men's Names, Qualities, D DD or R [discharged, discharged dead or run; also DS, discharged to sick quarters], Time of Discharge & Year, Whither or for What Reason [e.g. DD - fell from aloft].

The pay books, 1691-1856 (ADM 31-ADM 35), which duplicate much of the information of the musters, have one big advantage; they contain 'alphabets' (indexes of surnames in alphabetical order of first letter only) from about 1765, some fifty years before the musters had them. It may be worth checking through the alphabets in the pay lists before going on to look at the musters, 1667-1878 (ADM 36-ADM 41). The pay books were copied from the musters, and may contain more errors: in some cases, they may also include information about next-of-kin to whom remitted wages were paid.

When tracing men from ship to ship, it may be useful to consult the hospital musters, particularly if the name was marked DS (discharged to sick quarters): see **19.21**.

19.13 Naval ratings: certificates of service

The standard way of tracing a naval seaman or rating, before the introduction of continuous service in 1853, is to use the muster books and pay books (see **19.12**). However, this can take so long and is so dependent on getting the right ship, that it is sensible to investigate easier sources: if you are lucky, you will save yourself considerable time.

Ratings needed to have a certificate of service to support a claim to receive a pension, a gratuity or a medal. Thus there are certificates of service issued by the Navy Pay

Office, 1790-1865, among the papers of ratings and marines applying for entry to Greenwich Hospital as in-pensioners: although the certificates were issued from 1790, the services recorded go back at least forty years before then (ADM 73/1-35, arranged alphabetically).

Other such certificates issued between 1834 and 1894 are in ADM 29, for claims for pensions, medals, or admittance to Greenwich Hospital. This class also includes the entry books of certificates of service of warrant officers and ratings, 1836-1894, sent to Greenwich Hospital for the assessment of the claims of their children to be admitted to the Hospital Schools (ADM 29/17, 19, 25, 34, 43, 50, 59, 70 and 80-96: indexed by ADM 29/97-104). As orphans had priority, many of the certificates are of the service of men already dead, and, as always, the service predates the certificate by many years. The original certificates of service to which the entry books refer, together with supporting documentation such as baptismal and marriage certificates, are in ADM 73/154-389.

19.14 Naval ratings: continuous service records, 1853-c.1890

In 1853 began the first centralised registration of ratings, with the introduction of continuous service engagements. Each man had a continuous service number: the registers are arranged by these numbers, but there are alphabetical indexes. The first series covers ratings between 1853 and 1872 (ADM 139); the second, the complete careers of those who entered between 1873 and 1891, together with some continuations from ADM 139 (ADM 188/2-244, with indexes at ADM 188/245-267, on open access in the Reference Room). Both series give date and place of birth, physical characteristics on entry, and a summary of service. In the case of those who entered as boys, there is a form giving parental consent.

19.15 Naval officers and ratings: service records after 1891

The service records of officers who entered the service after the 1880s, and of ratings who enlisted after 1891, are not in the Public Record Office: for information, write to the Ministry of Defence, CS(R)2a, Bourne Avenue, Hayes, Middlesex, UB3 1RS. However, if they were serving in the 1890s or later, but entered the Navy before the above dates, their service records will be in the PRO. It may be worth checking the pensions to disabled ratings before 1914, in PIN 71 (see **19.22**).

There is a card index of naval officer casualties of the First World War (1914-1919) in the Reference Room at Kew. See also the indexes to the registers of naval war deaths, 1914-1921 and 1939-1948, at the General Register Office, St Catherine's House, mentioned in **4.2**.

19.16 Naval dockyard employees

Naval dockyards, situated all round the world, were run by civilian employees of the Navy Board, who were naval officers but not sea officers. However, there was considerable movement between the two branches of the service. The commissioners (in charge of the yards) and the masters attendant (in charge of ships afloat) were usually retired sea officers. Dockyard shipwrights, having served their apprenticeship, often became carpenters in the Navy, and might return to be master shipwrights, and in the same way the other master tradesmen and the boatswain were normally recruited from the sea service. The career of any skilled man may therefore have to be traced in the records of both services: naval pensioners often began a second career in the dockyards.

The main source for larger dockyards is the class of Yard Pay Books, 1660-1857 (ADM 42); for minor yards, treated as ships, try the pay books and musters in ADM 32, ADM 36, and ADM 37. In addition, ADM 106 contains some interesting sources, particularly the description books of artificers, 1748-1830; these include physical descriptions of the men in some yards.

There are other sources for dockyard employees given in the PRO information leaflet, *Dockyard Employees: Documents in* the *Public Record Office*: this also gives a summary of records relating to individual yards, arranged by place. For information on the policing of the dockyards, see **23.1**.

If you do find an ancestor who worked in one of the many naval dockyards, you may be interested in the photographs of work in dockyards, 1857-1961, in ADM 195.

19.17 Royal Navy apprentices

Information about dockyard and other naval apprentices may be found among the Admiralty and Secretariat Papers (ADM 1) and the Navy Board Records (ADM 106). In the Admiralty Digest (a subject index in ADM 12, relating to ADM 1 and other classes), it is worth checking under the heading 'Apprentices in Dockyards'. Examination results for dockyard and artificer apprentices, from 1876, are among the records of the Civil Service Commission (CSC 10).

There are apprenticeship registers for children from Greenwich Hospital School, 1808-1838, in ADM 73/421-448.

19.18 Sea Fencibles

The Sea Fencibles were a part-time organisation of fishermen and boatmen commanded by naval officers, formed for local defence, especially against invasion. Musters and pay lists, 1798-1810, are in ADM 28, together with the appointments of naval officers to the Sea Fencibles.

19.19 Royal Naval Reserve: service records

The Royal Naval Reserve was established in 1859; it was then a reserve force of merchant seamen, with a set limit of 30,000 men. By 1890, 20,000 had been enrolled. Service records of RNR officers, from 1862, are in ADM 240. A representative selection of service records of other ranks is in BT 164. For other records of merchant seamen, see **25**.

Records of the Royal Naval Volunteer Reserve, 1903-1958, have not yet been transferred to the PRO: contact the Ministry of Defence at the address given in **19.15**.

19.20 Naval medical services: surgeons and nurses

Surgeons and their mates were the only medical help available on individual ships, although nurses worked in naval hospitals and hospital ships from the seventeenth century.

Surgeons were warranted to ships by the Navy Board, having qualified by examination at the Barber-Surgeons' Company (until 1796). There is an incomplete collection of surgeons' passing certificates, c.1700-1800, issued by the Barber-Surgeons' Company in London, or by examining boards of surgeons at the outports or overseas (ADM 106/2592-2603, arranged alphabetically). There is an index to these in the Reference Room, Kew, giving dates and texts of the certificates, but no references to the documents.

There are several series of service registers for surgeons: the longest covers 1774-1886 (ADM 104/12-29, indexed in ADM 104/11). One particularly interesting series of registers of service contains correspondence on the merits of individual officers, 1829-1873 (ADM 104/31-40). Another interesting series of reports on questions of pay, half pay and promotion of surgeons, 1817-1832, includes much personal information about named officers (ADM 105/1-9, with internal indexes). For other sources, consult Rodger's book. The Medical Journals, 1785-1880 (ADM 101) can provide an insight into the daily lives of some of these surgeons: although they are mostly concerned with treatment of patients, some entries provide interesting details of life on ship.

There are full pay books of surgeons and nurses at Haslar Hospital, 1769-1819 (ADM 102/375-397) and at Plymouth Hospital, 1777-1819 (ADM 102/683-700). Other volumes in ADM 102 include the pay lists, often bound up with the musters, of many hospitals and stationary hospital ships in Britain and many other parts of the world; the musters of sea-going hospital ships will be found with the other musters in ADM 36 and ADM 37.

Greenwich Hospital, in its original form, paid no widows' pensions, but it employed the widows of seamen in its infirmary. Service registers of such nurses exist between 1704 and 1876 (ADM 73/83-88). Other surviving records include applications for this employment made by the widows of ratings, 1819-1842 (ADM 6/331), and 1817-1831 (ADM 6/329).

During the nineteenth century the Navy ceased to employ women as nurses, until the establishment of the professional Naval Nursing Sisters in 1883, renamed Queen Alexandra's Royal Naval Nursing Service (QARNNS) in 1902. From 1884, Head Nursing Sisters were included in the *Navy List*: other nursing officers were included from 1890. There are service records for nurses, 1884-1909 (ADM 104/43); succession books, listing nursing staff by hospital, are available for 1921-1939 (ADM 104/96).

For more detailed information on the history of naval nurses and the availability of records relating to them, see the PRO information leaflet *Nurses and the Nursing Services: Record Sources in the PRO*.

19.21 Naval medical services: hospital records

There are extensive muster lists of patients in naval hospitals and stationary hospital ships at Antigua, Ascension Island, Bermuda, the Cape of Good Hope, Chatham, Deal, Gibraltar, Halifax in Nova Scotia, Haslar, Jamaica, Madras, Malta, Plymouth, Woolwich, Yarmouth and for many other hospitals and hospital ships as well, dating from 1740 to 1880 (ADM 102). There are also several musters of lunatics at Hoxton House, 1755-1818 (ADM 102/415-420) and at Haslar, 1818-1854 (ADM 102/356-373); Yarmouth too was a major hospital for naval lunatics. Reports on the treatment of naval lunatics, 1812-1832, are in ADM 105/28. The musters of sea-going hospital ships will be found with the other musters in ADM 36 and ADM 37.

19.22 Pensions to naval officers and ratings

Until well into the nineteenth century, provision of pensions within the Navy was haphazard. There was no general entitlement to a pension for long service (although half pay was used to provide a kind of pension for officers), but there was a limited number of pensions available for particularly deserving cases, and there is usually a certain amount of personal information recorded in support of claims to pensions.

The Chatham Chest, set up about 1590, and funded by a deduction from seamen's wages, paid pensions to the dependants of warrant officers (including midshipmen and surgeons), ratings and dockyard workers killed in action or on service. The earliest payments are in the account books, 1653-1657. There are registers of payments to pensioners, 1675-1799, with alphabetical lists of the pensioners at Lady Day in each year. The indexes of pensions, 1744-1797, give names, amount of pension, particulars as to wounds, names of ships in which they served, and other information. All these records are in ADM 82; there are also other records of the Chatham Chest in ADM 80.

Disabled seamen were often petitioners to the crown for places as almsmen in the royal church foundations: there is a register of such petitions, 1660-1751, in SO 5/31.

The Royal Greenwich Hospital was founded in 1694 as a home for infirm seamen and marines: in-pensioners lived there until 1869. There are entry books of these in-pensioners, 1704-1869, which give very full particulars, and are mostly indexed. Admission papers, although dating from 1790-1865, relate to service going back to at least 1750; they give descriptions, with details of service and the nature of disablement. Both entry books and admission papers are in ADM 73. Papers of candidates for admission, 1737-1859 are in ADM 6/223-266. The church registers of the hospital, 1705-1864 (RG 4/1669-1679 and RG 8/16-18) can be very interesting: most entries relating to in-pensioners are of deaths, and occasionally include some comment as to manner of death.

The hospital also supported many more out-pensioners, who lived elsewhere: they received the out-pension as a form of superannuation, but were often still in full employment elsewhere. There are registers of candidates for out-pensions, 1789-1859, in ADM 6/271-320. Pay books of out-pensions, 1781-1809, are in ADM 73/95-131. For 1814-1846 they are in ADM 22/254-443, arranged alphabetically. From 1842-1883 they were paid by the War Office, through district pension offices, including many abroad: these records are arranged by place (WO 22).

Other pensions were available for wounds, or for meritorious service, or for medals and honours. Records of these are in ADM 23 and PMG 16.

A new class, PIN 71, contains the personal files on over 5,000 disabled ratings and soldiers who served before 1914 and who received disablement pensions: the information contained includes medical records, accounts of how injuries were incurred, and the men's own account of the incident, and conduct sheets. These conduct sheets give place of birth, age, names of parents and siblings, religion, physical attributes, marital and parental status. The class is alphabetically arranged: unfortunately it is a selection only, and does not cover all disabled soldiers and sailors of that date.

In 1853, ratings were given the prospect of receiving a pension after twenty years' continuous service: as many signed on at eighteen, naval pensioners were often much younger than the term suggests. Few records of superannuation to ratings survive.

A few officers also received Greenwich Hospital out-pensions: there are registers covering 1814 (ADM 22/254), 1815-1842 (ADM 22/47-9) and 1846-1921 (PMG 71). At various dates from 1836, officers became eligible for a retirement pension, or superannuation, either automatically on reaching a certain age, or upon application. Pension records for officers are extensive, and are fully listed by Rodger.

Warrant officers, and the civil establishment of the Navy, were paid pensions out of the Navy estimates; there are registers for 1694-1832 (ADM 7/809-822, indexed by ADM 7/823).

19.23 Pensions and other benefits to widows and orphans

The Chatham Chest also paid pensions to the widows of warrant officers, ratings and dockyard workers killed in action or on service: the registers of payment were shared with the pensions to wounded men (ADM 82, described in **19.22**). Before the mid nineteenth century, Greenwich Hospital paid no widows' pensions as such, but employed seamen's widows in its infirmary. They may be traceable through the establishment books (ADM 73: see **19.20** and **1.3**). Greenwich Hospital also provided a school for children of officers and men, to which orphans had priority of admission (see **19.24**).

The Charity for the Relief of Officers' Widows paid pensions to the poor widows of commissioned and warrant officers. Pay books, 1734-1835, are in ADM 22/56-237; for 1836-1929 they are in PMG 19/1-94. The papers submitted by widows applying for pensions between 1797 and 1829 include many marriage and death certificates (ADM 6/335-384): there is an index in the Reference Room at Kew. Similar papers for 1808-1830, referred for further consideration in doubtful cases, are in ADM 6/385-402.

The Compassionate Fund, voted by Parliament from 1809, was administered by the Admiralty: it dealt with pensions and grants to orphans and other dependents of officers killed in action or who had died in service, not otherwise eligible for assistance. The registers of applications for relief give the officer's rank, date of death, length of service and ship, date and place of marriage, the applicant's age, address and relationship to the dead officer, and other circumstances: they run from 1807 to 1836 (ADM 6/323-328). Pay books run from 1809 to 1921, giving the names and ages of recipients, and their relationship to the dead officer: from 1885 warrant officers' next-of-kin were eligible (1809-1836, ADM 22/239-250; 1837-1921, PMG 18).

The Admiralty's own pensions included pensions to the widows and orphans of commissioned officers, dating from 1673 (1673-1781, including widows of masters, ADM 18/53-118; 1694-1832, ADM 7/809-822, indexed by ADM 7/823; 1708-1818, ADM 181/1-27; later ones in ADM 22, ADM 23, PMG 16, PMG 19 and PMG 20). From 1830 warrant officers' widows were eligible for Admiralty pensions.

In addition to these pensions, a lump sum of one year's wages, known as the Royal Bounty, was payable to the widows, dependent children, or indigent mothers aged over 50, of officers and ratings killed in action. The papers submitted by dependants, in support of claims to the Bounty, consist mainly of marriage and death certificates, with other documents attesting the age, relationship or poverty of the applicants. There is a broken series of these running from 1672-1822 (ADM 16/3023-3025), with an index in the Reference Room, Kew. In addition, there are pay lists of the Bounty, 1739-1787, which give the name, address and relationship of the dependant, the name, quality and ship of the dead man, and the amount paid (ADM 106/3018-3020); these are not indexed.

These pension records are only the most important of those available: all are listed in detail in Rodger's book, which can be consulted at Kew. The exception is PIN 71, which contains over 1,000 personal files on the widows of naval ratings and Army other ranks whose service was before 1914. This is only a selection of such files, but it is alphabetically arranged, and very informative (see **19.22**).

19.24 Royal Hospital School, Greenwich

The school, attached to the Royal Greenwich Hospital, was established for the sons of seamen shortly after the hospital was founded. In 1805 it was joined by a similar

142

school for younger orphans (boys and girls), the Royal Naval Asylum. Orphans of officers and ratings killed in action or who had died in service had the prior claim for admittance, but entry was not restricted to them. The school admission papers, 1728-1870, include certificates of birth or baptisms for the children applying for entry, together with the marriage certificate of the parents, and details of the father's naval service (ADM 73/154-389: see also **19.13** for entry books). They are arranged by initial letter. The registers of applications, which are mostly indexed, include the same information, 1728-1883 (ADM 73/390-449). Registers of later claims are in ADM 161-ADM 163. The church registers, including many burials, for the Royal Hospital School and the Royal Naval Asylum are in RG 4/1669-1679, and RG 8/16-19.

19.25 Naval wills and powers of attorney

Copies or original wills made by officers and ratings are attached to many applications made after their deaths for their back pay: registers of these claims and wills can be used to find the names of next of kin.

There are two series of ratings' wills. Seamen's Wills (ADM 48) has wills, 1786-1882, alphabetically arranged: there are registers in ADM 142, which act as indexes, extending as far as 1909. These registers give the date of death and, for the first 14 volumes, name, address and relationship of the executor. The second series, Seamen's Effect Papers (ADM 44), covers 1800-1860, and contains the claims by executors and next of kin for the back pay of ratings who died in service. Some of these include wills, birth and marriage certificates and other supporting documents. Indexes are provided by the registers in ADM 141, using an odd system of alphabetisation.

Wills of commissioned and warrant officers, 1830-1860, may be found in similar claims for back pay in ADM 45: there is a card index to pieces 1-10 in the Reference Room at Kew.

Until 1815, seamen who died with over £20 of back wages owing to them (a frequent occurrence) had their wills proved in the Prerogative Court of Canterbury, whose records are in the PRO (see **6**). There is also a register of wills made at the naval hospital, Gibraltar 1809-1815 (ADM 105/40). Other wills of naval seamen, to c.1750, may be found in the records of the Commissary Court of London (London division) at the Guildhall Library.

Registers of powers of attorney, 1800-1899, often give details of next of kin, assigned to receive pay, or acting as executors (PMG 51). For c.1800-1839, they are arranged alphabetically (PMG 51/1-2).

19.26 Naval medals

Medal rolls do not give detailed information about individuals: before 1914, they are arranged by ship, and there are no name indexes.

Campaign medal rolls for the Navy are in ADM 171. This class, which is seen on microfilm, includes the award of the following, and some other, campaign medals: the Naval General Service Medal (1793), the China Medal (1840, 1857 and 1900), the Crimea Medal (1854), the Indian Mutiny Medal (1857), the Ashanti Medal (1873), the Arctic Medal (1875-1876), the Queen's South Africa Medal (1899), the King's South Africa Medal (1901), the Africa General Service Medal (1902), the Delhi Durbar Medal (1911), the British War Medal (1914-1920), and the Victory Medal and Stars (1914-1920). Lists of recipients of the Naval General Service Medal, 1793-1840, are given in the book by K Douglas-Morris.

Gallantry medals were first instituted during the Crimean War: others were added later, particularly during the First World War. Some surviving recommendations are in ADM 1 and ADM 116 (look under code 85 in both). Registers of gallantry awards to naval officers during the First World War are also in ADM 171; there is an index available, which gives the dates of entries in the *London Gazette*. Another index gives the dates of entries in the *London Gazette* for most awards to naval personnel from 1942 onwards. The PRO holds a complete set of the *London Gazette* at Kew, in the class ZJ 1. For more details, see the PRO information leaflets, *Records of Medals* and *First World War: Indexes to Medal Entitlements*.

19.27 The Royal Navy: bibliography and sources

[An * means this work can be seen at Chancery Lane; a # means it can be seen at Kew.]

Published works

***Navy Lists* etc., of personnel**
British Biographical Archive (London, 1984 continuing) #
J Campbell and W Stevenson, *Lives of the British Admirals* (London, 1917) #
J Charnock, *Biographia Navalis* (London, 1794-1798) #
Dictionary of National Biography (London, 1909 continuing) *#
K Douglas-Morris, *The Naval General Service Medal, 1793-1840* (Margate, 1982) #
A J Kealy, *Chaplains of the Royal Navy, 1626-1903* (Portsmouth, 1905) #
J Marshall, *Royal Naval Biography* (London, 1823-1830) #
National Maritime Museum, *Commissioned Sea Officers of the Royal Navy, 1660-1815* (London, 1954) #
Navy List (London, 1814 onwards) #
W R O'Bryne, *Naval Biographical Dictionary* (London, 1849) #
D Steele, *Steele's Navy List* (London, 1782-1817) #

General works
Calendar of State Papers Domestic, Charles I (London, 1858-1897) *
Calendar of State Papers Domestic, Charles II (London, 1860-1947) *
Calendar of State Papers Domestic, Commonwealth (London, 1875-1886) *
Public Record Office, *Admiralty Records as Sources for Biography and Genealogy* (Information Leaflet) *#
Public Record Office, *Dockyard Employees: Documents in the Public Record Office* (Information Leaflet) *#

Public Record Office, *First World War: Indexes to Medal Entitlement* (Information Leaflet) *#

Public Record Office, *Nurses and the Nursing Services: Record Sources in the Public Record Office* (Information Leaflet) *#

Public Record Office, *Records of Medals* (Information Leaflet) *#

Public Record Office, *Tracing an Ancestor in the Royal Navy: Officers* (Family Fact Sheet) #

Public Record Office, *Tracing an Ancestor in the Royal Navy: Ratings* (Family Fact Sheet) #

N A M Rodger, *Naval Records for Genealogists* (London, 1988) *#

Unpublished finding aids

ADM 1 Naval courts martial, 1680-1701: index #

ADM 6 Widows' pensions: index #

ADM 6 Naval chaplains: index #

ADM 6/15-23: Commission and warrant books: index #

ADM 6/193: Pursers: index #

ADM 6/223-247: Registers of out-pensioners, candidates for admission to Greenwich Hospital: index #

ADM 13 Officers' and warrant officers' marriage certificates: index #

ADM 20 Treasurers' ledgers, 1660-1699: index #

ADM 45/1-10: Officers and civilian effects papers: index #

ADM 48 Naval wills: index #

ADM 106 Naval surgeons: index #

ADM 171/78-88: Royal Naval Medal roll, First World War: index #

ADM 199 War history cases and papers: index #

ADM 242 Naval officers casualties and ships losses, First World War. Index only: records to which these relate do not survive. #

Awards of medals to foreign navy personnel, First World War: index. #

Royal Navy Russian honours and orders, First World War: index. #

Royal Navy service book index, applications and recommendations, First World War: index. #

Ships convoys, Second World War: index. #

Ships and submarines, Second World War: index. #

Operations/Code Names, Second World War: index. #

Records

Admiralty (at Kew)

[NB. Many of the following dates are the dates when entries were first or last made in registers; they are not the covering dates of the information included, which can extend on either side of the dates given].

ADM 1 Admiralty and Secretariat Papers. 1660-1976

ADM 6 Admiralty and Secretariat, Various Registers, Returns and Certificates. 1673-1960

ADM 7 Admiralty and Secretariat: Miscellanea. 1563-1953

ADM 9 Surveys of Officers' Services. 1817-1848

ADM 10 Officers' Services: Indexes and Miscellanea. 1660-1851

ADM 11 Officers' Service Records, Series I. 1741-1897

ADM 12 Admiralty and Secretariat Indexes and Compilations Series III. 1660-1938

ADM 13 Admiralty and Secretariat Supplementary. 1803-1917

ADM 18 Bill Books. 1642-1831

ADM 22 Registers of Salaries and Pensions. 1734-1934

ADM 23 Additional Pension Books. 1830-1934

ADM 24 Officers' Full Pay Registers. 1795-1905

ADM 25 Officers' Half Pay Registers. 1693-1924

ADM 28 Sea Fencibles Pay Lists. 1798-1810

ADM 29 Officers' Service Records, Series II and Ratings' Services. 1802-1919

ADM 31 Controllers Pay Books. 1691-1710

ADM 32 Ships' Pay Books, Ticket Office. 1692-1856

ADM 33 Ships' Pay Books, Treasurer's Series I. 1669-1778

ADM 34 Ships' Pay Books, Treasurer's Series II. 1766-1785

ADM 35 Ship's Pay Books, Treasurer's Series III. 1777-1832

ADM 36 Ships' Musters Series I. 1688-1808

ADM 37 Ships' Musters Series II. 1792-1842

ADM 38 Ships' Musters Series II. 1793-1878

ADM 39 Ships' Musters Series IV. 1667-1798

ADM 41 Ships' Musters, Hired Armed Vessels. 1794-1815

ADM 42 Yard Pay Books. 1660-1857

ADM 44 Seamen's Effect Papers. 1800-1860

ADM 45 Officers' and Civilians' Effects Papers. 1830-1860

ADM 48 Seamen's Wills. 1786-1882

ADM 51 Captains' Logs. 1669-1852

ADM 52 Masters' Logs. 1672-1840

ADM 53 Ships' Logs. 1799-1963

ADM 54 Supplementary Logs Series I: Masters' Logs. 1808-1871

ADM 55 Supplementary Logs Series II; Explorations. 1757-1904

ADM 73 Greenwich Hospital Miscellaneous Registers, etc. 1704-1981

ADM 80 Greenwich Hospital: Various. 1639-1957

ADM 82 Chatham Chest Records. 1617-1807

ADM 101 Medical Journals. 1785-188

ADM 102 Hospital Musters. 1740-1860

ADM 104 Medical Departments: Service Registers and Registers of Deaths and Injuries. 1742-1956

ADM 105 Medical Departments Miscellanea. 1696-1890

ADM 106 Navy Board Records. 1659-1837

ADM 107 Navy Board Passing Certificates. 1691-1848

ADM 116 Admiralty and Secretariat Cases. 1852-1960

ADM 139 Continuous Service Engagement Books. 1853-1872

ADM 141 Registers of Seamen's Effects Papers. 1802-1861

ADM 142 Registers of Seamen's Wills. 1786-1909

ADM 161 Greenwich Hospital Registers of Claims, Greenwich Hospital School. 1865-1930

ADM 162 Greenwich Hospital Registers of Claims, Orphans. 1882-1961

ADM 163 Greenwich Hospital Registers of Claims, Sons and Daughters of Commissioned Officers. 1883-1922

ADM 171 Medal Rolls. 1793-1972. (Most are seen on microfilm: some are open early.)

ADM 177 *Navy List* Confidential Edition. 1914-1945

ADM 181 Navy Estimates. 1708-1957

ADM 188 Registers of Seamen's Services. 1873-1895

ADM 195 Civil Engineer-in-Chief Photographs. 1857-1961

ADM 196 Officers' Service Records Series III. 1756-1954

ADM 240 Royal Naval Reserve: Records of Officers' Services. 1862-1960

Registrar General of Shipping and Seamen (at Kew)
BT 164 Registrar General of Shipping and Seamen: Royal Naval Reserve Representative Records of Service. 1840-1946

Chancery (at Chancery Lane)
C 213/385-389: oath of association sworn by officers of the fleet, 1696
C 215/6: oath of allegiance sworn by officers and men serving in the fleet, 1660

Civil Service Commission (at Kew)
CSC 10 Examination Tables of Marks and Results. 1876-1964

Exchequer (at Chancery Lane)
E 101 King's Remembrancer: Accounts Various. Henry II to George III

Admiralty Transport Department (at Kew)
MT 23 Admiralty Transport Department: Correspondence and Papers. 1795-1917

Ministry of Pensions and National Insurance (at Kew)
PIN 26 Selected War Pensions Awards Files: First World War. 1920-1972. (Many more files are expected to be transferred into this class in the near future. Most pieces are closed for 50 years.)

PIN 71 Selected War Pensions Awards Files, Pre 1914. 1854-1975. (This class is open immediately.)

Paymaster General's Office (at Kew)
PMG 15 Naval Establishment Half Pay, Retired Pay and Unattached Pay. 1836-1920

PMG 16 Naval Establishment, Miscellaneous Services, Wounds, Widows, etc., Pensions etc. 1836-1920

PMG 18 Naval Establishment Compassionate List. 1837-1921

PMG 19 Widows of Naval Officers Pensions. 1836-1929

PMG 20 Widows of Marine Officers, Relatives of Naval and Marine Officers, etc., Killed on Duty, Pensions, etc. 1870-1919

PMG 51 Power of Attorney Registers. 1800-1899

PMG 73/2: address book for commissioned officers, mates, masters, surgeons, pursers and chaplains, 1837

General Register Office (at Chancery Lane)

RG 4/1669-79: Royal Greenwich Hospital and School, registers of baptisms, marriages and burials

RG 8/16-18: Royal Greenwich Hospital and School, registers of baptisms, marriages and burials

Signet Office (at Chancery Lane)

SO 5/31: includes petitions from disabled seamen for places as almsmen, 1660-1751

Secretaries of State (at Chancery Lane)

SP 16 State Papers Domestic Charles I. 1625-1649

SP 18 Council of State, Navy Commission, and Related Bodies: Orders and Papers (*formerly* State Papers Interregnum). 1649-1660

SP 29 State Papers Domestic Charles II. 1660-1685

London Gazette (at Kew)

ZJ 1 *London Gazettes*. 1665-1986

20. The Royal Marines

20.1 Introduction

Soldiers formed part of the complements of ships of war from the earliest times, but the first British military unit to be raised specifically for sea service was the Lord Admiral's Regiment, formed in 1665. This subsequently became part of the Army establishment, and is the direct ancestor of the modern regiment, the Buffs. From 1690 additional Marine Regiments were raised in wartime for sea service, and disbanded at the end of the war, when the soldiers were discharged and the officers went on half pay. Oath rolls exist for the oath of association in support of William III taken by the First and Second Marine Regiments in 1696 (C 213/290-291).

Though intended for and usually employed in the sea service, these early Marine Regiments were part of the Army and were organised like other foot regiments. Parties serving at sea came under naval discipline and were borne on their ship's books (on a separate list) for wages and victuals (see **19.21**), but in other respects their administration and records did not differ from those of other foot regiments (see **18.20**). Marine Regiments sometimes served ashore as ordinary infantry, while other (non-Marine) infantry regiments contributed soldiers for sea service as necessary.

These Marine Regiments were disbanded for the last time in 1749. At the approach of war again in 1755, a new Corps of Marines was formed under Admiralty authority. This was not part of the Army, and it had no regimental structure, though it continued to use Army ranks and uniform. The fifty companies were divided for administrative and recruiting purposes between three divisions, with their depots at Portsmouth, Plymouth and Chatham. From 1805 to 1869, there was a fourth division, based at

Woolwich. Both divisions and companies were purely administrative entities and not fighting formations; officers and other ranks were drafted for sea service without regard to them, and each ship's party of Marines commonly included men of several companies. The Marine depots maintained records similar to those of foot regiments, while Marine detachments at sea were borne on the ships' books as before. Marines sometimes served ashore, particularly as landing parties, when they would be organised *ad hoc* into companies and battalions. If serving under military command in such circumstances they came under military discipline, but otherwise they were responsible solely to the Admiralty.

The duties of Marines afloat were, in action to lay down musketry on the enemy's decks; and otherwise to mount sentries and contribute to the unskilled labour of working the ship. From time to time they continued to be supplemented in these roles by infantrymen lent by the Army. Until the twentieth century the duties of the Royal Marines were almost entirely to provide detachments for ships. In 1914, however, a large force of Marines was landed to defend Antwerp, and some subsequently fought on the Western Front. In the 1930s the Marines developed a new role as part of the Mobile Naval Base Defence Organisation, and from 1942 they contributed units known as Commandos which operated under Combined Operations Headquarters, and specialised in raids on enemy coasts. After the war this became the principal duty of the corps.

Another category of troops serving afloat were the artillerymen who manned the mortars carried by bomb vessels. Disciplinary and other problems with them led the Admiralty in 1804 to form companies of marine artillery to man the bombs, which led to a formal division in 1859 between the Royal Marine Artillery (with barracks at Eastney, near Portsmouth) and the Royal Marine Light Infantry, which lasted until the two corps were amalgamated in 1923. They were known respectively as the Blue Marines and the Red Marines.

The Royal Marines Museum, at Eastney, is worth a visit: the address is in **48.6**.

20.2 Royal Marines: commissioned officers

Commissions in the Royal Marines, unlike commissions in the Army, were not sold, but were free appointments. The scattered nature of Marine forces meant that a considerable number of junior officers was required, and that there was little chance for promotion within the Marines as the number of senior officers needed was so small. Some Marine officers went on to buy further promotion in the Army.

Commissions and appointments, 1703-1713, are recorded in ADM 6/405; for 1755-1814, they are in ADM 6/406. There is no index, and they contain no genealogical information. There are some lists of officers' services, 1690-1740, in ADM 96/1-2. There are two incomplete sets of *Lists of Marine Officers*, 1757-1850 and 1760-1886 (ADM 118/230-336 and ADM 192 respectively), which can be used to discover the outline of an officer's career: they are indexed from 1770. The *Navy List*, published annually from 1814, also includes Marine officers. There is a register of commissions issued between 1849 and 1858 (ADM 201/8).

There is a separate service register for officers of the Royal Marine Artillery, 1798-1855, in ADM 196/66. Marine officers' service records from 1837 to 1915, with some from 1793 onwards, will be found in ADM 196/58-65 and ADM 196/83. These dates are the dates of commission, and not of subsequent service; the last details available come from 1954. All enquiries concerning officers appointed after 1915 should be sent to the Commandant General, Royal Marines, at the address given in **48.7**.

There are some other sources which may be worth investigation. Pay records in ADM 96 can give some extra information. There are lists of half pay officers for 1789-1793 and 1824-1829 in ADM 6/410-413. The survey of officers conducted in 1822 (as for the Navy: see **19.9**) can provide details of age (ADM 6/409). For 1837, there is an address book for Marine officers on half pay (PMG 73/2). Confidential letters on officers' affairs, 1868-1889, are in ADM 63/27-30; they are indexed. The general administrative papers in ADM 193 and ADM 201 may provide more information on individuals.

20.3 Royal Marines: warrant officers

There are few separate records of warrant officers, many of whom went on to become commissioned officers. The only separate register relating to warrant officers' services covers 1904-1912 (ADM 196/67). For Woolwich division, 1812, there is an alphabetical list of warrant officers and ratings, entered for limited service (ADM 6/407).

20.4 Royal Marines: other ranks

Records relating to Royal Marines other ranks are abundant, but at the moment individual Marines are hard to trace. Until 1884, there was no system of numbering individuals, and the records are arranged by division. However, a card index to the attestation forms will shortly be made available, which should help considerably.

The attestation forms, 1790-1901 (ADM 157) were completed at the time of enlistment, but are now filed in order of discharge date (except for those of the Chatham division) up to 1883. They can include details of discharge or death. Each division also kept its own discharge books (ADM 81 and ADM 183-ADM 185). For the Woolwich division there is an alphabetical list of warrant officers and ratings who had entered for limited service, dated 1812 (ADM 6/407).

The description books, c.1750-1940 (ADM 158) consist of several different, though related, types of register, arranged by date of enlistment, and then by first letter of surname. They provide similar information to the Army's description books (see **18.20**); age on enlistment, parish of birth, and a brief physical description. They do not give details of service.

Marines aboard ship (provided that their ship is known) should appear in the ship's muster books and pay lists: see **19.12**.

In 1884, a system of divisional numbers was introduced, with each man having a unique number in his division. Unfortunately, there is no key to the numbers, so that a search in the service registers in ADM 159 may be lengthy. However, the information contained in these registers is useful: date and place of birth, trade, religion, date and place of enlistment, physical description, a full record of service, and comments on conduct, promotions etc. The registers so far available cover men who enlisted up to 1901, some of whom served up to the Second World War; they are open to inspection.

For records of service of men enlisted after 1901, write to the Royal Marines, Drafting and Record Office, at the address given in **48.7**.

20.5 Royal Marines: medals

Medal records for the Royal Marines are the same as those for the Navy: see **19.26**. For correspondence on good conduct medals and gratuities, 1849-1884, which includes individual service records, see ADM 201/21.

20.6 Pension records

Pension records for the Royal Marines and their families are fairly extensive, but in general the records are the same as those for Naval pensions: the Royal Hospital Greenwich was founded to aid both the Navy and the Marines. For more details, see **19.22-19.24**. There are two alphabetical registers of Marine officers receiving Greenwich pensions, 1862-1908, which give considerable details (ADM 201/22-23).

20.7 Royal Marines: wills

There is a collection of Royal Marines wills and administrations, 1740-1764, in ADM 96/524. Wills were later deposited in the Navy Pay Office by Royal Marines other ranks, 1786-1909 (ADM 48, indexed by ADM 142). There is also a register of probates affecting the payment of pensions, 1836-1915, in PMG 50.

20.8 Royal Marines: families

Each division of the Royal Marines kept its own registers of births, marriages and deaths, of children and wives borne on the strength. These registers give the Marine's rank, and some information on posting from the division to a ship or station, under the heading 'disposal'. The registers for Chatham division cover 1830-1913 (ADM 183/114-120); for Plymouth, 1862-1920 (ADM 184/43-54); for Woolwich (marriage rolls only), 1822-1869 (ADM 81/23-25); and for the Royal Marine Artillery, 1810-1853 (ADM 193/9), and 1866-1921 (ADM 6/437). For Portsmouth division, there appear to be none surviving.

Pensions to the widows of Marine officers will be found in ADM 96/523 (1712-1831), PMG 16 (1836-1870), PMG 20 (1870-1919), and PMG 72 (1921-1926). The last class, PMG 72, appears to relate to other ranks as well. For pensions to officers' children, 1837-1921, see PMG 18. More information on families may perhaps be found in the registers of powers of attorney, 1800-1899 (PMG 51).

For details of pensions and other help provided to families by the Royal Greenwich Hospital, which catered for the Marines as well as the Navy, see **19.23-19.24**.

20.9 The Royal Marines: bibliography and sources

[An * means this work can be seen at Chancery Lane: a # means it can be seen at Kew.]

Published works

C Field, *Britain's Sea Soldiers* (Liverpool, 1924)
J A Good, *A Register of Royal Marine War Deaths, 1939-1945* (Southsea, 1987)
Public Record Office, *Royal Marine Records in the Public Record Office* (Information Leaflet) *#
Royal Marine Museum, *The Royal Marines: a Short Bibliography* (Southsea, [1978])
P C Smith, *Per Mare Per Terram: A History of the Royal Marines* (St Ives, 1974)

Records

Admiralty (at Kew)
ADM 2 Admiralty and Secretariat Out-Letters: for Royal Marines letters,1703-1845
ADM 6 Admiralty and Secretariat: Various Registers, Returns and Certificates. 1673-1960
ADM 23 Additional Pension Books. 1830-1834
ADM 48 Seamen's Wills. 1786-1882
ADM 63 Royal Marines: Royal Marines Office Letter Books, Miscellaneous. 1834-1889
ADM 81 Royal Marines, Woolwich Division. 1805-1869
ADM 96 Royal Marines Pay Office Records. 1688-1862
ADM 142 Registers of Seamen's Wills. 1786-1909
ADM 157 Royal Marines Attestation Forms. 1790-1901
ADM 158 Royal Marines Description Books. c.1750-1940
ADM 159 Royal Marines Registers of Service. 1842-1905
ADM 165 Greenwich Hospital Registers of Pensions to Naval and Marine Officers and Greenwich Hospital Staff. 1871-1961
ADM 166 Greenwich Hospital Registers of Pensions to Widows and Seamen and Marines, etc., 1882-1949
ADM 175 Coastguard Records of Service. 1816-1947. (Includes service records of Royal Marines, 1900-1923.)
ADM 183 Royal Marines, Chatham Division. 1755-1941
ADM 184 Royal Marines, Plymouth Division. 1760-1941
ADM 185 Royal Marines, Portsmouth Division. 1763-1941
ADM 192 Royal Marines, Lists of Officers. 1760-1886
ADM 193 Royal Marines, Miscellaneous. 1761-1918
ADM 196 Officers' Service Record Series III. 1756-1954

ADM 201 Royal Marines Office: Correspondence and Papers. 1761-1971

Paymaster General's Office (at Kew)

PMG 16 Naval Establishment Miscellaneous Services, Wounds, Widows, etc., Pensions etc. 1865-1920

PMG 18 Naval Establishment Compassionate List. 1837-1921

PMG 20 Widows of Marine Officers, Relatives of Naval and Marine Officers, etc., Killed on Duty, Pensions etc. 1870-1919

PMG 50 Probate Registers. 1836-1915

PMG 51 Power of Attorney Registers. 1800-1899

PMG 72 Widows and Dependants of Seamen and Marines Pensions etc. 1921-1926

PMG 73 Naval Establishment Miscellanea. 1821-1837

21. The Royal Air Force

21.1 Operational and service records

The Royal Air Force was formed on 1 April 1918, by the amalgamation of the Army's Royal Flying Corps and the Navy's Royal Naval Air Service, founded in 1912 and 1914 respectively. Before the amalgamation, service records will be either Army (and therefore not yet in the PRO) or Navy (registers of officers' service records are in ADM 273, but they are not informative and are closed until the mid 1990s). Operational records of the Royal Flying Corps during the First World War are available (AIR 1, AIR 23, AIR 25, AIR 27-AIR 29). Medals awarded for First World War service are in WO 329 for the Royal Flying Corps and Royal Air Force, and in ADM 171 for the Royal Naval Air Service: for more information see the PRO information leaflet *Records of Medals*. Pensions to disabled airmen and gratuities for the First World War may be found in PMG 42.

The only complete muster list of the Royal Air Force was compiled on the amalgamation of these two forces, on 1 April 1918 (AIR 1/819 and AIR 10/232-237).

The PRO holds no RAF personnel records. The Air Ministry records that it does hold consist of central office papers and operational records, which often include the names of serving men and women. Personnel records of all RAF ranks will be released, to relatives only, on application to RAF Personnel Management. Queries about officers are dealt with by RAF Barnwood and about other ranks by RAF Innsworth: the addresses are given in **48.7**. Other records, such as notification of casualties and honours, are held by RAF Officers' Records.

Officers' careers can be traced in the *Air Force List*: a complete set is available at Kew. For 1939-1954 the *Confidential Air List* is kept separately (in AIR 10). Correspondence with officers, recommendations for awards and promotions, confidential reports and combat reports are found in AIR 1: indexes are available. For records of RAF prisoners of war, see AIR 20/2336, and **36.3**.

Operations Record Books (AIR 24-AIR 29) are the diaries of the RAF and do not contain much personal detail, apart from promotions, transfers and awards. Crashes and casualties incurred during operations are recorded here. For those which happened on non-operational flights, apply to the Air Historical Branch, Ministry of Defence (address in **48.7**).The General Register Office, St Catherine's House, has indexes to RAF war deaths, 1939-1948, and also to RAF births, marriages and deaths abroad, from 1920: see **4.2**.

The RAF Museum at Hendon has photographs, air log books and a huge collection of privately-deposited officers' records, as well as planes. Its archive includes a card index of every aircraft that flew in the RAF. The Imperial War Museum at Duxford is another place to see early RAF planes. The addresses are given in **48.6**.

21.2 The Royal Air Force: bibliography and sources

[An * means this work can be seen at Chancery Lane: a # means it can be seen at Kew.]

Published works

Air Force List (from 1918) #
Public Record Office, *Air Records as Sources for Biography and Family History* (Information Leaflet) *#
Public Record Office, *Records of Medals* (Information Leaflet) *#

Records

Admiralty (at Kew)
ADM 171 Medal Rolls. 1793-1972
ADM 273 Royal Naval Air Service: Registers of Officers' Services. 1914-1918

Air Ministry (at Kew)
AIR 1/819 and AIR 10/232-237: muster of all RAF personnel on 1 April 1918
AIR 2 Correspondence. 1887-1980
AIR 10 Air Publications. 1913-1976
AIR 20/2336: list of all aircrew held prisoner by the Germans in late 1944
AIR 24 Operation Records Books: Commands. 1920-1960
AIR 25 Operation Records Books: Groups. 1914-1962
AIR 26 Operation Records Books: Wings. 1920-1963
AIR 27 Operation Records Books: Squadrons. 1911-1967
AIR 28 Operation Records Books: RAF Stations. 1913-1961
AIR 29 Operation Records Books: Miscellaneous Units. 1912-1967

Paymaster General's Office (at Kew)
PMG 42 War of 1914-1918 Disability Retired Pay, Gratuities, etc. 1916-1920
PMG 44 War of 1914-1918 Pensions to Relatives of Deceased Officers. 1916-1920

War Office (at Kew)
WO 329 Service Medal and Award Rolls: War of 1914-1918. 1917-1926

22. The Coastguard and the preventive services

22.1 Introduction

The Coastguard was formed in 1822 by the amalgamation of three of the services for the prevention of smuggling. These were the Revenue Cruisers, the Riding Officers (both dating from 1698) and the Preventive Water Guard, set up in 1809. These three services were part of the Customs, although from 1816 the officers and men of the Revenue Cruisers were appointed by the Admiralty, and the Riding Officers were often appointed from the Army. The Riding Officers operated in Kent and Sussex: the Revenue Cruisers were largely confined to the Kent, Sussex and East Anglian coasts and the Thames estuary, until the end of the eighteenth century, when they covered the English and Welsh coasts. Scotland had its own fleet. In 1831 another preventive service, the Coastal Blockade (set up by the Admiralty in 1816) was also amalgamated into the Coastguard. These four preventive forces employed nearly 6,700 men at the time of amalgamation.

Confusingly, the Board of Excise had its own Revenue Cruisers and its own officers called Riding Officers: these covered the entire country, not just the coasts of Kent and Sussex, and were concerned with the collection (and preventing the evasion) of excise duty.

The Board of Customs had overall control of the Coastguard, despite the active role of the Admiralty, from 1822 until 1856, when the Admiralty was granted control by the Coastguard Service Act. After 1856, the duties of the Coastguard continued to be the defence of the coast, the provision of a reserve for the Navy, and the protection of the revenue against evasion by smuggling: over the next seventy years new responsibilities were added, stressing assistance to shipping. The Coastguard as run by the Admiralty consisted of three distinct bodies; the Shore Force, the Permanent Cruiser Force and the Guard Ships, naval ships which lay at major ports to act as headquarters of Coastguard districts.

22.2 The preventive forces: service records

For information relating to the (Customs) Riding Officers and the Preventive Water Guard, try the records of the Board of Customs (see **24.4**); for the (Excise) Riding Officers and (Excise) Revenue Cruisers, try the Excise records (see **24.4**); for the Coastal Blockade, try the Admiralty records (see **19**); and for the Revenue Cruisers, try both the Admiralty and the Customs records.

A good place to start may be with the published reports made to Parliament about the operation of the various preventive services; these can include genealogical information such as name, age, place of birth, date of appointment, etc. The reports cover officers and men appointed to the Preventive Boat Service (i.e. the Preventive Water Guard), November 1816-March 1819 (ZHC 1/693), and Coastal Blockade men killed in conflicts with Kent and Sussex smugglers, 1821-1825 (ZHC 1/822). Later reports on the Coastguard can give details of earlier service in the preventive services (see **22.3**). Pension records for c.1818-1825 are in CUST 40/28.

Administration of the Revenue Cruisers was split between the Customs and the Admiralty, with the latter appointing the officers and men after 1816; this system continued when the Revenue Cruisers were merged into the Coastguard in 1822. Officers serving in Revenue Cruisers are given in the *Navy List* from 1814. Admiralty appointments to Revenue Cruisers of lieutenants, masters and boatswains for 1816-1831 are in ADM 6/56; for later appointments see **22.3**.

22.3 The Coastguard: service records

The published Parliamentary Papers on the Coastguard can provide information such as name, age, place of birth, date of appointment, etc., for commanders of Revenue Cruisers in Scotland, 1822-1823 (ZHC 1/773); captains and commanders in the Preventive or Coastguard service and Revenue Cruisers on 1 July 1833 (ZHC 1/1092); and chief (warrant) officers of the Coastguard, with previous service, 1853 (ZHC 1/2390).

There are registers of Admiralty nominations of officers and ratings to the Coastguard in England, 1819-1866 (ADM 175/74-80, with indexes in ADM 175/97-98 for 1823-1866); in Ireland, 1820-1849 (ADM 175/74, 81, 99-100); and in Scotland, 1820-1824 (ADM 175/74). Nominations for England may also be found in ADM 6/199 (1831-1850), and in ADM 175/101 (1851-1856). Discharge records for 1858-1868 are in ADM 175/102. Many people from the Bengal Marine entered the Coastguard after 1856, when the East India Company gave up its navy (see also **18.26**). Between 1866 and 1886 there is an unexplained gap in the records. For Coastguard officers, 1886 to 1947, there are indexed Service Registers (ADM 175/103-107, 109-111). For Coastguard ratings, 1900-1923, there are service record cards (ADM 175/82A-84B, alphabetical, 1900-1923; ADM 175/85-89, with an index in ADM 175/108, 1919-1923; and ADM 175/90, 1919-1923). Discharge registers for 1919, when large numbers of Coastguards were paid off after the First World War, are in ADM 175/91-96.

Officers serving in Revenue Cruisers (part of the Coastguard since 1822) are given in the *Navy List* from 1814. Admiralty appointments to Revenue Cruisers of lieutenants, masters and boatswains for 1816-1831 are in ADM 6/56; for 1822-1832 they are in ADM 2/1127. Quarterly musters of Revenue Cutters, 1824-1857, are in ADM 119. Men serving on the Revenue Cruisers can also be traced in the ship's Establishment and Record Books, 1816-1879 (ADM 175/24-73). For the establishment of the Revenue Cruisers between 1827 and 1829, try CUST 19/52-61.

Among the Customs records are some other items relating to the Coastguard. Coastguard minute books, 1833-1849, are in CUST 29/40-42; Coastguard statistics are in CUST 38/32-60; and CUST 39/173 contains the salaries and incidents of the Thames Coastguard, 1828-1832. Pension records, 1857-1935, are in PMG 23; other records of pensions, 1855-1935, are in ADM 23. Chief officers were also entitled to receive Greenwich pensions after 1866 (PMG 70).

22.4 The Coastguard and the preventive services: bibliography and sources

[An * means this work can be seen at Chancery Lane: a # means it can be seen at Kew.]

Published works

E Carson, *The Ancient and Rightful Customs* (London, 1972)
Public Record Office, *Customs and Excise Records as Sources for Biography and Family History* (Information Leaflet) *#
Public Record Office, *Records of H M Coastguard* (Information Leaflet) *#
N A M Rodger, *Naval Records for Genealogists* (London, 1988) *#
G Smith, *Something to Declare! 1,000 Years of Customs and Excise* (London, 1980)
W Webb, *Coastguard: An Official History of HM Coastguard* (London, 1976)

Records

Admiralty (at Kew)
ADM 2/1127: appointments to Revenue Cruisers, 1822-1832
ADM 6/56: appointments to Revenue Cruisers, 1816-1831
ADM 6/199: Admiralty nominations to the Coastguard in England, 1831-1850
ADM 23 Additional Pension Books
ADM 119 Ships' Musters: Coastguard and Revenue Cruisers. 1824-1857
ADM 175 Coastguard Records of Service. 1816-1947

Board of Customs and Excise (at Kew)
CUST 19/52-61: establishment of Revenue Cruisers, Michaelmas 1827 - Christmas 1829
CUST 29/40-42: Coastguard minute books, 1833-1849
CUST 38/32-60: Coastguard statistics, 1828-1912
CUST 39/173: Thames Coastguard salaries and incidents, 1828-1832
CUST 40/28: Preventive Service: pensions, c.1818-1825

Paymaster General's Office (at Kew)
PMG 23 Coastguard Civil Pensions. 1857-1935

Parliament (at Kew)
ZHC 1/693: *A Return of Officers and Men Appointed to the Preventive Boat Service between November 1816 and March 1819*
ZHC 1/773: *Names of Commanders of Revenue Cruisers in Scotland, 1822-1823*
ZHC 1/822: *Names of Men Killed on the Kent and Sussex Coasts in Conflicts between the Coast Blockade and Smugglers 1821-1825*
ZHC 1/1092: *A Return of Captains and Commanders in the Preventive or Coastguard Service and Revenue Cruisers on 1 July 1833*
ZHC 1/2390: *Return of Names, Age, Date of Appointment, Gross Pay and Allowances of All Chief Officers of the Coastguard, with Previous Service*

23. Police forces

23.1 Metropolitan Police

Records of early attempts to police London, 1756-1835, are in T 38/671-694.

The Metropolitan Police Act, 1829, set up the force and defined its district as an area of about seven miles radius from Charing Cross (excluding the City of London): in 1839, this was extended to fifteen miles radius. In 1835 the Bow Street Horse Patrol was incorporated into the force, followed by the Bow Street Foot Patrol and the River Thames Force in 1839. The City of London Police has successfully resisted any attempts at amalgamation with the Metropolitan Police. The Metropolitan Police also had responsibility for the police of the royal dockyards and military stations at Portsmouth, Chatham, Devonport, Pembroke and Woolwich, from 1860 to 1934.

The Metropolitan Police District was composed of seventeen divisions (twenty after 1865), each under the charge of a superintendent: maps of the divisions and their changing boundaries can be found in MEPO 15. Divisional records have not been transferred to the PRO. Incomplete divisional records are held by the Records Section at New Scotland Yard, but those of the Thames division are held at the Wapping Police Station Museum. Neither of these is open to the public, but both will try to answer written enquiries: the addresses are given in **48.6**.

Recruits were supposed to be between twenty and thirty-five, well built, at least 5' 7'' in height, literate and of good character. Scotsmen were well represented in both the Metropolitan and City Police Forces. Staff records are good, but have not survived in full: in particular, there are none between May 1857 and November 1869. Nearly all provide name, rank, warrant number, division and dates of appointment and removal: other information given is noted in square brackets:

numerical registers, September 1829 - March 1830 (MEPO 4/31-32) [gives also the officer's height and cause of removal from the force].
alphabetical register, 1829-1836 (HO 65/26) [gives also the dates of promotion or demotion].
pensions and gratuities, 1829-1859 (MEPO 5/1-90) [mentioned in general correspondence and papers].
returns of death whilst serving, 1829-1889 (MEPO 4/2), with an index (MEPO 4/448) [cause of death].
alphabetical register of joiners, September 1830 - April 1857, July 1878-1933 (MEPO 4/333-338) [the earliest volumes give the name and addresses of referees].
register of pensions to widows of officers killed on duty, 1840-1858 (MEPO 4/33).
attestation ledgers, February 1869 - May 1958 (MEPO 4/352-360) [signatures of recruit and witnesses: there is a section at the back for police stationed at the royal dockyards and military stations: arranged by warrant number].
certificate of service records, January 1889 - November 1909 (MEPO 4/361-477) [arranged by warrant number: includes a description of the recruit, date of birth,

trade, marital status, residence, number of children, name and place of last employer, previous public service, surgeon's certificate, postings to divisions, dates of promotion or demotion, and causes of removal].
registers of leavers, March 1889 - January 1947 (MEPO 4/339-351) [indexed].

There is also a register of local constables sworn to act within the Metropolitan Police district, 1839-1876 (MEPO 4/3-5): there is no index.

It is unfortunate that the very full certificate of service records should cover such a short period: it seems that no earlier or later records of this type survive. It also appears that the service records of policewomen (first appointed in 1919) do not survive. Joining papers and particulars of service of certain distinguished officers have been preserved among the Special Series of correspondence and papers from the Commissioner's Office (MEPO 3/2883-2921): these personnel files are subject to closure for at least seventy-five years.

An index of names of officers is now being made available at Kew as it is being compiled by the Metropolitan Police. So far this is largely drawn from the registers of joiners, 1829-1836. It is not a complete index of all officers who have served in the Metropolitan Police, and does not necessarily include all the information about an individual officer which is to be found in the staff records.

Another index is available at Kew, covering officers who joined between 1880 and 1889. This had been compiled from those years' annual Police Orders, which give details of officers pensioned, promoted, dismissed and transferred (MEPO 7). The Police Orders are subject to fifty year closure.

Pension records, dating back to 1853, are still held by the Pensions Branch of the Metropolitan Police: they are willing to answer written enquiries (address in **48.7**). Many of these records will shortly be transferred to the PRO, into MEPO 21.

The Metropolitan Police were among the first to apply photography for practical purposes: as a result there are two sets of photographic records of police life. The photographs of police stations, 1857-1983 (MEPO 14), have brief histories of the stations attached to the earlier pictures, while MEPO 13 contains photograph albums compiled from earlier prints, documents etc., illustrating the development of the Metropolitan Police from about 1770 to the present day. Both these classes are open to inspection without waiting for the usual thirty years from creation.

Other information on the early years of the Metropolitan Police can be found in *Hue and Cry* and the *Police Gazette*, 1828-1845 (HO 75).

23.2 Royal Irish Constabulary

A single peace-keeping force, the Irish Constabulary, was created in 1836 when the local groups of sub-constables were united under the command of an Inspector-General. It was given the title Royal Irish Constabulary in 1867. The RIC was responsible for the whole of Ireland with the exception of Dublin (policed by the Dublin Metropolitan Police, founded in 1786), and so was disbanded in August 1922.

For the earlier local forces, a list of superannuations awarded was published by order of Parliament in 1832, giving names, period of service, amount granted, and the nature of the injury which was the cause of the superannuation (ZHC 1/1045).

The service records of members of the Royal Irish Constabulary are very full (HO 184). The registers are arranged by service number, but there are separate alphabetical indexes. They normally give name, age, height, religious affiliation, native county, trade, marital status, native county of wife (but not her name), date of appointment, counties in which the man served, length of service and date of retirement or death, but no information about parentage. Separate registers, with integral indexes, were compiled for officers and for members of the auxiliary forces (HO 184).

Pensions and allowances granted to officers, men and staff, and to their widows and children are recorded among the Paymaster General's records (PMG 48), and usually give the recipient's address. There are also registers of deceased pensioners (1877-1918) and of awards of pensions made on the disbandment of the force in this class. Among the Colonial Office records are files on pension options at the time of disbandment, arranged by county (CO 904/175-6).

There are more records relating to the activities of the Irish police, but although there are references among them to individual officers there is no way of finding them short of reading through great numbers of files (CO 903, CO 906, HO 45, HO 100, T 1, T 160-T 164, T 192).

Records relating to the Irish Revenue Police, 1830-1857, are in CUST 111.

23.3 South African Constabulary

The PRO has the original correspondence and registers of in- and out-letters of the Colonial Office, relating to the South African Constabulary, 1902-1908 (CO 526, CO 639 and CO 640). A large proportion of this correspondence relates to individuals: however, much of the correspondence that is noted in the registers has in fact been destroyed. The registers have name indexes, and can provide some information even if the correspondence noted has not survived.

Although there are no service records, information on individuals can be found. The general orders give appointments, postings, leave on medical grounds and resignations. There are some pension returns, supplying the name of the widow and place of payment (Britain or South Africa). There are also nominal rolls of various kinds: casualties, men taken on (sometimes supplying the name and address of next-of-kin), men placed on the married establishment, and men taken off the strength. In addition, individuals are sometimes mentioned in correspondence.

There appears to have been some confusion between the South African Constabulary and the various local armed forces: men who joined the Constabulary sometimes served with other forces (see **18.28**).

23.4 Other police forces

Police records of other forces are not public records. Those which survive are held either by the appropriate local record office (or national archive in the case of colonial police forces), or by the force itself.

The City of London Police have registers listing every member of the force since warrant numbers were introduced on 9 April 1832, together with personal files on 95% of the officers who have served since that date: for further information, write to the City of London Police Record Office at the address given in **48.6**.

The Royal Military Police keep their own records: write to the address given in **48.7**.

For railway police, see **26.2**.

23.5 Police forces: bibliography and sources

[An * means this work can be seen at Chancery Lane: a # means it can be seen at Kew]

Published works

Police Historical Society, *Notes for Family Historians* (Police Historical Memo No 1, 1987)
Public Record Office, *Metropolitan Police Records of Service* (Information Leaflet) *#
Public Record Office, *Records of the Royal Irish Constabulary* (Information Leaflet)*#
R Whitmore, *Victorian and Edwardian Crime and Punishment from Old Photographs* (London, 1978)

Records

Colonial Office (at Kew)
CO 526 South African Constabulary: Original Correspondence. 1902-1908
CO 639 South African Constabulary: Register of Correspondence. 1902-1908
CO 640 South African Constabulary: Register of Out-letters. 1902-1908
CO 903 Ireland, Confidential Print. 1885-1919
CO 904 Dublin Castle Records. 1795-1926
CO 906 Irish Office. 1796-1924

Board of Customs and Excise (at Kew)
CUST 111 Irish Revenue Police. 1830-1857

Home Office (at Kew)
HO 45 Registered Papers. 1839-1971

HO 65/26: alphabetical register of Metropolitan Police, 1829-1836
HO 75 *Hue and Cry* and *Police Gazette*. 1828-1845
HO 100 Ireland, Correspondence and Papers. 1782-1851
HO 184 Royal Irish Constabulary. 1816-1922

Metropolitan Police (at Kew)
MEPO 2 Office of the Commissioner: Correspondence and Papers. 1799-1984
MEPO 4 Office of the Commissioner: Miscellaneous Books and Papers. 1829-1981.
    (Partial index available.)
MEPO 5 Office of the Receiver: Correspondence and Papers. 1829-1972
MEPO 7 Police Orders. 1829-1983
MEPO 13 Public Information Department: Photographs. c.1770-1980
MEPO 14 Photographs of Police Stations. 1857-1983
MEPO 21 Metropolitan Police: Records of Police Pensioners. (To be transferred to
    the PRO in the near future.)

Paymaster General's Office (at Kew)
PMG 48 Royal Irish Constabulary, Pensions. 1873-1925

Treasury (at Kew)
T 1 Treasury Board Papers. 1557-1920
T 38/671-694: financial and administrative records of early attempts to police
    London, 1756-1835
T 160 Finance Files. 1887-1948
T 161 Supply Files. 1905-1961
T 162 Establishment Files. 1890-1948
T 163 General Files. 1888-1948
T 164 Pensions (Superannuation Files). 1893-1970
T 192 Ireland Files. 1920-1922

House of Commons
ZHC 1/1045 *House of Commons Sessional Papers, 1831-1832*, vol. XXVI, p. 465 (list
    of superannuations of local Irish forces)

24. Crown employees and civil servants

24.1 Royal household officials and servants

The Royal Archives has a card index of members of the royal household, 1660-1837 (compiled from the records of the Lord Chamberlain and the Lord Steward, which are in the PRO, and from other sources elsewhere), and is prepared to answer postal enquiries. The address is given in **48.6**.

The Lord Chamberlain was broadly responsible for 'upstairs': the chambers, the wardrobe, the office of robes, ceremonies, revels, musicians, chapels, housekeepers, messengers, yeomen of the guard, watermen, physicians, artists, craftsmen and other offices such as keeper of the lions at the Tower. There are records of appointments, 1660-1851 (LC 3/61-71) and 1851-1901 (LC 5/237-241). Records of payments, 1516-1782 are in LC 5/11-83: there is a partial index to these and other documents in LC 5, including entry books of wills and letters of attorney, 1750-1784 (LC 5/104-106).

The Lord Steward was responsible for 'downstairs', until 1854, when his office was abolished, and its functions were taken over by the Master of the Royal Household, whose records are not public records. The Lord Steward, and later the Master, had responsibility for the kitchen offices, the counting house, the wood and coal yards, the gardens and stables, and a whole host of other offices such as keeper and repairer of the buckets. Warrants of appointments, 1660-1820, are in LS 13/246-267.

There are many other sources for royal household servants, such as the accounts in E 101, E 351, LC 9, LS 1, LS 2, LS 3 and T 38: see the PRO information leaflet, *Royal Warrant Holders and Household Servants*.

24.2 Royal warrant holders

The issue of royal warrants to tradesmen, with the right to use the royal coat of arms and the phrase 'By Appointment', was recorded systematically from the 1830s. Warrants to tradesmen supplying ceremonial items (e.g. peruke makers) and to those supplying more personal items (e.g. combs, perfumes and corset stays) to the office of robes, 1830-1901, are in LC 13/1-5. Warrants to tradesmen supplying such items as furnishings, linens and stationery for Queen Victoria are in LC 5/243-246. Each volume has an internal index. The original bills presented by tradesmen, whether warrant holders or not, are in LC 11.

Before the 1830s, the situation was not so well-regulated. Trademen's appointments, 1660-1837, appear with the appointment of household servants in LC 3/61-70.

For other possible sources, see the PRO information leaflet, *Royal Warrant Holders and Household Servants*.

24.3 Civil servants

There are a number of printed sources available at Kew on the postings of senior civil servants, but they do not provide personal information. The main one is the *British Imperial Calendar*, which runs from 1810 to 1972, when it became the *Civil Service Year Book*. From 1852 there is the *Foreign Office List*, and from 1862 the *Colonial Office List*. Sainty and Collinge's lists of *Office Holders in Modern Britain* cover the period 1660-1870, and include officials of the Admiralty, the Board of Trade, the Colonial Office, the Foreign Office, the Home Office, the Navy Board, Royal Commissions of Inquiry, the ,ecretaries of State, and the Treasury.

There are few personal details about civil servants in the public records, and it is quite difficult to trace them. If you know the office or department, it is worth looking through its records to find establishment lists, etc., which may possibly be useful. To discover where to find the records of a particular small or defunct office, look in Part 3 (the index) and Part 1 of the *Current Guide*.

Another possibility, for nineteenth century departments, would be to explore the parliamentary papers, which contain annual reports from the various branches of the civil service, and also include many reports on aspects of its work. There is a full set available at Kew (ZHC 1 and ZHL 1), and there are indexes at both Kew and Chancery Lane. From the indexes it is not clear if some of the returns are statistical, or if they contain personal information of some kind. Some certainly do: for example, there is a complete list of civil staff in post at the Ordnance Survey in England on 31 March 1863 (ZHC 1/2817), and another for the Ordnance Survey in Scotland, 1854-1858, in ZHC 1/2451.

If you do find such lists as a result of exploring the parliamentary papers, please could you inform the staff at the Reference Desk, so that the information can be shared.

Other possible sources outside the particular department's own records may be among the records of the Treasury (e.g. the Departmental Accounts in T 38), the pension records of the Paymaster General (PMG 27 and PMG 28), and the records of the Civil Service Commission, although details given there are mostly to do with passing the qualifying examination (CSC 8 and CSC 10). One useful class of Civil Service Commission records, which used to be at the PRO but is now kept by the Society of Genealogists, is CSC 1, the evidences of age submitted by candidates for appointment between 1855 and 1880.

24.4 Customs officers and Excise men

In contrast to other civil servants, there is a fair amount of material for the employees of the two separate Boards of Customs and Excise: the PRO information leaflet *Customs and Excise Records as Sources for Biography and Family History*, which contains many useful guidelines as to the contents of particular types of record, should be consulted.

Warrants for the appointment of Customs officers, 1714-1797, are in C 208, indexed by C 202/267-269. The Customs Board minute books, in CUST 28, contain information on the first and later postings of Customs officers, with details of any praise or censure: they contain no family details, but they can be used to work out the details of a man's career. For Ireland, there are registers of officers' appointments, 1761-1823, in CUST 20/154-159.

For the Customs, there are pay lists and staff lists, arranged by place, in PRO 30/32/15-29 (1673-1689), CUST 18 (1675-1813), CUST 19 (1814-1829), CUST 39 (1671-1922) and T 42 (1716-1847). There is a separate series for Scotland, 1714-1829, in T 43. Similar records for Ireland (but also including some Excise men), 1684-1826, are in CUST 20. However, in general these give little personal detail, although very occasionally details of marriage might be given.

Some family details can be found in the pension records in CUST 39/145-151, which cover 1803 to 1922: these are closed for 75 years from the date of the record. For Ireland, there are pension records covering 1785-1851 in CUST 39/161. The most useful for family historians are, as always, the sections relating to widows' pensions, which give details of any children. Applications for pensions can be found in T 1, using the indexes in T 2 and T 108. Other family details can be found among the correspondence of the individual ports ('outports' in the Customs service) with the Customs Board. To use the outport records and the pension records to their best advantage, first consult *Customs and Excise Records as Sources for Biography and Family History*.

Many of the sources for tracing Excise men are similar to the Customs records. There are pay lists for the English Excise, 1705-1835 (T 44) and the Scottish Excise, 1708-1832 (T 45). The Excise Board minute books, 1695-1867 (CUST 47) contain the same kinds of information as those of the Customs Board, as do the Excise pension records, 1856-1922 (CUST 39/157-159).

However, there are also the Excise Entry Papers, 1820-1870 (CUST 116). There is an alphabetical index to these, in the Reference Room Kew. The Entry Papers usually consist of two letters, folded together. The first is a letter of recommendation, giving the name of the applicant, his age, place of birth, marital status (but no details of his wife), and a character reference. The second letter is from the Excise officer responsible for the applicant's training: this states whether he is proficient in writing, spelling and arithmetic.

Records relating to the Irish Excise men, 1824-1833, and the Irish Revenue Police, 1830-1857, are in CUST 110 and CUST 111.

24.5 Crown employees and civil servants: bibliography and sources

[An * means this work can be seen at Chancery Lane: a # means it can be seen at Kew.]

Published works

The British Imperial Calendar (London, 1810-1972) #
Colonial Office List (London, annually from 1862) #
Court & City Register (London, 1742-1808)
Foreign Office List (London, annually from 1852) #
E B Fryde ed., *Handbook of British Chronology* (London, 3rd edn 1986) (Lists monarchs, officers of state, archbishops and bishops, dukes, marquesses and earls, in chronological sequence.) *#
Public Record Office, *Customs and Excise Records as Sources for Biography and Family History* (Information Leaflet) *#
Public Record Office, *Royal Warrant Holders and Household Servants* (Information Leaflet) *#
Royal Kalendar (London, 1746-1849)
J C Sainty and J M Collinge, *Office Holders in Modern Britain* (London, 1972-1984) *#
G Smith, *Something to Declare!: 1000 years of Customs and Excise* (London, 1980)

Records

Chancery (at Chancery Lane)
C 202/267-269: indexes to C 208
C 208 Warrants for Customers' Patents. 1714-1797

Civil Service Commission (at Kew)
CSC 8 Commissioners' Minute Books. 1835-1962
CSC 10 Examination Tables of Marks and Results. 1876-1964

Board of Customs (at Kew)
CUST 18 Establishments, Series I. 1675-1813
CUST 19 Establishments, Series II. 1814-1829
CUST 20 Salary Books and Establishments (Ireland). 1682-1826
CUST 28 Board and Secretariat: Minute Books. 1734-1885
CUST 39 Establishments: Staff Lists. 1671-1922

Board of Excise (at Kew)
CUST 47 Excise Board and Secretariat: Minute Books. 1695-1867
CUST 110 Board of Excise: Irish Board and Establishment. 1824-1833
CUST 111 Irish Revenue Police. 1830-1857
CUST 116 Entry Papers of Excise Men. 1820-1870

Exchequer (at Chancery Lane)
E 101: includes Royal Wardrobe and Household accounts, Richard I to 1816
E 351: includes Royal Wardrobe and Household accounts, 1533-1810

Lord Chamberlain (at Chancery Lane)
LC 3 Registers. 1641-1902
LC 5 Miscellanea. 1516-1920
LC 9 Accounts. 1483-1901
LC 11 Bill Books Series IV. 1784-1900

Lord Steward (at Chancery Lane)
LS 1 Accounts Comptroller of the Household. 1640-1761
LS 2 Accounts Lord Steward, Salaries. 1761-1854
LS 3 Accounts Ledgers. 1761-1851
LS 13 Miscellaneous Books. 1598-1870

Paymaster General's Office (at Kew)
PMG 27 Civil Establishment Consolidated Fund, etc. 1811-1929
PMG 28 Civil Establishment Superannuation and Retired Allowances. 1834-1925

Public Record Office (at Kew)
PRO 30/32/15-29: pay lists for Customs officers, England and Wales, 1673-1689

Treasury (at Kew)
T 1 Treasury Board Papers. 1557-1920
T 2 Registers of Papers. 1777-1920

T 38 Departmental Accounts. 1558-1937. (For Household accounts, 1575-1820.)
T 42 Registers, English Customs Establishments. 1716-1847
T 43 Registers, Scottish Customs Establishments. 1714-1829
T 44 Registers, English Excise Establishments. 1705-1835
T 45 Registers, Scottish Excise Establishments. 1708-1832
T 108 Subject Registers. 1830-1920

25. Merchant seamen

25.1 Seamen's registers, 1835-1857

The Merchant Shipping Act 1835, ordered the registration of merchant seamen with the aim of creating a reserve for manning the Royal Navy in time of war. An index or register of seamen was created from the information in the crew lists, also set up at the same time (see **25.2**). The registration of seamen lasted from 1835 to 1857.

The registers of seamen are in four separate series, which overlap to some extent, and which represent different methods of registration. The first (BT 120) consists of alphabetically arranged entries, 1835-1836: it is available on film in the search rooms at Kew. The second series (BT 112) covers 1835 to 1844: it is roughly alphabetical, with an index (BT 119) and cross-references to the crew lists (see **25.2**). In 1845 a ticket system was introduced, which lasted until October 1853: the third series of registers (BT 113) gives full genealogical details as well as a physical description and service record. Use the index (BT 114) to find the ticket number, by which the registers are arranged. The last series (BT 116), which started after the ticket system was abolished, lists seamen alphabetically, giving age, place of birth, and details of the voyage.

The registration of seamen was stopped in 1857, and after this there is no easy method of discovering the career of a merchant seaman, although the crew lists continue. The Royal Naval Reserve, which was established in 1859, was officered and manned by merchant seamen, and there are some service records: see **19.19**. The Modern Records Centre at the University of Warwick has some National Union of Seamen material: the address is given at **48.6**.

25.2 Musters, agreements and crew lists, 1747-1860

From 1747, the masters or owners of merchant ships had to keep muster rolls for each voyage, containing the names and addresses of officers and seamen employed on the ship, dates of engagement and discharge, and the name of the ship in which they last sailed (BT 98): there are no indexes. The only surviving rolls from before 1800 came from Shields, Dartmouth, Liverpool and Plymouth.

In 1835 a new system of crew lists and agreements was introduced, which provided more information. Under the Merchant Shipping Act 1835, masters of any ships belonging to UK subjects undertaking a foreign voyage, and masters of any British registered ships of 80 tons or more employed in the coastal trade or the fisheries, had to enter into a written agreement with every seaman on conditions of service. On return to the home port, the master had to deliver a list of the crew and the original agreements to the Registrar General of Shipping and Seamen (also in BT 98). Before 1854 these are arranged by port of registry: from 1854 they are arranged by the ship's official number. To discover the official number, use BT 111, *Lloyds Register of Shipping*, or the *Mercantile Navy List*. There are only incomplete sets of *Lloyds Register* and the *Mercantile Navy List* at Kew, but there are full sets at the Guildhall Library.

The crew lists in BT 98 should provide name, age, place of birth, quality (i.e. rank), previous ship, date and place of joining, and time and date of death or leaving the ship. The crew lists were supposed to be handed in at the *end* of the voyage, and they are arranged by the date they were handed in. To get the right crew list (if you want to trace an individual seaman), you must first refer to the appropriate seamen's register (see **25.1**). Between 1835 and 1844, make a note of the number of the port and the name of the ship given in the register entry (ignore the port rotation number): there is a key to the port numbers in the list of BT 98, and the crew lists are arranged by these numbers, by year and, internally, by ship. Between 1845 and 1856, you will still need to start with the appropriate seamen's register, but the procedure is more complicated. Watts' and Watts' article and book give a sample entry, for one James Watts, from the seamen's register of 1846 (BT 113/24) to illustrate the procedure:

OUT	HOME
1140-75-2	1140-75-2
75-6-4	64-31-7

The top number 1140-75-2 identifies the ship, which is no longer named in the seamen's register: 75 is the port registry number for Newcastle, and indicates that the vessel was registered there. The bottom line of the 'OUT' column shows that the ship left Newcastle (75) on 6-4 [1846] - that is, on 6 April. The bottom line of the of the 'HOME' column shows that Watts left the ship in London (port number 64) on 31-7 [1846] - 31 July. Unfortunately, as the ship's name is not given in the register, it may be necessary to search through all the boxes of crew lists for the appropriate port and year to find the right ship, identifiable by its number (1140-75-2 in this example).

After 1857 you can no longer go through the seamen's registers to use the crew lists in BT 98, which henceforth were arranged each year by ships' official numbers: these numbers can be found by consulting the *Mercantile Navy List*. Since there is no longer an index of seamen indicating which ship they were on, it can take a great deal of hard work and good luck to trace individual seamen through the crew lists.

25.3 Location of agreements and crew lists, from 1861

After 1860, only a random 10% sample of agreements and crew lists was selected for permanent preservation in the PRO (BT 99), together with those of certain well-known ships (BT 100): the rest have been preserved elsewhere. For the years 1861, 1862, 1865, 1875, 1885, 1895 and 1905, 10% are at the PRO, Kew, and 90% at the

National Maritime Museum at Greenwich. The largest collection (about 70% of the total) is at the Memorial University of Newfoundland: there is a microfiche index to ships' numbers (not names) at Kew, and the University has a research and reprographic service for which it normally charges a fee. Crew lists of local interest are held by some county record offices: there is a location list attached to the class list of BT 99. A 10% sample of similar records for fishing vessels of under 80 tons, compiled under the Merchant Shipping (Fishing Boats) Act 1883, is also available at Kew (BT 144 and BT 99).

25.4 Certificates of competency and service: masters, mates and engineers

By an order of 1845, the Board of Trade authorised a system of voluntary examinations of competency for men intending to become masters or mates of foreign-going and home-trade British merchant ships (BT 122-BT 127). These later became compulsory. From 1862 there are also certificates for engineers (BT 139-BT 142), and from 1883 for skippers and mates of fishing boats (BT 129, BT 130, BT 138). Colonial certificates were entered separately (BT 128). The certificates give name, place and date of birth, date and place of issue of the certificate, and rank examined or served in. Deaths, injuries and retirements have also been noted.

25.5 Merchant seamen: apprenticeships

A register of apprentices from all over England, bound to fishermen in the south-east, survives for 1639-1664 (HCA 30/897). For the port of Colchester, there is a register of seamen's indentures covering 1704-1757, and 1804-1844 (BT 167/103).

There are indexes of apprentices registered in the merchant fleet between 1824 and 1953 (BT 150). The earlier volumes give name, age, date and term of indenture and the name of the master: entries in later volumes include the port where the apprentice signed on and the ship's name. In addition, specimens of copy indentures, taken at five-yearly intervals, are preserved in the Apprentices' Indentures, 1845-1950 (BT 151) and the Apprentices' Indentures for Fishing, 1895-1935 (BT 152).

25.6 Merchant seamen: births, marriages and deaths at sea

By the Seamen's Fund Winding-up Act 1851, the masters of British ships were required to hand over the wages and effects of any seamen who had died during a voyage. Registers (BT 153) were maintained until 1889-1890, and provide useful information: the name, Register Ticket number, date of engagement, and the place, date and cause of the man's death, with the name and port of his ship, the master's name, the date and place of payment of wages, the amount of wages owed and the date they were sent to the Board of Trade. The indexes to these registers (BT 154, BT 155) are by seamen and by ship, and give simple page references. Associated with the registers are printed monthly lists of dead seamen (BT 156) giving name and age, rating, nationality or birth place, last address, and cause and place of death. There are also nine manuscript registers (BT 157), containing half yearly lists of deaths, classified by cause.

Following the Merchant Shipping Act of 1854, registers were compiled from the official logs, of births, marriages and deaths at sea. All three are recorded from 1854-1883, births and deaths only from 1883-1887, and deaths only from 1888 (BT 158). Masters were further required by the Registration of Births and Deaths Act of 1874 to report births and deaths on board ships to the Registrar General of Shipping and Seamen, where they were entered in two separate registers (BT 159, BT 160). All these records end between 1888 and 1891. See also **4.2** and **4.4**.

For further biographical information on ordinary seamen after 1870, and on officers after 1913, write to the Registrar General of Shipping and Seamen.

There are many wills of merchant seamen from the late seventeenth century to 1857 among the records of the Commissary Court of London (London Division) at the Guildhall Library. A visit to, for example, the Historic Ships Collection (**48.6**) would add life to the facts.

25.7 Medals for gallantry at sea

Records of medals awarded for saving lives at sea, 1839-1882, are in FO 83/769. The Albert Medal was awarded for gallantry at sea: the medal register, 1866-1913, also includes awards to sailors in the Royal Navy until 1891. Records of other awards for gallantry at sea, 1856-1981, are in BT 261.

25.8 Merchant seamen: bibliography and sources

[An * means this work can be seen at Chancery Lane: a # means it can be seen at Kew.]

Published works

N G Cox, 'The Records of the Registrar General of Shipping and Seamen' *Maritime History*, vol. II, pp. 168-188
Index to Crew Lists, Agreements and Official Logs at the Memorial University of Newfoundland, microfiche #
Lloyds Register of Shipping (London, annually from 1764) #
K Matthews 'Crew Lists, Agreements and Official Logs of the British Empire 1863-1913, now in possession of the Maritime History Group, Memorial University', *Business History*, vol. XVI, pp. 78-80
Mercantile Navy List (London, annually from 1857) #
Public Record Office, *Records of the Registrar General of Shipping and Seamen* (Information Leaflet) *#
C T and M J Watts, 'Unravelling Merchant Seamen's Records', *Genealogists' Magazine*, vol. XIX, pp. 313-321
C T and M J Watts, *My Ancestor was a Merchant Seaman* (Society of Genealogists, 1986) #

Records

BT 154 Indexes to Names of Seamen. 1853-1889
BT 155 Indexes to Names of Ships. 1855-1889
BT 156 Monthly Lists of Deaths of Seamen. 1886-1890
BT 157 Registers of Seamen's Deaths, Classified by Cause. 1882-1888
BT 158 Registers of Births, Deaths and Marriages of Passengers at Sea. 1854-1890.
    (On microfilm.)
BT 159 Registers of Deaths at Sea of British Nationals. 1875-1888
BT 160 Registers of Births at Sea of British Nationals. 1875-1891
BT 165 Ships' Official Logs. 1902-1919
BT 167/103: Colchester: register of apprentice seamen, 1704-1757, 1804-1844
BT 261 Marine Divisions: Gallantry at Sea Awards. 1856-1981. (Registers of awards
    for gallantry at sea made, or proposed, by British authorities and foreign
    governments, to British seamen. This class is open immediately.)

Foreign Office (at Kew)
FO 83/769: British medals awarded for saving life at sea, 1839-1882

High Court of Admiralty (at Chancery Lane)
HCA 30/897: register of apprentice fishermen, 1639-1664

26. Railway workers

26.1 Railway staff records

The records of the nationalised railway companies, together with those of the canal,
dock and shipping companies owned by them, were collected by the British Transport
Historical Commission, and were formerly housed in London, York and Edinburgh.
The Edinburgh collection has now gone to the Scottish Record Office, and the York
and London collections have come to the PRO. The core of the collection is formed
by the extensive records of the Great Western Railway, but the records of several
hundred railway, canal and dock companies have also ended up at Kew.

However, comprehensive staff records have survived from relatively few railway
companies, and there are no union indexes to the names of employees. Staff records
of a kind exist: the covering dates given can be very misleading. Before ordering
these staff records, you must sign an undertaking to respect the confidentiality of any
personally sensitive information.

Another possible source of information on individuals may be the large collection of
railway periodicals and staff magazines, kept under the lettercode ZPER.

26.2 Railway police

Records for the railway police of the various railway companies do not appear to be
amongst the railway staff records in the PRO. Information about the numbers and

organisation of the railway police c.1900 can be found in RAIL 527/1036. The occasional reference to 'Police Department' in the railway staff records relate to signalmen, etc.

26.3 Railway workers: bibliography and sources

[An * means this work can be seen at Chancery Lane: a # means it can be seen at Kew.]

Published works

Public Record Office, *British Transport Historical Records* (Information Leaflet)*#
T Richards, *Was Your Grandfather a Railwayman?* (FFHS, 2nd edn 1989) #

Unpublished finding aids

Card index of subjects to British Transport Historical Commission Records #

Records

British Transport Historical Commission (at Kew)

(Staff records, arranged alphabetically by name of railway company)

Barry Railway Company. 1886-1922. RAIL 23/46-60, 64-65
Brecon and Merthyr Tydfil Junction Railway Company. 1880-1922. RAIL 65/31-35
Cambrian Railways Company. 1898-1944. RAIL 92/142-148
Cardiff Railway Company. 1869-1923. RAIL 97/32-44
Chester and Holyhead Railway Company. 1862. RAIL 113/53
Cleator and Workington Junction Railway Company. 1879-1923. RAIL 119/13
Furness Railway Company. 1852-1922. RAIL 214/97-104
Great Central Railway Company. 1857-1949. RAIL 226/193-235, 637
Great Eastern Railway Company. 1855-1930. RAIL 227/445-490
Great Northern Railway Company. 1848-1943. RAIL 236/727-745
Great Western and Midland Railway Companies Joint Committee. 1865-1915. RAIL 241/28
Great Western Railway Company. 1835-1954. RAIL 264/1-463
Hull and Barnsley Railway Company. 1885-1927. RAIL 312/77-81
Hull and Selby Railway Company. 1845-1875. RAIL 315/30
Isle of Wight Central Railway Company. 1860-1963. RAIL 328/16-18
Lancashire and Yorkshire Railway Company. 1853-1941. RAIL 343/827-845
Lancashire, Derbyshire and East Coast Railway Company. 1904-1906. RAIL 344/56
Liverpool and Manchester Railway Company. 1845. RAIL 371/23
London and Birmingham Railway Company. 1833-1847. RAIL 384/284-291
London and North Eastern Railway Company. 1920-1942. RAIL 397/1-11
London and North Western and Great Western Railway Companies Joint Committee. 1871-1897. RAIL 404/177-180
London and North Western and Midland Railway Companies Joint Committee. 1861-1911. RAIL 406/16

London and North Western Railway Company. 1831-1927. RAIL 410/1217-1218, 1797-1986

London and South Western Railway Company. 1838-1944. RAIL 411/483-537

London Brighton and South Coast Railway Company. 1837-1925. RAIL 414/750-796

London Midland and Scottish and London and North Eastern Railway Companies Joint Committee. 1891-1938. RAIL 417/16

London Midland and Scottish Railway Company. RAIL 427/1-15

London, Tilbury and Southend Company. 1871-1923. RAIL 437/44-57

Manchester, Sheffield and Lincolnshire Railway Company. 1847-1926. RAIL 463/177, 210-215

Midland and Great Northern Railways Joint Committee. 1879-1893. RAIL 487/115

Midland and South Western Junction Railway Company. 1891-1921. RAIL 489/21

Midland Railway Company. 1864-1924. RAIL 491/969-1081

Neath and Brecon Railway Company. 1903-1921. RAIL 505/13

Newcastle upon Tyne and Carlisle Railway Company. 1845-1848. RAIL 509/96

North and South Western Junction Railway Company. 1883-1916. RAIL 521/19

North Eastern Railway Company. 1843-1957. RAIL 527/1895-1965

North London Railway Company. 1854-1920. RAIL 529/130-138

North Staffordshire Railway Company. 1847-1923. RAIL 532/58-67

North Sunderland Railway Company. 1893-1948. RAIL 533/75-76

North Union Railway Company. 1841-1856. RAIL 534/29

Otley and Ilkley Joint Line Committee (Midland and North Eastern Railway Companies). 1865-1901. RAIL 554/24-25

Port Talbot Railway and Docks Company. 1883-1918. RAIL 574/13

Rhondda and Swansea Bay Railway Company. 1882-1922. RAIL 581/36-37

Rhymney Railway Company. 1860-1922. RAIL 583/41-65

Sheffield District Railway Company. 1897-1916. RAIL 611/25-26

Shropshire Union Railways and Canal Company. 1844-1897. RAIL 623/66-68

Somerset and Dorset Joint Line Committee. 1877-1928. RAIL 626/44-53

Somerset and Dorset Railway Company. 1863-1877. RAIL 627/6

South Eastern and Chatham Railway Companies Managing Committee. 1850-1944. RAIL 633/343-382

South Eastern Railway Company. 1845-1944. RAIL 635/302-310

South Wales Railway Company. 1844-1864. RAIL 64/45, 47, 52, 55-56

Southern Railway Company. 1923-1957. RAIL 651/1-10

Stockton and Darlington Railway Company. 1835-1856. RAIL 667/1283-1291

Stratford upon Avon and Midland Junction Railway Company. 1873-1923. RAIL 674/11

Taff Vale Railway Company. 1890-1924. RAIL 684/94-120

Trent Valley Railway Company. 1845-1946. RAIL 699/5

Wirral Railway Company. 1884-1926. RAIL 756/10-11

York and North Midland Railway Company. 1848, 1843-1850. RAIL 770/77-81

York, Newcastle and Berwick Railway Company. 1845. RAIL 772/106

British Transport Historical Collection Library (at Kew)
ZPER For railway periodicals with this lettercode, see the *Current Guide* Part 2.

27. Apprentices

27.1 Civilian apprenticeships

The training of working people was not usually a matter of public record and indentures of apprenticeship were private documents. If they survive at all they will normally be in private hands: there is a small collection at the Society of Genealogists. Between 1710 and 1811, however, apprenticeship indentures were subject to tax and the records relating to this tax are in the PRO, Kew (IR 1, indexes in IR 17). Duty was payable by the master at the rate of 6d for every pound under £50 which he received for taking on the apprentice, and 1s for every £1 above that sum. The deadline for payment was one year after the expiry of the indenture; it may therefore be necessary to search the records of several years' payments in order to find a particular entry, even when the date of the indenture is known.

These Apprenticeship Books record the names, addresses and trades of the masters, the names of the apprentices and dates of their indentures. Until 1752 the names of apprentices' parents are given, but rarely after that year. There are indexes of masters' names from 1710 to 1762, and of apprentices' names from 1710 to 1774. These were made on behalf of the Society of Genealogists and copied from their originals in the Guildhall Library, London. Further indexes, for later dates, are in preparation. Where the stamp duty was paid in London, entries will be found in the 'City' registers in this series; where it was paid elsewhere, entries will be found in the 'Country' registers.

It is important to note that masters did not have to pay stamp duty for apprentices taken on at the common or public charge of any township or parish, or by or out of any public charity (8 Anne, c.5, s.59). This means that very many apprentices were never subject to the duty, and are therefore not mentioned in the registers. In such cases, local or charity records, if they survive, are likely to be the only source of information on individuals. The PRO has records of the apprenticeship of children from the Royal Naval Asylum, Greenwich, and the Duke of York's Military School, Chelsea: see **19.17** and **18.24** respectively. London livery companies often kept full records of membership, which give places of birth, previous residences and other details. For these, apply to the Guildhall Library. For Royal Navy and Merchant Navy apprenticeships, see sections **19.17** and **25.5**. Among the War Office records there is a list of apprentices who enlisted in the Army but had to return to their masters until their indentures expired, 1806 to 1835 (WO 25/2962).

27.2 Apprentices: bibliography and sources

[An * means this work can be seen at Chancery Lane: a # means it can be seen at Kew]

Published works

I Maxted, *The British Book Trades, 1710-1777: an index of Master's and Apprentices' Records in the Inland Revenue Registers at the PRO, Kew* (Exeter, 1983)

Public Record Office, *Alphabetical Guide to War Office & Other Material* (Lists and Indexes, vol. LIII) *#

Public Record Office, *Apprenticeship Records* (Information Leaflet) *#

W B Stephens, *Sources for English Local History* (Manchester, 2nd edn 1981) *

University of Warwick, *Trade Union and Related Records* (Coventry, 1988)

Records

Inland Revenue (at Kew)
IR 1 Apprenticeship Books. 1710-1811
IR 17 Indexes to Apprenticeship Books. 1710-1774

War Office (at Kew)
WO 25/2962: recruits claimed as apprentices, 1806-1835

28. Lawyers

28.1 Lawyers: printed sources

The published *Law Lists*, produced annually from 1775, are the easiest place to start. There is a set running from 1799-1976 at Chancery Lane, and the Guildhall Library has a full set. However, there are some problems with the coverage of the *Law Lists*. Between 1775 and 1789, they contain the names of some men never actually admitted to a court, whereas from 1790 they only give the names of those who had taken out the annual certificate to practise that year. Until 1861 they do not give the date of admission.

Lists of attorneys and solicitors admitted in 1729 and 1730 were printed for presentation to Parliament: a copy is available at Chancery Lane.

28.2 Judges and serjeants-at-law

The PRO does hold some records of the appointment of judges and of the creation of serjeants-at-law (an obsolete degree, which had the monopoly of pleading in the court of Common Pleas until 1846, and which, for several centuries, was the usual route to judgeship). However, these are widely scattered and not very informative. As there is a great deal of biographical information in print on the judges and the serjeants-at-law, you would be well advised to investigate the published sources first: the main ones are listed in **28.8**.

28.3 Barristers

The PRO is not the place to look for records relating to barristers: entry to this degree was and is controlled by the Inns of Court (Lincoln's Inn, Gray's Inn, the Inner Temple and the Middle Temple). The Inns of Court have published many of their records of genealogical interest: see the printed sources listed in **28.8**. For further information, contact the libraries of the particular Inn of Court: the addresses are given in **48.6**.

However, the PRO does have records of the oaths of allegiance sworn by barristers: swearing of this oath was required before a barrister could practice in the courts. Signatures to the oath, 1673-1944, are in KB 24, and 1858-1982, in KB 4.

28.4 Solicitors and attorneys: the central courts

There are two main sources of information on attorneys and solicitors in the PRO, as a result of statutory controls operated by the courts on this branch of the legal profession. The various central and regional courts regulated the admission of new solicitors and attorneys, and each court kept its own records of clerks so admitted to work within that court's jurisdiction. For the details of the records of each court, see **28.8**. Before 1838, an attorney or solicitor had to be admitted to each court separately, if he wished to practice in more than one. Before 1750, most practised in the Common Pleas, and you should start a search there; after 1750, King's Bench had more admissions.

Attorneys' and Solicitors' Rolls or Books begin in 1729, when attorneys and solicitors were ordered to serve five years as clerks under articles, take the prescribed oath, and have their names entered on a roll kept by the court to which they were seeking admittance. Affidavits of Due Execution of Articles of Clerkship begin in 1749. The new solicitor or attorney had to file an affidavit that he had properly completed his articles of clerkship, within three months of admittance to the court. The registers of these affidavits, which are indexed, show to whom the new entrant had been articled, while the affidavits themselves give the name of the parent or guardian, if any, who had arranged the articles.

28.5 Solicitors and attorneys: the Palatine and Welsh courts

Records of attorneys admitted to the Palatinate courts of Chester, 1697-1830, are in CHES 36; for those admitted to the Palatinate courts of Durham, 1660-1843, see DURH 3 and DURH 9. Records of attorneys admitted to the Palatinate courts of Lancaster, 1730-1875, are in PL 23. After 1830, attorneys practising in the Courts of Sessions and Great Sessions in Chester and Wales were allowed to enrol in the courts at Westminster. For attorneys enrolled in the court of Common Pleas, 1830-1844, see IND 1/4608; for those enrolled in King's Bench, 1830-1834, see IND 1/4592(1). This privilege was also extended to attorneys and solicitors working in the courts of the Palatinate of Lancaster and the Palatinate of Durham.

28.6 Solicitors and attorneys: records elsewhere

The Law Society has the records of the Registrar of Attorneys and Solicitors, established in 1843. These include lists of admissions from 1845 onwards, with additional lists of admissions back to about 1790. They also have some registers of articles of clerkship from about 1860 onwards. These records are kept at the Law Society, Ipsley Court, Redditch, Hereford and Worcester. The Law Society also has, at its office in Chancery Lane, four volumes of the PRO's Chancery Solicitors' Roll, covering 1722-1858 (C 216/22-25), which are on loan to the librarian of the Law Society.

28.7 Civil lawyers

For civil lawyers (i.e. those who practised the civil law used in the church courts and the High Court of Admiralty, and the High Court of Delegates), there is a selective index of advocates and proctors, at Chancery Lane. Civil lawyers were also listed in *Law Lists* (**28.1**). There are short biographies of London advocates (the civilian equivalent of barristers) in the book by G D Squibb. The admission of proctors (the civilian equivalent of attorneys) in London - that is, those practising from Doctors' Commons - is recorded in the registers of the Archbishop of Canterbury, at Lambeth Palace Library. Records of civil lawyers who practised in provincial church courts are best sought locally, in diocesan record offices.

28.8 Lawyers: bibliography and sources

[An * means this work can be seen at Chancery Lane: a # means it can be seen at Kew.]

Published works

J H Baker, *The Order of Serjeants at Law*, Selden Society, Supplementary Series vol. V (London, 1984)
E H W Dunkin, C Jenkins and E A Fry, *Act Books of the Archbishop of Canterbury, 1663-1859* (British Record Society, Index Library 1929)
E Foss, *A Biographical Dictionary of the Judges of England* (London, 1870) *
J A Foster, *Men-at-the-Bar: A Biographical Handlist of the Members of the Various Inns of Court including Her Majesty's Judges etc.* [as at 1885] (London, 1885)
J A Foster, *The Register of Admissions of Gray's Inn, 1521-1889* (London, 1889)
J Hutchinson, *A Catalogue of Notable Middle Templars* (London, 1902)
F A Inderwick and R A Roberts, *A Calendar of Inner Temple Records, 1505-1800* (London, 1896-1936)
Law List (London 1775, continuing) Volumes for 1799-1976 are available at Chancery Lane
Lincoln's Inn, *Admissions, 1420-1799* (London, 1896)
Lincoln's Inn, *The Black Books, 1422-1914* (London, 1897-1968)
Public Record Office, *Records of Attorneys and Solicitors in the Public Record Office* (Information Leaflet) *#
Parliament, *List of Attorneys and Solicitors Admitted in Pursuance of the Late Act for the Better Regulation of Attorneys and Solicitors, 1729-1730* (London, 1729-1731) *
John Sainty, *A List of English Law Officers, King's Counsel and Holders of Patents and Precedence*, Selden Society, Supplementary Series vol. VII (London, 1987)

G D Squibb, *Doctors' Commons* (Oxford, 1977)

C Trice Martin, *Minutes of Parliament of the Middle Temple, 1501-1703* (London, 1904-1905)

Unpublished finding aids

Index to proctors and other officials of Doctors' Commons *

Records

Court of Bankruptcy (at Chancery Lane)

B 2/8-11: admission roll and registers of town and country solicitors, 1832-1883

Court of Chancery (at Chancery Lane)

C 216/22-26: solicitors rolls, 1729-1875. Pieces 22-25 (1729-1858) are on loan to the Law Society.

Palatinate of Chester (at Chancery Lane)

CHES 36 Chester Attorneys' Records. 1697-1830

Court of Common Pleas (at Chancery Lane)

CP 5 Common Pleas Articles of Clerkship. 1730-1838. This class includes Articles of Clerkship, Affidavits of Due Execution of Articles, etc. There are various contemporary means of reference: the most useful are the Admission Books, 1724-1848 (IND 1/4599-4602), which are alphabetical, giving the addresses of the attorneys and the exact date of admission.

CP 8 Common Pleas Attorneys' Admission Rolls. 1838-1860

Palatinate of Durham (at Chancery Lane)

DURH 3/217-21: oath roll, 1730-1843, and admission rolls, 1660-1803

DURH 9 Affidavits of Attorneys' Clerks. 1750-1834. There is a register of certificates, 1785-1842, giving dates and addresses (IND 1/10152).

Exchequer of Pleas (at Chancery Lane)

E 3 Exchequer of Pleas: Attorneys' Oath Rolls. 1830-1872

E 4 Exchequer of Pleas: Books of Attorneys, etc 1830-1855

[This was the common law side of the Exchequer: until 1832 only the officers of the court were allowed to act as its attorneys. There is a register of Affidavits of Due Execution of Articles 1833-1855 (IND 1/18671), and rolls of attorneys, 1830-1875 (IND 1/461-462 and IND 1/29719-29721).]

Exchequer: Equity Side (at Chancery Lane)

E 108 Solicitors' Certificate Book. 1785-1843

E 109 Rolls of Books of Solicitors. 1729-1841

E 200 Solicitors and Commissioners for Oaths: Oath Rolls. 1730-1841

Court of King's Bench (at Chancery Lane)

KB 4 King's Bench and Supreme Court of Judicature: Barristers' Rolls. 1868-1982

KB 24 Swearing or Oath Rolls. 1673-1944
KB 105 Affidavits of Due Execution of Clerkship Series I. 1775-1817
KB 106 Affidavits of Due Execution of Clerkship Series II. 1817-1834
KB 107 Affidavits of Due Execution of Clerkship Series III. c.1830-1875
Chronological registers, 1749-1877, are in IND 1/4568-4573, and IND 1/29722-
29728. The Rolls of Attorneys, 1729-1875, are arranged by first letter of the surname
and give the county (IND 1/4583-4592, IND 1/29714-29717, and IND 1/29737-
29738). The Attorneys' Residence Books, 1790-1829, are alphabetical by surname
and give the address: IND 1/4593-4595.

Palatinate of Lancaster (at Chancery Lane)
PL 23 Palatinate of Lancaster: Court of Common Pleas: Records of the Admission of
       Attorneys. 1730-1875

29. The medical professions

29.1 Records of doctors and nurses in the PRO

In general, the PRO is not the place to look for records of doctors (or nurses until
1921), except as they were engaged upon government service. Records of doctors and
nurses in the Army and Navy, however, are quite extensive: see **18.25** and **19.20 - 21**.
There are a number of published lists of doctors: see **29.3**. For detailed information
on records relating to civilian and military nurses see *Nursing and the Nursing
Services: Record Sources in the Public Record Office*. This gives information on the
period before registration began.

Before 1919, the individual nurse training schools kept records: these are often still
with the hospital records (see **29.2**). The Nightingale Training School records and the
Nightingale collection are at the Greater London Record Office.

The registration of civilian nurses began in 1921, following the foundation of the
General Nursing Council in 1919. From 1921, State Registered Nurses were entered
on the Register of Nurses (DT 10): the Register included nurses who were currently
active, and who may therefore have qualified well before that date. From 1947, State
Enrolled Nurses were entered on the Roll of Nurses (DT 11). After 1973, information
on various categories of nurses can be found in DT 12. The information given in the
Register and Roll includes name and maiden name, qualifications and training,
address, change of name, date of marriage, and date of death.

29.2 Hospital records

The PRO and the Wellcome Institute for the History of Medicine have compiled a
computerised data base of the location in records offices of the records of over a
thousand hospitals in England and Wales. There is little of direct relevance to the
genealogist, but if you are interested in finding the records of a particular hospital,

write to the Hospital Records Project, care of the Records Administration Division, Public Record Office, Ruskin Avenue, Kew, Richmond, Surrey TW9 4DU.

29.3 The medical professions: bibliography and sources

[An * means this work can be seen at Chancery Lane: a # means it can be seen at Kew.]

Published works

J Harvey Bloom and R Rutson Jones, *Medical Practitioners in the Diocese of London, Licensed Under the Act of 3 Henry VIII, c.11: An Annotated List 1529-1725* (Cambridge, 1935)

W Munk, *The Roll of the Royal College of Physicians of London, 1518-1825* (London, 1861-1878)

Public Record Office, *Nurses and the Nursing Services: Record Sources in the Public Record Office* (Information Leaflet) *#

J H Raach, *A Directory of English Country Physicians, 1603-1643* (London, 1962)

C H Talbot and E A Hammond, *The Medical Practitioners of Medieval England: A Biographical Register* (London, 1965)

P J Wallis and R V Wallis, *Eighteenth Century Medics (Subscriptions, Licences, Apprenticeships)* (Newcastle-upon-Tyne, 2nd edn 1988) - lists about 35,000 individuals

Records

General Nursing Council for England and Wales (at Kew)
DT 10 Registration: The Register of Nurses. 1921-1973
DT 11 Registration: The Roll of Nurses. 1944-1973
DT 12 Registration: Computerised Register and Roll. 1973-1983. Most pieces are open.

30. Teachers and school records

30.1 Teachers and school records

The history of teacher training is succinctly described in *Education: records of teachers*. However, the PRO holds policy papers on teacher training and registration, rather than staff records themselves. Detailed information about staff or pupils of individual schools may be found in the appropriate local record office, together with school log books and building plans.

Deeds relating to the foundation of schools, and other charitable foundations, were enrolled in Chancery (C 54) until 1902, and then in the Supreme Court (J 18). There are indexes to these trust deeds, arranged by place, covering 1736 to 1904: although most of the trust deeds appear to relate to the founding of building of nonconformist chapels, very many concern schools.

30.2 Teachers and school records: bibliography and sources

[An * means this work can be seen at Chancery Lane: a # means it can be seen at Kew.]

Published works

Public Record Office, *Education: records of teachers* (Information Leaflet) *#
Public Record Office, *Education: records of special services* (Information Leaflet) *#
Public Record Office, *Records relating to elementary and secondary schools* (Information Leaflet) *#
Public Record Office, *Records relating to technical and further education* (Information Leaflet) *#

Unpublished finding aids

Indexes to trust deeds, by place. 1736-1904 *

Records

Chancery (at Chancery Lane)
C 54 Close Rolls. 1204-1903

Supreme Court of Judicature (at Chancery Lane)
J 18 Supreme Court Enrolment Books. 1903-1983

31. The established church

31.1 Introduction

Until the break with Rome in 1534, the established religion of England and Wales was (Roman) Catholic; after this, with the brief exception of Mary I's reign (1553-1558), the established religion was that of the Church of England, covering a wide range from high church to low church, Anglo-Catholic to Calvinist.

The PRO is not the obvious place to look for ecclesiastical records: see Owen's book on the records of the established church, and Bourne and Chicken's guide to Anglican records. In fact, the PRO does have considerable holdings on the administration of the church in relation to the state, and particularly on the monasteries, but relatively little of this contains information of interest to the genealogist.

However, there are some sources in the PRO which can provide information on the clergy and the lay members of the church, before and after the Reformation.

31.2 Anglican clergymen

Descent from pre-Reformation clergy, in theory, should not be possible, as they were vowed to celibacy: however, the Church of England allowed priests to marry.

Before using any documentary sources, you should consult the following printed works, which should be available in a good reference library. *Crockford's Clerical Directory*, published annually from 1858, is the place to start, followed by the lists of Oxford and Cambridge *Alumni* [students]. For the higher clergy, down to archdeacons, try the *Fasti Ecclesiae Anglicanae, 1066-1857*; not all dioceses have been covered up to 1857. There is a card index of clergy, the Fawcett Index, in the library of the Society of Genealogists.

The ordination records in the appropriate diocesan archives can be a very useful source of genealogical information: they usually include a certified copy of the baptismal entry, or a letter explaining why there was none, details of education, and character references.There were several life insurance companies catering solely for the clergy: the Guildhall Library has a collection of London insurance company records, which can provide a wealth of personal details.

Most PRO documents relating to the appointment of Anglican clergymen to benefices are very formal, and do not include any information of great use to genealogists. The bishops' certificates of institutions to benefices, 1544-1912 (E 331) are usually approached through the Institution Books, 1556-1838, which are available in the Round Room at Chancery Lane. These are arranged firstly by county (1556-1660) or diocese (1661-1838), then by place: they give the name of the clergyman instituted to the benefice, the date, and the name of the patron of the benefice. They can be useful for tracing the ecclesiastical career of the clergyman, but they do not provide any personal details.

For the Commonwealth period, the surveys of church livings provide the name of the incumbent, and details of the value of the living as assessed by the parishioners (C 94).

If you have an ancestor who was a clergyman in 1801 or 1851, you may like to investigate two series of records composed of returns made by the parish clergy on conditions in their parish. The Acreage Returns of 1801 (HO 67), although intended to provide factual information on the state of agriculture at a village level, can include some very individualistic comments made by the parish priest on his parishioners. A later survey of places of worship, the Ecclesiastical Census of 1851 (HO 129), can also provide an interesting picture of life at the parish level, and sometimes personal details on the clergy as well.

31.3 Excommunicates, 1280s-1840s

The PRO holds the requests (technically, known as *significavits* or significations) from the bishops for the 'secular arm' (i.e. the power of the state) to be used against people excommunicated by the church: excommunication was a punishment imposed for a wide variety of offences. These significations survive from the 1220s to

1611 (C 85), and again from George II to the 1840s (C 207). It is not clear what has happened to the intervening requests.

The earliest significations usually provide little more than the name of the person excommunicated, but the later ones in C 85 can include reference to occupation, place of residence, father, nature of the offence, etc. About 7,600 significations survive from C 85, and there is a card index to these, first by diocese and then alphabetically by name of the person excommunicated. The documents themselves are in Latin. The significations in C 207 are in English, but have not yet been indexed: as a result, they are less easy to use than the earlier ones.

Significations for the county palatine of Chester were issued by Chester officials, and are in CHES 38. Those for the counties of Flint, Henry VIII to Elizabeth I, and for Pembroke, George II, have been transferred with the rest of WALE 28 to the National Library of Wales.

31.4 Sacrament certificates

From the Test Act of 1672 onwards, various statutes required that office-holders and aliens seeking naturalisation should take certain oaths in support of the crown and against papal supremacy; to afforce these oaths, the swearer was required to take the sacrament of the Lord's Supper according to the Anglican rites. Evidence of this was provided by a certificate completed and signed by the minister and churchwardens of the parish with the signatures of two witnesses appended. The certificates were presented when the oath was sworn, at one of the central courts if within thirty miles of Westminster, and at the quarter sessions if further away. As a result, the majority of sacrament certificates in the PRO are from Middlesex, Hertfordshire, Surrey and Kent, within the thirty mile radius of Westminster.

Certificates presented to Chancery, 1673-1778, are in C 224; those presented in the Exchequer, 1700-1827, are in E 196. Certificates presented in King's Bench survive from 1676 and from 1728-1828 (KB 22). Certificates presented in the Cheshire courts, 1673-1768, are in CHES 4: many of them date from the 1715 Jacobite Rising. Of these four classes, only E 196 has been well listed, by county, and the documents cleaned: the documents in the other classes are still in large sacks or boxes, but can be seen. Sacrament certificates presented to the quarter sessions should be in local record offices.

31.5 The established church: bibliography and sources

[An * means this work can be seen at Chancery Lane: a # means it can be seen at Kew]

Published works

S Bourne and A H Chicken, *Records of the Church of England: A Practical Guide for the Family Historian* (Maidstone, 1988)
Crockford's Clerical Directory (Oxford, annually from 1858)
J Foster, *Alumni Oxonienses, 1500-1886* (Oxford, 1891)

184

J Le Neve and others, *Fasti Ecclesie Anglicanae* (London, 1716). There is a revised
    and updated version, covering 1066-1857 (London, 1962 continuing). *

F D Logan, *Excommunication and the secular arm in medieval England* (Toronto, 1968)

D M Owen, *The records of the established church in England, excluding parochial
    records* (British Records Association, 1970)

Public Record Office, *Records relating to the dissolution of the monasteries: sources
    in the PRO* (Information Leaflet) *#

Public Record Office, *Sources for the history of religious houses and their lands
    c.1100-1530* (Information Leaflet) *#

L F Salzman, 'Sussex excommunicates', *Sussex Archaeological Collections*, vol.
    LXXXIII, pp. 124-140

J and J A Venn, *Alumni Cantabrigienses, from the Earliest Times to 1900* (Cam-
    bridge, 1922-1927)

Unpublished finding aids

Card index to C 85 *
Card index to E 135 *

Records

Chancery (at Chancery Lane)
C 85 Significations of Excommunication. 1220-1611
C 207 Cursitor's Records (Petty Bag Office). Elizabeth I to Victoria
C 224 Petty Bag Office Sacrament Certificates. 1673-1778

Palatinate of Chester (at Chancery Lane)
CHES 4 Sacrament Certificates.1673-1768
CHES 38/25/4-6: significations of excommunications, 1378-1690

Exchequer (at Chancery Lane)
E 196 King's Remembrancer Sacrament Certificates. 1700-1827

Home Office (at Kew)
HO 67 Acreage Returns. 1801
HO 129 Ecclesiastical Census Returns. 1851

Court of King's Bench (at Chancery Lane)
KB 22 Sacrament Certificates. 1676-1828

32. Protestant nonconformists

32.1 Nonconformist church records

The PRO holds the majority of nonconformist registers of births or baptisms,
marriages, and deaths or burials for the period before 1837, and also a considerable

number after that date: these are discussed in **3**. However, in some cases, these registers contained other records of the church or chapel as well. The General Register Office, to whom they had been surrendered, adopted the practice of tearing out the other records where this could be done easily, and returning them to the church. To discover their present location, you need to consult a guide to the particular denomination's archives (see **32.3**). In a few cases, the information was spread throughout the volume, and this piece of archival vandalism was not carried out, so that some of the registers discussed in **3** still include more general records.

32.2 Nonconformist chapels and charities

From 1736, deeds involving the inalienable transfer of land for charitable purposes had to be enrolled on the Close Rolls (C 54 and, from 1902, J 18). The great majority of these deeds involved the establishment of nonconformist chapels, schools, burial grounds and charities: between 1736 and 1870 over 35,000 deeds were enrolled. There are two indexes to these deeds, both to places: for 1736-1870 there are volume indexes to trust deeds, and for 1870-1904 there are card indexes. In addition, C 54 and J 18 also have annual indexes to their whole contents. These deeds are a very valuable source for local history and for the involvement of individual nonconformists in establishing their chapels and setting up schemes for self improvement.

32.3. Nonconformists: other records

There are a number of oath or affirmation rolls for nonconformists in the PRO. The Association Oath of 1696, in support of William III, was sworn or affirmed by London and Hampshire dissenters (C 214/9-10), Quakers in Colchester (C 213/473), nonconformist ministers in Cumberland (C 213/60-61) and Baptist ministers in London (C 213/170). There are also affirmation rolls for Quaker attorneys, 1831-1835 (E 3) and 1836-1842 (CP 10).

The Recusant Rolls, 1592-1691 (E 376 and E 377) are annual returns of both Protestant nonconformists and of Catholics, who had property forfeited or who were fined for dissenting from the Church of England.

32.4 Huguenots

Huguenots were French protestants fleeing from religious persecution from the 1550s onwards, and in large numbers after the Revocation of the Edict of Nantes (which reversed the previous policy of toleration of them) in 1685. It is quite possible, however, for a Huguenot ancestor to appear in England some time after this, as many fled first to Holland or Germany and only later moved to England. The Central Bureau of Genealogy of Holland may be able to assist in these cases. There are often strong family traditions of Huguenot descent, and names with a French flavour are usually a good indication of such a background.

The main Huguenot settlements were in London, Norwich, Canterbury, Southampton, Rye, Sandwich, Colchester, Bristol, Plymouth, Thorney and various places in

Ireland. There are no known records of any communities in the Midlands or the North of England, and there is little on settlement in Scotland. It is, naturally, more difficult to trace a family which struck out on its own to a new part of the country where no French church existed, and which used the local parish church for baptisms. Huguenot burial records are rare at all times, and by the nineteenth century almost non-existent, except for the records of deaths of the inmates of the London Huguenot Hospital, which are in the Huguenot Library.

A great deal has been published by the Huguenot Society of London and the search should begin by looking at that readily available material. There is a Huguenot Library in London: no personal callers can be seen but the staff will undertake a brief search for a fee. Huguenot material is to be found in other areas of settlement: in the Cathedral Library at Canterbury, the County Record Office at Norwich and the City Record Office at Southampton, for instance.

Most of the sources for Huguenot genealogy in the PRO (see **3** and **12**) have been included in Huguenot Society publications in some form. The published *Calendars of State Papers* are also useful, as are the various lists in print of aliens resident in England, naturalised, or taking oaths of allegiance (see **12** and **15**).

32.5 Protestant nonconformists: bibliography and sources

[An * means this work can be seen at Chancery Lane: a # means it can be seen at Kew.]

Published works

G R Breed, *My Ancestor was a Baptist* (Society of Genealogists, 1986) *
N Currer-Briggs and R Gambier, *Huguenot Ancestry* (Chichester, 1985) *
Dr Williams's Trust, *Nonconformist Congregations in Britain* (London, 1973) *
N Graham, *The Genealogists' Consolidated Guide to Nonconformist and Foreign Registers in Inner London, 1538-1837* (Birchington, 1980)
Huguenot Society, *Publications* (1885 continuing) *
W Leary and M Gandy, *My Ancestor was a Methodist* (Society of Genealogists, 1982) *
E H Milligan and M J Thomas, *My Ancestors were Quakers* (Society of Genealogists, 1983) *
P Palgrave-Moore, *Understanding the History and Records of Nonconformity* (Norwich, 2nd edn 1989) *
D J Steel, *Sources of Nonconformist Genealogy and Family History* (London, 1973)*
H G Tibbutt, 'Sources for Congregational Church Records', *Transactions of the Congregational History Society*, vol. XIX, pp. 147-155, 230-236
E Welch, 'The Early Methodists and their Records', *Journal of the Society of Archivists*, vol. IV, p. 210

Unpublished finding aids

Indexes to trust deeds. 1736-1904 *

Index to C 54 *
Index to J 18 *

Records

Chancery (at Chancery Lane)
C 54 Close Rolls. 1204-1903
C 213 Association Oath Rolls. 1696-1697
C 214 Various Oath Rolls. Charles II - Victoria

Court of Common Pleas (at Chancery Lane)
CP 10 Oath Rolls. 1779-1847

Exchequer (at Chancery Lane)
E 3 Attorneys' Oath Rolls. 1830-1872
E 376 Exchequer: Pipe Office: Recusant Rolls (Chancellor's Series). 1591-1691
E 377 Exchequer: Pipe Office: Recusant Rolls (Pipe Office Series). 1591-1691

Supreme Court of Judicature (at Chancery Lane)
J 18 Supreme Court Enrolment Books. 1903-1983

33. Roman Catholics

33.1 Roman Catholic registers

The registers of Catholic churches are either in the PRO (see **3.7**) or with the congregation. The relevant diocesan archivist or the Catholic Central Library may be able to assist in tracing them. The *English Catholic Ancestor* aims at acquiring and disseminating information about Catholic families. The Catholic Record Society has published a great deal of useful material. Burials of Catholics often took place in the parish churchyard and are therefore recorded in the parish registers. For much fuller information on Catholic genealogy, see the book by Steel and Samuel.

33.2 Records of persecution

In the PRO, records of Catholics are largely the records of their persecution, and the bulk of these accordingly varies with fluctuations in anti-popery. The Recusant Rolls (E 376 and E 377) are annual returns of dissenters (Protestant and Catholic) who had property forfeited or were fined, 1592-1691. County record offices hold much material on persecutions of Papists. Most Catholics supported the King in the Civil War, so their estates may be referred to in *Calendars of the Committee for Compounding with Delinquents*. There are many inventories of Catholic possessions in the State Papers for the Interregnum (SP 28). From the reign of George I and the Jacobite risings, there are lists of Catholics who forfeited their estates (E 174, KB 18, FEC 1, and FEC 2). There is a PRO information leaflet on Jacobite sources.

33.3 Oath rolls

There are lists of Catholic solicitors and attorneys for the period 1790-1836 (CP 10), 1791-1813 (DC 217/180/5) and 1830-1875 (E 3). The 'Papists' oaths of allegiance etc. in E 169/79-83 give names and addresses for 1778-1857 (with gaps).

33.4 Roman Catholics: bibliography and sources

[An * means this work can be seen at Chancery Lane: a # means it can be seen at Kew.]

Published works

J Bossy, *The English Catholic Community, 1570-1850* (London, 1975)
Calendar of State Papers, Domestic, Committee for Compounding with Delinquents, 1643-1660 (London, 1889-1893)
Catholic Directory (London, annually from 1837)
Catholic Record Society, *Bibliographical Studies*, vols I-III, changed to *Recusant History*, from vol. IV (Bognor Regis, 1951 to date)
Catholic Record Society, *Publications* (1905, continuing)
The English Catholic Ancestor (Aldershot, 1983-1989; Ealing, 1989 continuing)
Public Record Office, *Sources for the History of the Jacobite Risings 1715 and 1745* (Information Leaflet) *#
D J Steel and E R Samuel, *Sources for Roman Catholic and Jewish Genealogy and Family History* (London, 1974) *

Records

Chancery (at Chancery Lane)
C 217/180/5: Catholic solicitors, 1791-1813

Court of Common Pleas (at Chancery Lane)
CP 10 Attorneys Oath Rolls. 1779-1847
CP 43 Recovery Rolls. 25 Elizabeth I to 1837. (Indexes in IND 16943-16949, 17183-17216.)

Exchequer (at Chancery Lane)
E 3 Exchequer of Pleas, Attorneys' Oath Rolls. 1830-1972
E 169 Oaths of Allegiance etc. 1709-1868
E 174 Returns of Papists' Estates. George I
E 376 Exchequer: Pipe Office, Recusant Rolls, Chancellor Series. 1591-1691
E 377 Exchequer: Pipe Office, Recusant Rolls, Clerk of the Pipe Series. 1591-1691

Forfeited Estates Commission (at Kew)
FEC 1 Papers. 1552-1744
FEC 2 Books. 1715-1726

Court of King's Bench (at Chancery Lane)
KB 18 Returns of Papists in Lancaster. George I

Secretaries of State (at Chancery Lane)
SP 28 Commonwealth Exchequer Papers. 1642-1660 (see SP 28/217A and B)

34. Orthodox Christians

34.1 Records of the Russian Orthodox Church in London

The archive of the Russian Orthodox Church in London (sometimes known as the Orthodox Greco-Russian Church), 1721-1951, is in RG 8/111-304. Most of the archive is in Russian, with some documents in Greek, English, French and German: there is a descriptive list, in English.

The records are of various kinds to do with the organisation of the church, and the Russian community in England, including Russian prisoners-of-war during the Crimean War. There are also registers and other records of baptisms, marriages and deaths as well as communicants and conversions, dating from 1721 to 1927. Some of these relate to Greeks and other non-Russians.

34.2 Orthodox Christians: bibliography and sources

Records

General Register Office (at Chancery Lane)
RG 8/111-304: records of the Russian Orthodox Church in London, 1721-1951

35. Jews

35.1 Jewish genealogy

For specific guides to Jewish genealogy see the books by Gandy, and by Steel and Samuel. There were Jews in England in the early Middle Ages, but no line of descent has been traced from members of this early community, which was expelled in 1290. The Jewish community was re-established in the mid 17th century, from which time there has been a steady rate of assimilation into the gentile population.

The immigrants were two sorts: Sephardim (Portuguese, Spanish and Italian), arriving from 1656 onwards; and Ashkenazim (Central and East European), first coming in the 1680s from Holland and Bohemia. The main influx of Ashkenazim, however, was of Russians and Poles in the last two decades of the nineteenth century (about 120,000 in the period up to 1914).

The registers of the London Spanish and Portuguese Synagogue are partly published. The registers of the Ashkenazim contain a high proportion of entries totally in Hebrew before 1840. Some earlier entries are included in the *International Genealogical Index*. Later records are not easily accessible as most are held by the congregations concerned. The names and addresses of synagogues throughout the British Isles are, from 1896, in the *Jewish Year Book*. For help, apply to the Information Department of the Board of Deputies. There are registers in the archives of the United Synagogue for the three principal London synagogues founded before 1837, and they will search these for a fee. For help on the London Sephardic community apply to the Honorary Archivist at the Spanish and Portuguese Synagogue, where the records are kept.

The Anglo-Jewish Archives in the Mocatta Library, University College, have an invaluable collection of Jewish pedigrees compiled by Sir Thomas Colyer Fergusson as well as many other Jewish sources.

The most productive sources for specifically Jewish genealogy at the PRO are wills (see **6**), naturalisation papers (see **12.3**) and records of change of name (see **17**).

35.2 Jews: bibliography

[An * means this work can be seen at Chancery Lane: a # means it can be seen at Kew.]

Published works

M Gandy, *My Ancestor was Jewish* (Society of Genealogists, 1982)
Jewish Year Book (London, annually from 1896)
D J Steel and E R Samuel, *Sources for Roman Catholic and Jewish Family History and Genealogy* (London, 1974) *

36. Prisoners of war

36.1 Prisoners of war 1793-1914

Most records in the PRO about prisoners of war before 1914 relate to the costs of holding foreign prisoners, and do not provide lists of names or any detailed information. Before 1793, some correspondence and accounts survive; these are detailed in the PRO information leaflet *Prisoners of War 1660-1919: Documents in the PRO*, which should also be consulted for more information on the following subjects.

For the period of the French Revolutionary and Napoleonic Wars (1793-1815), there are lists and accounts of British prisoners in France and elsewhere, transmitted by the agent for prisoners in Paris, in ADM 103. Most of the prisoners appear to have been naval and civilian internees. There is no general index of names. Registers of French prisoners in Britain are also in ADM 103, arranged by depot, prison ship or parole town: again, there is no central index. Lists of enemy prisoners on parole are in HO 28. There is a register of American prisoners of war in Britain, compiled in 1813 (ADM 6/417), and ADM 103 also has records relating to such men.

For the Crimean War, 1853-1855, there is some official material relating to Russian prisoners in British hands, in the headquarters papers in WO 28/182 and in naval hospital musters in ADM 102. The records of the Russian Orthodox Church in London include lists of Russian prisoners (in Russian) with correspondence in Russian, English and French relating to the distribution of money to them (RG 8/180).

For the Boer War, 1899-1902, there are registers of Boer prisoners, recorded in prisoner number order and arranged by area of confinement (e.g. Natal) in WO 108/ 303-305. Correspondence about their confinement in Ceylon, St Helena and elsewhere is in CO 537/403-409 and 453. Correspondence concerning Dutch, German and French prisoners is in FO 2/824-826.

36.2 Prisoners of war 1914-1919

The International Committee of the Red Cross in Geneva keeps lists of all known prisoners of war and internees of all nationalities for the First World War. Enquiries within the United Kingdom should be sent to The Director, International Welfare Department, British Red Cross Society, 9 Grosvenor Crescent, London SW1X 7EJ.

The PRO holds no comprehensive lists of prisoners of war on either side. Lists of prisoners and internees in Britain were compiled, but were largely destroyed by bombing in 1940. Two specimen lists survive, of German subjects interned as prisoners of war in 1915-1916 (WO 900/45-46). For British and Dominion subjects in German hands, there is a list compiled in July 1915 in ADM 1/8420/124; it is mainly concerned with the Giessen camp. There are also lists of British and Dominion subjects (mostly army personnel) held in Germany, Turkey and Switzerland in 1916, in AIR 1/892/204/5/696-698.

Deaths of prisoners of war and internees occurring in military and non-military hospitals and in enemy and occupied territory were notified to the British authorities by foreign embassies, legations, registration authorities and American authorities in charge of British internees: these certificates may be found in RG 35.

36.3 Prisoners of war 1939-1945

The International Committee of the Red Cross keeps lists for the Second World War as for the First: write to the address given in **36.2**. In the PRO, there are a few lists of prisoners and a wide range of general and policy documents. An alphabetical list of British and Dominion Air Force prisoners of war in German hands in 1944-1945 is in AIR 20/2336. Nominal rolls of Air Force prisoners for individual camps, principally Japanese, are in AIR 49/383-388. A nominal list of all Royal Marines known to have been held in German camps between 1939 and 1945 is in ADM 201/111. Lists of naval personnel interned in enemy camps may be found in ADM 116, code 79, although these are not identifiable from the class list. There is also a great deal of other material, including camp histories and escape reports, which is detailed in the PRO information leaflet *Prisoners of War and Displaced Persons 1939-1953: Documents in the Public Record Office*.

36.4 Prisoners of war 1950-1953

There are lists of British and Commonwealth servicemen who were known or believed to be prisoners of war in Korea, January 1951 - July 1953, in WO 208/3999. Another list of Commonwealth prisoners of war, compiled in January 1954, is in WO 308/54.

36.5 Prisoners of war: bibliography and sources

[An * means this work can be seen at Chancery Lane: a # means it can be seen at Kew.]

Published works

Public Record Office, *Prisoners of War 1660-1919: Documents in the Public Record Office* (Information Leaflet) #
Public Record Office, *Prisoners of War and Displaced Persons 1939-1953: Documents in the Public Record Office* (Information Leaflet) *#

Records

Admiralty (at Kew)
ADM 1/8420/124: list of British and Dominion prisoners in German hands, 1915
ADM 6/417: list of American prisoners in Britain, 1813
ADM 102 Hospital Musters. 1740-1860
ADM 103 Registers of Prisoners of War. 1755-1831
ADM 116 Admiralty and Secretariat Cases. 1852-1960. (Code 79 includes lists of naval prisoners held in enemy hands, 1939-1945.)
ADM 201/111: Royal Marines prisoners in German hands, 1939-1945

Air Ministry (at Kew)
AIR 1/892/204/5/696-699: lists of British and Dominion Subjects held in Germany, Turkey and Switzerland, 1916
AIR 20/2336: Air Force prisoners in German hands, 1944-1945
AIR 49/383-388: Air Force prisoners in Japanese hands, 1940-1945

Colonial Office (at Kew)
CO 537/403-409, 453: correspondence about Boer prisoners, 1899-190

Foreign Office (at Kew)
FO 2/824-826: correspondence on Dutch, German and French prisoners, 1899-1902

Home Office (at Kew)
HO 28 Admiralty correspondence, 1782-1840

General Register Office (at Chancery Lane)
RG 8/180: lists of Russian prisoners in Britain, 1854-1857
RG 35 Miscellaneous Foreign Deaths. 1830-1921

War Office (at Kew)
WO 28 Headquarters Records, 1746-1909
WO 108/303-305: registers of Boer prisoners, 1899-1902
WO 208/3999: British and Commonwealth prisoners in Korean hands, 1951-1953
WO 308/54: Commonwealth prisoners in Korean hands, 1954
WO 900 Specimens of Classes of Documents Destroyed. (Includes records relating to enemy prisoners of war, 1914-1918 and 1939-1945.)

37. Coroners' inquests

37.1 Introduction

Coroners have been holding inquests on the bodies of people who died in suspicious circumstances ever since the twelfth century. Most coroners' records are held locally, but the PRO does have a substantial number of them. The most useful introduction is *Coroners' Records in England and Wales*, by Gibson and Rogers, which lists the location of records available, by county, and also has a section on sources in the PRO. Not all deaths investigated by the coroner and his jury were cases of homicide: many were accidental deaths, or deaths of people in custody, or unexpected deaths. The inquest verdict gives the cause of death: if depositions survive, they are very much fuller. Verdicts were in Latin until 1733, after which English was used. Incidentally, a coroner's inquest and the modern post mortem medical examination are not the same as an inquisition post mortem: the latter is concerned with establishing the identity of the heir, not the cause of death (see **41.6**).

37.2 Coroners' records in the PRO

The PRO has coroners' records from coroners across the country who handed in their inquests to the assize justices: in addition, there are the records of coroners in the palatinates of Chester and Lancaster, and of inquests on prisoners who died in the King's Bench prison, and the Millbank Penitentiary.

The PRO has many coroners' rolls for the late thirteenth to the early fifteenth centuries: they are arranged by county (JUST 2). Few other records survive until the sixteenth century. Inquests were handed in to the assize judges by local coroners in large numbers from about the 1530s: some were used for murder or manslaughter trials, others gave details of accidental deaths or deaths in custody from sickness. Although these records are numerous, they are not very easy to find, as there are no indexes. They were filed with local indictments of crimes, also handed in to the assize judges: the inquests look different from the other records in the same file, because they are indentures, with a zigzag top. All these records were handed in to the court of King's Bench by the assize judges, and they were filed according to the law term in which they were handed in. For the period 1485-1675, the inquests are filed in KB 9, and for 1675-1845 in KB 11; London and Middlesex have separate files for 1675-1845 (KB 10). However, the general practice of handing in inquests appears to have stopped on most circuits in about 1750, although inquests continued to be handed in to the assize judges of the Western circuit, c.1740-1820 (KB 13). Hunnisett has produced two calendars of inquests, one for Nottinghamshire and one for Sussex, both covering 1485-1558: other publications can be found from Gibson and Rogers.

The Palatinates of Chester and Lancaster have extensive coroners' records. The Chester records cover Flint as well. Inquests from 1714 to 1851, with a few earlier ones, are in CHES 18: from 1798 to 1891 they are in ASSI 66. For the period of overlap, you will need to look in both classes, as the division appears to be haphazard. Inquests from the Palatinate of Lancaster, 1626-1832, are in PL 26/285-295, continued for 1804-1894 in DL 46: there are also very informative depositions about accidental deaths and homicides in PL 27.

Other sources in the PRO relate to the deaths of prisoners. The inquests of prisoners (usually debtors) held in the King's Bench prison, 1747-1750, and 1771-1839 (KB 14), can be informative about previous occupations. There is also a register of deaths of prisoners and of inquests upon them for the Millbank Penitentiary, 1848-1863 (PCOM 2/165).

37.3 London murders, 1891-1966

There are police registers of murders and of deaths by violence (including the deaths of women by illegal abortion) in the Metropolitan Police area, for 1891-1909, 1912-1917, and 1919-1966. These give the name, address and occupation of the victim, date and place of death, and subsequent charges or convictions (MEPO 20).

37.4 Coroners' inquests: bibliography and sources

[An * means this work can be seen at Chancery Lane: a # means it can be seen at Kew.]

Published works

J S W Gibson and C Rogers, *Coroners' Records in England and Wales*   (FFHS, 1988) *
R F Hunnisett, *Calendar of Nottinghamshire Coroners' Inquests, 1485-1558*, Thoroton Society, Record Series, vol. XXV
R F Hunnisett, 'Medieval Coroners' Rolls', *American Journal of Legal History*, vol.III, pp. 95-221, and 324-359 *

R F Hunnisett, *Sussex Coroners' Inquests, 1485-1558*, Sussex Record Society, vol. LXXIV

R F Hunnisett, *Wiltshire Coroners' Bills, 1752-1796*, Wiltshire Record Society, vol. XXXVI *

Records

Assizes (at Chancery Lane)
ASSI 66 Assizes: North and South Wales Circuit, Chester and North Wales Division: Coroners' Inquisitions. 1798-1891

Palatinate of Chester (at Chancery Lane)
CHES 18 Chester Coroners' Inquisitions. Edward III to Victoria

Duchy of Lancaster (at Chancery Lane)
DL 46 Coroners' Inquests and Returns. 1804-1896

Itinerant Justices (at Chancery Lane)
JUST 2 Coroners' Rolls. Henry III to Henry VI

Court of King's Bench (at Chancery Lane)
KB 9 Ancient Indictments. Edward I to 1675
KB 10 Indictments London and Middlesex. 1675-1845
KB 11 Out Counties Indictments Files. 1675-1845
KB 13 Court of King's Bench: Crown Side: Coroners' Inquisitions. 1748-1808
KB 14 Court of King's Bench: Crown Side: Coroners' Inquisitions on Prisoners in the King's Bench. 1746-1839

Metropolitan Police Office (at Kew)
MEPO 20 Metropolitan Police: General Registry: Registers of Murders and Deaths by Violence. 1891-1966

Prison Commission (at Kew)
PCOM 2/165: register of deaths and inquests at the Millbank Penitentiary, 1848-1863

Palatinate of Lancaster (at Chancery Lane)
PL 26 Palatinate of Lancaster: Crown Court: Indictments. 1424-1868
PL 27 Palatinate of Lancaster: Crown Court: Depositions. 1663-1867

38. Criminal trials

38.1 Introduction

There is an enormous amount of documentation on crime, but the records are not easy to use. Unless you already have firm evidence of the date and place of an ancestor's trial, or of a crime in which an ancestor was the victim, you should be prepared for a long and possibly unrewarding search. Futhermore, the records are in Latin until 1650, and again from 1660 to 1733; they do not give reports of proceedings in court; and the procedures can be difficult to follow (although Baker's article gives a good description of the criminal process before the modern period). Except for celebrated criminals, people transported for felony are probably the easiest to trace (see **40**), and the eighteenth and nineteenth century sources are fuller than others. From about 1750 onwards, newspaper reports of crimes often give considerably more detail than can be found in surviving court records, and if either a date or a place is known it may be better to start there. Newspapers also contain reports of crimes which never came to trial, and they can be useful in providing the family background of victims; they also include good reports of coroners' inquests (see **37**).

38.2 Quarter sessions

Until the sixteenth century, many manorial courts exercised jurisdiction in cases of petty theft, affray, drunkenness, and other offences (see **41.2**), but from the fourteenth century until 1971 quarter sessions, held in each county by lay justices of the peace, were the main courts at which minor crimes were tried and at which major crimes were heard in the first instance. For the fourteenth and fifteenth centuries the few surviving records are in the PRO, mostly in JUST 1; they are listed in Putnam's edition, and many have been published by local record societies. From the sixteenth century onwards, quarter sessions survive in increasing quantities, and they are deposited in local record offices; Gibson's *Quarter Sessions Records* gives details and locations, while Ratclif's *Warwick County Records* gives a very full indication of the nature of the records and the sort of information they contain.

38.3 Assizes records

From the thirteenth century until 1971, most serious crimes were tried before professional judges acting as justices of gaol delivery; pairs of justices went on circuits through groups of counties, holding 'assizes' sessions in each county twice a year. Assizes records are in the PRO. For the fourteenth and fifteenth centuries they are mostly in JUST 3, with some others in JUST 1, JUST 4 and KB 9; after 1559 they are in the ASSI classes. Certain areas had special jurisdictions serving much the same function as assizes; the Palatinate of Chester, primarily comprising Cheshire and Flint (CHES 17, CHES 19, CHES 20, CHES 21, CHES 22, CHES 24, CHES 25, CHES 26, CHES 27, fourteenth century to 1830); the Palatinate of Durham covering County Durham and certain areas beyond (DURH 15, DURH 16, DURH 17, DURH 18, DURH 19, sixteenth century to 1876), and the Palatinate of Lancaster, covering Lancashire (PL 15, PL 25, PL 26, PL 27, PL 28, fifteenth century to 1876). In Wales, the equivalent jurisdiction was exercised from 1542 to 1830 by the Great Sessions of Wales, whose records are in the National Library of Wales; from 1830 to 1971 the Welsh counties were included among the assizes circuits. Scotland had a very different legal system, whose surviving records are in the Scottish Record Office and local record offices.

The nature and quality of the assizes records varies considerably from period to period and from circuit to circuit. Among the principal and most useful records, if they survive, are the indictments, which set out the charge against the defendant; the depositions or witness statements; and gaol books or crown books, in which the defendants at each session were listed, with a brief note of the charges and annotations indicating verdict and sentence.

In all these records the genealogical details are usually disappointing. Ages of defendants are not given; there are no details of family relationships unless the victim was related to the accused (and not always then); and the alleged parish of residence is quite unreliable, since it was normally made identical with the parish in which the crime took place (it is common to find a defendant described as being 'of' two or more quite different places, corresponding to the scenes of the crimes cited in different indictments at the same sessions). More guidance on using assizes records is in the PRO information leaflet *Assizes Records*, and there is a very detailed explanation of procedures and the contents of records in the *Introduction* volume of the *Calendar of Assize Records*.

The assize circuits were as follows:
Home circuit 13th century-1876: Essex, Hertfordshire, Kent, Surrey, Sussex.
Midland circuit 13th century-1863: Derbyshire, Leicestershire, Lincolnshire, Northamptonshire, Nottinghamshire, Rutland, Warwickshire.
Midland circuit 1864-1876: Derbyshire, Lincolnshire, Nottinghamshire, Warwickshire, Yorkshire.
Midland circuit 1876-1971: Bedfordshire, Buckinghamshire, Derbyshire, Leicestershire, Lincolnshire, Northamptonshire, Nottinghamshire, Rutland, Warwickshire.
Norfolk circuit 13th century-1863: Bedfordshire, Buckinghamshire, Cambridgeshire, Huntingdonshire, Norfolk, Suffolk.
Norfolk circuit 1864-1876: Bedfordshire, Buckinghamshire, Cambridgeshire, Huntingdonshire, Leicestershire, Norfolk, Northamptonshire, Rutland, Suffolk.
North and South Wales circuit 1830-1876: Cheshire and all Welsh counties.
North and South Wales circuit, North Wales Division 1876-1945: Anglesey, Caernarvon, Cheshire, Denbigh, Flint, Merioneth, Montgomery.
North and South Wales circuit, South Wales Division 1876-1945: Brecknock, Cardigan, Carmarthen, Glamorgan, Pembroke, Radnor.
North Eastern circuit 1876-1971: Durham, Northumberland, Yorkshire.
Northern circuit 13th century-1863: Cumberland, Northumberland, Westmorland, Yorkshire.
Northern circuit 1864-1876: Cumberland, Northumberland, Westmorland.
Northern circuit 1876-1971: Cumberland, Lancashire, Westmorland.
Oxford circuit 13th century-1971: Berkshire, Gloucestershire, Herefordshire, Monmouthshire (added 1543), Oxfordshire, Shropshire, Staffordshire, Worcestershire.
South Eastern circuit 1876-1971: Cambridgeshire, Essex, Hertfordshire, Huntingdonshire, Kent, Suffolk, Surrey, Sussex
Wales and Chester circuit 1945-1971: Cheshire, and all Welsh counties.
Western circuit 13th century-1971: Cornwall, Devon, Dorset, Hampshire, Somerset, Wiltshire.

38.4 London

In London, there were sessions of oyer and terminer and gaol delivery for the city of London and the county of Middlesex, held before the lord mayor at the Old Bailey, which performed very much the same functions as the assize sessions in the counties. In 1834, these sessions were replaced by the Central Criminal Court (at the Old Bailey), whose records are at the PRO, in CRIM classes (see also **38.7**). The jurisdiction of this court extended beyond London, to include Middlesex and parts of Essex, Kent and Surrey.

The original records of these sessions are not in the PRO: the London records are at the Corporation of London Record Ofice, and the Middlesex records are at the Greater London Record Office. The main source for trials at the Old Bailey, however, is the printed series of *Old Bailey Sessions Papers*, which are available at the Guildhall Library; they are substantial but incomplete sets in the PRO (PCOM 1, for 1801 to 1904, and CRIM 10, for 1834 to 1912). These are verbatim reports of the proceedings in court, giving the name of the accused, the charges, the evidence of witnesses, the verdict (with the prisoner's age if found guilty), and the sentence; the report will also indicate whether the case was a London or a Middlesex one. The reports are roughly indexed in each volume. For the period 1815 to 1849 only, there is additional information (the prison to which a convicted person was sent, and the final judgment in cases where this was not given at the trial) in HO 16.

38.5 King's Bench

The Court of King's Bench exercised the highest jurisdiction in criminal matters until the reorganisation of the courts in 1876. Relatively few cases were heard each term, and they were mostly cases where the defendant was rich and influential, cases where the crown had a particular interest, or cases which presented some special difficulty. The main records (KB 9, KB 10, KB 11, KB 12, KB 27, KB 28) are difficult to use and have no itemised lists or indexes. The exception is the so-called '*Baga de Secretis*' (KB 8), which contains records of certain treason trials and other special cases. Some other records of, or relating to, treason trials, including lists of prisoners and convicts, are in KB 33, TS 11 and TS 20; see the PRO information leaflet *The Jacobite Risings of 1715 and 1745*. Many of the most celebrated cases in King's Bench are reported in detail in the published *State Trials*.

38.6 High Court of Admiralty

From 1535 to 1834 jurisdiction in cases of piracy and other crime on the high seas was exercised by the High Court of Admiralty. Its criminal records in HCA 1 are indexed; they include death warrants as well as other procedural records.

38.7 Central Criminal Court

From 1834 the Central Criminal Court at the Old Bailey exercised both a London jurisdiction (see **38.4**) and a wider jurisdiction including crimes on the high seas or abroad and cases removed to the court because of local prejudice or other factors. Consequently many of the most notorious trials took place here. The records are in CRIM classes.

38.8 Criminal trial registers, 1791-1892

Most records of criminals and criminal trials are not easy to use, as they are not usually arranged by name. If the date and place of trial are known the Criminal Registers can be helpful. There are two series: HO 26, which covers Middlesex only, 1791-1849; and HO 27, which covers all England and Wales, 1805-1892 (including Middlesex from 1850). The registers are returns from the counties, bound up in alphabetical order of county. They show all persons charged with indictable offences, giving the date and result of the trial, sentence in the case of conviction, and dates of execution.

38.9 Criminal trials: bibliography and sources

Published works

J H Baker, 'Criminal courts and procedure at common law 1550-1800', in *Crime in England 1550-1800*, ed J S Cockburn (London, 1977)
J S Cockburn ed, *Calendar of Assize Records, Home Circuit Indictments, Elizabeth and James I*(London, 1975 continuing) *
J S W Gibson, *Quarter Sessions Records for Family Historians: a Select List* (FFHS, 2nd edn 1986)
T B Howell and T J Howell eds, *A complete collection of state trials...* (London, 1816-1826)
J McDonell ed, *Reports of State Trials, New Series* (London, 1858-1898, reprinted Abingdon 1982)
Public Record Office, *Assize Records* (Information Leaflet) *#
Public Record Office, *The Jacobite Risings of 1715 and 1745* (Information Leaflet) *#
B H Putnam ed, *Proceedings before the Justices of the Peace in the Fourteenth and Fifteenth Centuries* (1938)
S C Ratclif and others eds,*Warwick County Records* (Warwick, 1935-1964)

Records

Assizes (at Chancery Lane)
ASSI 2 Oxford Circuit: Crown Books. 1656-1972
ASSI 3 Oxford Circuit: Second Court Crown Books. 1847-1951
ASSI 5 Oxford Circuit: Indictments. 1650-1968
ASSI 6 Oxford Circuit: Criminal Depositions and Case Papers. 1719-1968
ASSI 10 Oxford Circuit: Miscellanea Returns. 1732-1890
ASSI 11 Midland Circuit: Crown Minute Books. 1818-1945
ASSI 12 Midland Circuit: Indictments. 1860-1968
ASSI 13 Midland Circuit: Criminal Depositions and Case Papers. 1862-1968
ASSI 16 Norfolk Circuit: Indictments and Subsidiary Documents. 1606-1699
ASSI 21 Western Circuit: Crown Minute Books. 1730-1971

ASSI 23 Western Circuit: Gaol Books. 1670-1824
ASSI 24 Western Circuit: Miscellaneous Books. 1611-1932
ASSI 25 Western Circuit: Indictments. 1729-1968
ASSI 26 Western Circuit: Criminal Depositions and Case Papers. 1861-1968
ASSI 31 Home and South Eastern Circuits: Agenda Books. 1735-1943
ASSI 32 Home, Norfolk and South Eastern Circuits: Minute Books. 1783-1971
ASSI 33 Norfolk Circuit: Gaol Books. 1734-1863
ASSI 35 Home, Norfolk and South Eastern Circuits: Indictments. 1559-1968
ASSI 36 Home, Norfolk and South Eastern Circuits: Depositions. 1813-1968
ASSI 40 Home and South Eastern Circuits: Index to Crown Minute Books. 1859-1911
ASSI 41 Northern and North Eastern Circuits: Crown Minute Books. 1714-1971
ASSI 42 Northern Circuit: Gaol Books. 1658-1811
ASSI 44 Northern and North Eastern Circuits: Indictments. 1607-1968
ASSI 45 Northern and North Eastern Circuits: Depositions. 1613-1968
ASSI 47 Northern and North Eastern Circuits: Miscellanea. 1629-1950
ASSI 51 Northern Circuit: Indictments. 1863-1968
ASSI 52 Northern Circuit: Criminal Depositions and Case Papers. 1877-1968
ASSI 53 Northern Circuit: Orders. 1879-1890
ASSI 61 Chester and North Wales Circuit: Crown Minute Books. 1831-1938
ASSI 62 Chester and North Wales Circuit: Crown Books. 1835-1883
ASSI 64 Chester and North Wales Circuit: Indictments. 1831-1945
ASSI 65 Chester and North Wales Circuit: Criminal Depositions. 1831-1944
ASSI 71 South Wales Circuit: Indictments. 1834-1945
ASSI 72 South Wales Circuit: Criminal Depositions. 1835-1944
ASSI 73 South Wales Circuit: Miscellanea. 1839-1937
ASSI 74 South Wales Circuit: Judgment Rolls. 1841-1842
ASSI 76 South Wales Circuit: Minute Books (Crown Court). 1844-1942
ASSI 77 South Wales Circuit: Miscellaneous Books. 1837-1884
ASSI 79 Wales and Chester Circuit: Crown Minute Books. 1945
ASSI 80 Midland Circuit: Indictments (second series). 1652-1688
ASSI 81 Midland, Oxford and Western Circuits: Pardons. 1866-1958
ASSI 82 Western Circuit: Criminal Case Papers. 1951-1953
ASSI 83 Wales and Chester Circuit: Indictments. 1945-1968
ASSI 84 Wales and Chester Circuit: Criminal Depositions and Case Papers. 1945-1968

Palatinate of Chester (at Chancery Lane)
CHES 17 Chester Eyre Rolls. 1306-1500
CHES 19 Chester Sheriffs' Tourn Rolls. 14th to 16th centuries
CHES 20 Chester Calendar Rolls. 14th to 16th centuries
CHES 21 Chester Crown Books. 16th to 19th centuries
CHES 24 Chester Gaol Files, Writs, etc. 1329-1831
CHES 25 Chester Indictment Rolls. 1293-1497
CHES 26 Chester Mainprise Rolls. 1344-16th century
CHES 27 Chester Outlawry Rolls. 1461-1483

Central Criminal Court (at Chancery Lane)
CRIM 1 Depositions. 1835-1949
CRIM 2 Calendars of Depositions. 1923-1940

CRIM 4 Indictments. 1834-1957
CRIM 5 Calendars of Indictments. 1833-1971
CRIM 6 Court Books. 1834-1949
CRIM 10 Minutes of Evidence. 1834-1912

Palatinate of Durham (at Chancery Lane)
DURH 15 Crown Minute Books. 1770-1876
DURH 16 Crown Books. 1735-1876
DURH 17 Indictments. 1582-1877
DURH 18 Depositions. 1843-1876
DURH 19 Crown Miscellanea. 1471-1815

High Court of Admiralty (at Chancery Lane)
HCA 1 Admiralty Court Oyer and Terminer Records. 1535-1834

Home Office (at Kew)
HO 16 Returns of Committals for Trial at the Old Bailey and Central Crminal Court.
    1815-1849
HO 26 Criminal Registers, Middlesex. 1791-1849
HO 27 Criminal Registers, England and Wales. 1805-1892

Justices Itinerant (at Chancery Lane)
JUST 1 Eyre and Assize Rolls etc. 1201-1482
JUST 3 Gaol Delivery Rolls and Files. 1271-1476
JUST 4 Eyre and Assize Files. 1248-c.1450

Court of King's Bench (at Chancery Lane)
KB 8 *Baga de Secretis*. 1477-1813
KB 9 Ancient Indictments. Edw I to 1675
KB 10 Indictments London and Middlesex. 1675-1845
KB 11 Out Counties Indictments Files. 1675-1845
KB 12 Indictments London, Middlesex and Out Counties, Amalgamated. 1846-1926
KB 27 *Coram Rege* Rolls. 1273-1702
KB 28 Crown Rolls. 1702-1911
KB 33 Crown Side Precedents. c.1600-1907

Prison Commission (at Kew)
PCOM 1 Old Bailey Sessions Papers. 1801-1904

Palatinate of Lancaster (at Chancery Lane)
PL 15 Court of Common Pleas: Plea Rolls. 1400-1848
PL 25 Crown Court: Assize Rolls. 1422-1843
PL 26 Crown Court: Indictments. 1424-1868
PL 27 Crown Court: Depositions. 1663-1867
PL 28 Crown Court: Miscellaneous Records. 14th to 19th centuries

Treasury Solicitor (at Chancery Lane)
TS 11 Treasury Solicitor and HM Procurator General, Papers. 1584-1856
TS 20 The 1745 Rebellion Papers. 1745-1753

39. Remanded and convicted prisoners

39.1 Introduction

Many prisoners are most easily traced from the records relating to their trials (see **38**) or those relating to their subsequent history if they were transported overseas (see **40**), and a number of the sources cited there give information about the periods of imprisonment. There are, however, other records which can be used to supplement this information or to provide clues when the dates and places of trials are unknown. It should be remembered that before the late eighteenth century there was no co-ordinated policy on the use of imprisonment as a punishment, especially since relatively minor felonies carried the death penalty, commutable to transportation; prisons were largely used for remand awaiting trial.

39.2 Conviction and sentence

For Middlesex, 1791-1849, and for England and Wales, 1805-1892, there are criminal trial registers with information about the execution of sentences (see **38.8**). The court orders for imprisonment or transfer, with details of the convict's penal history, 1843-1871, are in PCOM 5, with indexes in PCOM 6. Correspondence and other papers, including judges' recommendations for mercy, are in HO 42 (1782-1820), HO 47 (1784-1829), HO 6 (1816-1840), and HO 44 (1820-1861). Petitions by prisoners for remission or reduction of sentence or for free pardon, and related registers, papers and warrants, 1797-1921, are in HO 17, HO 18, and HO 19, with related correspondence in HO 11, HO 13, HO 15, HO 147 and PC 1. There are some petitions on behalf of prisoners, 1779-1790, 1805-1841, and 1854, in PRO 30/45/1.

39.3 Registers of prisoners

Not all prison records were collected or retained centrally, and many are still kept by the prisons, or by the authorities who took them over. Nevertheless the PRO has registers of various prisons, included prison ships or hulks (imprisonment in a hulk did not necessarily imply transportation overseas; the hulks were floating prisons permanently moored in coastal waters). There are many such registers, including details of the individual prisoners (and, in some cases, photographs), 1770-1916 in PCOM 2 and HO 9. There are sworn lists of convicts, with particulars of each, 1824-1876, in HO 8. There are quarterly returns relating to the hulks, 1802-1831, in T 38. Other registers, also including detailed descriptions of the prisoners, 1838-1875, are in HO 23 and HO 24, while KB 32/23 has a return of convicts in the Millbank Penitentiary in 1826.

39.4 Registers of habitual criminals

From 1869, prisoners who would previously have been transported were instead imprisoned and released in England and Wales: there was much worry about the effect on the crime rates. Local prisons were required to compile registers of prisoners convicted of any of the many crimes specified by the Habitual Criminals Act 1869, or by the Prevention of Crime Act 1871, before their release. Printed forms were supplied with these registers: these required name and alias, age, description, trade, prison from which released, date of liberation, offence, sentence, term of supervision, intended residence, distinguishing marks and any previous convictions. In addition photographs were pasted onto the forms. These local registers were supposed to be sent to the central Habitual Criminals Registry, where an alphabetical national register of habitual criminals was compiled, of people thought likely to reoffend: the idea was to distribute the printed national register to police stations. The national register did not include the photographs.

The first national register of habitual criminals covered December 1869 to March 1876, and included 12,164 people under 22,115 names, out of a total of 179,601 submitted in the local registers (PCOM 2/404). These registers are such an unused source, and so useful as an index to aliases, that a typical entry is worth quoting:
Smith, Benjamin, alias Jackson, Charles; [age] 27; [height] 5'4''; [hair] br; [eyes] gr; [face] fr; [trade or occupation] hammerman; [prison and date of liberation] Wandsworth 11/1/75; [offence] uttering; [sentence] 12 months; [supervision] 7 years; [intended residence] 3 Williams-place, Great Guildford-street, Southwark; [marks and remarks] scars on forehead, nose right thumb and arm. Two previous convictions for felony.

The PRO does not have a full set of these national registers, but since they were compiled for local distribution, others may well survive elsewhere. The registers in the PRO are to be found in PCOM 2/404 (1869-1876) and in MEPO 6/1-52 (1881-1882, 1889-1940); they are closed for 75 years from the date of creation. The PRO also has the local prison registers of habitual criminals for Birmingham, 1871-1875 (PCOM 2/296-299, 430-434) and Cambridge, 1875-1877 (PCOM 2/300). Other local registers are still in the custody of the prisons and constabularies which took over their responsibilities. There are also similarly informative registers of habitual drunkards, 1903-1914 (MEPO 6/77-88).

39.5 Licences

There are notes of licences to convicts to be at large, and of revocations of such licences, 1853-1887, in PCOM 3 (male convicts) and PCOM 4 (female convicts), indexed in PCOM 6.

39.6 Remanded and convicted prisoners: bibliography and sources

Published works

W B Johnson, *The English Prison Hulks* (revised edn, 1970)
R Whitmore, *Victorian and Edwardian Crime and Punishment* (London, 1978)

Records

Home Office (at Kew)
HO 6 Judges' and Recorders' Returns. 1816-1840

HO 8 Convict Prisons: Quarterly Returns of Prisoners. 1824-1876
HO 9 Convict Prison Hulks: Miscellaneous Registers. 1802-1849
HO 11 Convict Transportation Registers. 1787-1870
HO 13 Criminal Entry Books. 1782-1871
HO 15 Criminal and Miscellaneous Warrant Books. 1850-1898
HO 17 Criminal Petitions, Series I. 1819-1839
HO 18 Criminal Petitions, Series II. 1839-1854
HO 19 Registers of Criminal Petitions. 1797-1853
HO 23 Registers of County Prisons. 1847-1866
HO 24 Prison Registers and Returns. 1838-1875
HO 42 Domestic Correspondence, George III. 1787-1820
HO 44 Domestic Correspondence, George IV and later. 1820-1861
HO 47 Judges' Reports. 1784-1829
HO 147 Criminal Warrant Books. 1887-1921. (Records closed for 100 years.)

Court of King's Bench (at Chancery Lane)
KB 32 Crown Side Miscellanea. James I to 1889

Metropolitan Police Office (at Kew)
MEPO 6 Criminal Record Office: Habitual Criminals Registers, etc. 1834-1959

Privy Council Office (at Chancery Lane)
PC 1 Unbound Papers. 1481-1946. (Convict establishment papers, 1819-1844.)

Prison Commission (at Kew)
PCOM 2 Prisons Records, Series I. 1770-1940
PCOM 3 Male Licences. 1853-1887
PCOM 4 Female Licences. 1853-1887
PCOM 5 Old Captions and Transfer Papers. 1843-1871
PCOM 6 Registers and Indexes. 1824-1929

Public Record Office (Gifts and Deposits)
PRO 30/45 Hatton Papers. 1779-1854

Treasury (at Kew)
T 38 Departmental Accounts. 1558-1937

40. Convicted prisoners transported abroad

40.1 Transported convicts: general sources

Limited and informal forced emigration of convicts, vagrants, destitute orphans, and political rebels to the colonies commenced soon after the colony of Virginia was founded in 1607. In 1655 a formal system was introduced which enabled death sentences to be reduced to transportation, and two years later justices of the peace were empowered to transport vagrants. In 1718 assize courts were given the power to impose sentences of transportation for a range of petty and more serious crimes.

Records for the earlier period are not easy to use but much of the information about named convicts which they contain has been published. For any period or destination you are advised to start your search with the published sources discussed below. A particularly useful book is Hawkings's *Bound for Australia*, which provides transcripts and facsimiles of a wide range of records relating to imprisonment and transportation: it is available at both Kew and Chancery Lane.

Many of the records relating to voluntary emigration (see **14**) may also contain details of convicts or ex-convicts. For records of trials resulting in transportation, see **38**. For records of prisons and prison hulks, in which convicts were housed for various periods prior to transportation, see **39**. Names and parishes of those condemned to hang but subsequently pardoned on condition of transportation are listed in the Patent Rolls, 1654-1717 (C 66, written in Latin: contemporary indexes are available), and in the State Papers Domestic until 1782 (SP 35, SP 36, SP 37, SP 44).

Home Office warrants for pardons and reprieves are in HO 13 (1782-1849) and HO 15 (1850-1871). Home Office records also include petitions on behalf of prisoners for commutation of death sentences (HO 17, 1819-1840; HO 18, 1839-1854), as well as justices' returns (HO 6, 1816-1940) and judges' reports (HO 47, 1784-1829) giving information about commutations. These can all be very informative.

Some wives applied to accompany their convicted husbands. Their petitions survive for 1819-1844 (PC 1/67-92) and from 1849 (HO 12, identified via the registers in HO 14). Privy Council correspondence, 1819-1844 (PC 1/67-92) contains additional material about transportation as do the Privy Council registers (PC 2), which also give lists of convicts transported for 14 years or less.

40.2 Transportation to America and the West Indies

If you are looking for an individual who may have arrived in America or the West Indies as an unfree emigrant, a good starting point is P W Coldham's *Complete Book of Emigrants in Bondage, 1614-1775*, based on records in the PRO as well as in local record offices. This lists transported convicts and gives, where known, date and place of trial, occupation, month of embarkation and landing, name of ship, and destination. An earlier version of Coldham's research findings, published as *Bonded Passengers to America* (but also covering transportation to the West Indies) includes a readable history of the system.

In addition to the more general records noted above, the PRO holds Treasury money books (T 53) which include details of payments by the Treasury to contractors engaged to arrange transportation between 1716 and 1772. Until October 1744 names of all those to be transported from the home counties are listed, together with names of ships and their captains. Thereafter only totals for each county are given. Until 1742 the colony of destination is usually recorded. Similar information is given in a broken run of transportation lists, 1747-1772, in T 1.

Colonial Office correspondence with America and the West Indies (CO 5) includes material on all aspects of transportation to the American colonies. For other records relating to the American and West Indian colonies which may include details of convicts or ex-convicts, as well as free emigrants, see **14.3**. For records in the United States see **14.2**.

40.3 Transportation to Australia

The American War of Independence curtailed transportation to the American colonies and, following investigation of other possible destinations, it was decided in 1786 to found a penal colony in New South Wales. The PRO information leaflet, *Australian Convicts: Sources in the Public Record Office*, provides details of records relating to trials, transportation and settlement. Microfilm copies of many PRO documents are available in Australia at the National Library in Canberra, and at the Mitchell Library in Sydney.

The first fleet of convict ships left England in May 1787, reaching Australia in January 1788. The names of the convicts are listed by P G Fidlon and R J Ryan in *The First Fleeters*. A list of convicts transported on the second fleet of ships, which left in 1789, is in R J Ryan's *The Second Fleet Convicts*. Most transportation to Australia was from the British Isles, but some convicts arrived in Australia from other parts of the Empire. Transportation to Australia came to an end in 1868.

A search for an individual may begin with the court records (see **38**) if the place of trial is known. Otherwise, the Convict Transportation Registers, 1787-1867 (HO 11) provide the name of the ship on which the convict sailed as well as the date and place of conviction and the term of the sentence. Contracts with agents to transport the prisoners, with full lists of ships and convicts, 1842-1867, are in the Treasury Solicitor's Department general series papers (TS 18/460-525 and 1308-1361).

Reports on the medical condition of the convicts while at sea may be found in the Admiralty medical journals, 1817-1856 (ADM 101), and in the Admiralty Transport Department surgeon-superintendents' journals, 1858-1867 (MT 32).

40.4 Settlement in Australia

Musters or censuses, primarily but not exclusively concerned with the convict population, were taken periodically in New South Wales and Tasmania between 1788 and 1859 (HO 10). The New South Wales census of 1828 (HO 10/21-27) is the most complete, and is available in a published edition by Sainty and Johnson. It contains the names of more than 35,000 people with details of age, religion, family, place of residence, occupation and stock or land held. Whether each settler came free, or as a convict (or was born in the colony) is recorded; and date of arrival and the name of the ship are given. The papers relating to convicts in New South Wales and Tasmania (HO 10) also contain material about convicts' pardons and tickets of leave from New South Wales and Tasmania, 1835-59. Home Office records also include some information about deaths of convicts in New South Wales, 1829-1834 (HO 7/2).

Colonial Office records relating to Australia sometimes note individual convicts as well as policy decisions, but they are not easy to search for particular named individuals. There are, however, lists of convicts, together with emigrant settlers, 1801-1821, in New South Wales Original Correspondence (CO 201). Names can also be traced in New South Wales entry books from 1786 (CO 202), and registers from 1849 (CO 360 and CO 369). Records of the superintendent of convicts in New South Wales, 1788-1825, are now held in the State Archives of New South Wales; the PRO holds microfilm copies (CO 207). Some of the lists from these records have been printed in L L Robson, *The Convict Settlers of Australia*.

For other records which may provide relevant information, see **14.5**.

40.5 Convict transportation: bibliography and sources

[An * means this work can be seen at Chancery Lane: a # means it can be seen at Kew.]

Published works

C Bateson, *The Convict Ships, 1787-1868* (Glasgow, 2nd edn 1969) #

P W Coldham, *Bonded Passengers to America, 1615-1775* (Baltimore, 1983) *#

P W Coldham, *The Complete Book of Emigrants in Bondage, 1614-1775* (Baltimore, 1987) *

P G Fidlon and R J Ryan ed, *The First Fleeters* (Sydney, 1981) *#

Friends of the East Sussex Record Office, *East Sussex Sentences of Transportation at Quarter Sessions, 1790-1854* (Lewes, 1988)

D T Hawkings, *Bound for Australia* (Chichester, 1987) *#

R Hughes, *The Fatal Shore: A History of Transportation of Convicts to Australia, 1781-1868* (London, 1987)

Public Record Office, *Australian Convicts: Sources in the Public Record Office* (Information Leaflet) *#

L L Robson, *The Convict Settlers of Australia* (Melbourne, 1981)

R J Ryan, *The Second Fleet Convicts* (Sydney, 1982) *#

M R Sainty and K A Johnson ed, *New South Wales: Census...November 1828* (Sydney, 1980) #

I Wyatt ed., *Transportees from Gloucester to Australia, 1783-1842* (Bristol and Gloucester Archaeological Society, 1988)

Records

Admiralty (at Kew)
ADM 101 Medical Journals. 1785-1880

Chancery (at Chancery Lane)
C 66 Patent Rolls. 1201-1962

Colonial Office (at Kew)
CO 5 America and West Indies Original Correspondence, etc. 1606-1822

CO 201 New South Wales Original Correspondence. 1783-1900
CO 202 New South Wales Entry Books. 1786-1873
CO 207 New South Wales Entry Books Relating to Convicts. 1788-1868.
CO 360 New South Wales Register of Correspondence. 1849-1900
CO 369 New South Wales Registers of Out-letters. 1873-1900

Home Office (at Kew)
HO 7 Convicts, Miscellanea. 1785-1835
HO 10 Settlers and Convicts, New South Wales and Tasmania: Records. 1787-1859
HO 11 Convict Transportation Registers. 1787-1870
HO 12 Criminal Department: Old Criminal (OC) Papers. 1849-1871
HO 13 Criminal Entry Books. 1782-1871
HO 14 Criminal Department: Registers of Papers. 1849-1870
HO 15 Criminal and Miscellaneous Warrant Books. 1850-1898
HO 17 Criminal Petitions, Series I. 1819-1839
HO 18 Criminal Petitions, Series II. 1839-1854
HO 47 Judges' Reports on Criminals. 1784-1829

Admiralty Transport Department (at Kew)
MT 32 Surgeon Superintendents' Journals of Convict Ships. 1858-1867

Privy Council (at Chancery Lane)
PC 1/67-92: Convict establishment papers, 1819-1844
PC 2 Registers. 1540-1978

Secretaries of State (at Chancery Lane)
SP 35 State Papers Domestic, George I. 1714-1727
SP 36 State Papers Domestic, George II. 1727-1760
SP 37 State Papers Domestic, George III. 1760-1782
SP 44 Secretaries of State: State Papers: Entry Books. 1661-1828

Treasury (at Kew)
T 1 Treasury Board Papers. (Contains transportation lists, 1747-1772.)
T 53 Warrants Relating to Money. 1676-1839

Treasury Solicitor (at Chancery Lane)
TS 18/460-525, 1308-1361: contracts to transport named prisoners, 1842-1867

41. Land ownership

41.1 Introduction

In England and Wales, records of the ownership and transfer of particular lands are difficult to locate, as there was no national system of registration before the nineteenth century. The PRO has hundreds of thousands of property records, but there is no general index and searching is difficult without some idea of when, where and why a conveyance took place. Some understanding of the different methods of land holding (e.g. freehold, copyhold) and of land transfer is also useful.

The records of tithe redemption, enclosures and land valuation, discussed in **42**, as well as the rentals and surveys discussed in **41.5** can also provide information on land owners in a particular place.

41.2 Court rolls

Before the nineteenth century, a high proportion of people held land by a form of tenure called copyhold. Such land was transferred by surrendering it to the lord of the manor from whom it was held, who then regranted it. Conveyances of copyhold property and the admissions of heirs on the death of tenants were entered on manorial court rolls. These are potentially a valuable source for confirming or expanding information found in parish registers which, in some cases, they predate.

Court rolls, however, have a limited value for two reasons. First, there might be several manors in one parish or the property of a manor could be scattered through several parishes and consequently it is not always easy to discover of which manor, if any, a man was tenant. Second, the survival of court rolls has not been good; only a small proportion of rolls survive from before the sixteenth century.

Court rolls are held in the PRO and in many other repositories. Most of the PRO's holdings of court rolls come from manors which formed part of the crown lands (DL 30, SC 2, ADM 74, C 116, CRES 5, LR 3, MAF 5, WARD 2). A register of all known surviving manorial documents is held by the Historical Manuscripts Commission.

In the nineteenth century, much copyhold property was converted to freehold, and copyhold was finally abolished by the Law of Property Acts, 1922 and 1924. The PRO holds lists of copyholders who converted to freehold and files relating to such cases (MAF 9, MAF 13, MAF 20, MAF 27).

41.3 Fines and recoveries

Other ways to transfer the ownership of land involved the common law and the King's courts: the most usual, fines and recoveries, were methods of conveying property by means of fictitious legal actions. The intended purchaser, as plaintiff, claimed the property from the vendor; the property was then transferred by a legally sanctioned agreement in the case of a fine, or by judgement of the court in the case of a recovery. Fines were used from the twelfth century until 1833, recoveries from the fifteenth century until the same date.

The largest series of records are the Feet of Fines (CP 25) and Common Recoveries (CP 40 and CP 43). Other series are in CHES 31, for the Palatinate of Chester; PL 17 for the Palatinate of Lancaster; and DURH 12 for the Palatinate of Durham. There are manuscript lists of fines and recoveries arranged by date: some have place indexes. Many early fines have been published, mainly by local record societies.

41.4 Deeds

There are many original deeds in the PRO. Most came into the crown's hands when it acquired property, or were produced as evidence in law suits. There is no union (i.e. combined) list or index of them and a search would have to be made through a large number of individual class lists.

Until the nineteenth century it was common practice to enrol private deeds in the central courts; certain types of deed continued to be enrolled up to 1925 (see **32.2** for trust deeds). The greatest number of deeds was enrolled in the Chancery (C 54); others were enrolled in the Exchequer (E 13, E 159, E 315 and E 368), the Court of Common Pleas (CP 40 before Easter 1583 and 1834-1875 and CP 43, 1583 to 1834) and the Court of King's Bench (KB 26, KB 27 before 1702 and KB 122, 1702-1875). In many cases, there are lists and indexes of such deeds. Deeds were sometimes used as evidence in law suits and their texts can be found on the plea rolls or pleadings.

There are also large collections of individual deeds, which came from private or monastic muniments. Many of these have been calendared or descriptively listed. The major classes are C 146-C 149; DL 25-DL 27; DURH 21; E 40-E 44; E 210-E 213; E 325-E 330; LR 14-LR 16; PL 29; WALE 29-WALE 31; and WARD 2.

Registries of deeds were established in the three Ridings of Yorkshire and in Middlesex early in the eighteenth century; the one in Middlesex closed in 1940, but those in Yorkshire continued to operate until the 1970s. The Middlesex register can be seen at the Greater London Record Office; those for the North, East and West Ridings of Yorkshire are in the county record offices at Northallerton, Beverley and Wakefield. In the City of London and in many other cities and boroughs, transfers of property were often entered on the hustings rolls or in the records of the municipal courts. These should be sought in the relevant local record offices.

In 1862 a national Land Registry was established, but registration was voluntary and was little used. Compulsory registration on sale was introduced in London in 1899 and now covers all the major conurbations, although some rural areas are still excluded and there are still many unregistered properties in the compulsory registration areas. The Land Registry does not normally hold original deeds once property has been registered and cannot give details about the property without the permission of the current owner.

41.5 Rentals and surveys

Information about properties, including the names of owners and tenants, can often be discovered from rentals and surveys in the PRO. Surveys of crown property were taken for the purpose of estate management, and private property was sometimes surveyed if it was the subject of litigation. Rentals and surveys are found among the records of the Exchequer (E 36, E 142, E 164 and E 315) and the State Paper Office (SP 10-SP 18 and SP 46) and in the Special Collections (SC 11 and SC 12). They range from the thirteenth to the nineteenth centuries, but most are from the sixteenth and seventeenth centuries. Of special interest are the detailed Parliamentary Surveys

(E 317) of the crown lands taken in the Commonwealth period. Surveys taken as a result of litigation or for other reasons will be found in Depositions by Commission (E 134) and Special Commissions (E 178), which exist for the sixteenth to the nineteenth centuries. There are published lists of all the surveys.

41.6 Inquisitons post mortem, homage and wardship

Before 1660, on the death of any holder of land who was thought to have held that land direct from the crown (called a tenant in chief by knight service), an inquiry was held by the escheator of the county involved. A local jury had to swear to the identity and extent of the land held by the tenant at the time of his death, by what rents or services they were held, and the name and age of the next heir. If there was no heir, the land escheated (reverted) to the crown: if the next heir was under age, the crown claimed rights of wardship and marriage over the lands and the heir until he or she came of age. If the heir was adult, livery and seisin of the lands was granted on performance of homage to the king, and payment of a reasonable fine or relief. If the heir's age was in doubt, there might have been a separate inquiry to produce proof of age. These proofs often record memories of other events (eg. birth of the witness's child) to fix the heir's year of birth. All this finished in 1660, when feudal tenures were abolished.

The documents produced by these inquiries, the inquisitions post mortem, filed with some proofs of age, are a very valuable source for both family and local history: however, not all the information given is reliable. The main series are those returned into Chancery (C 132-C 142): unfortunately they are often illegible. Transcripts of some were sent to the Exchequer (E 149 and E 150) and the Court of Wards (WARD 7), and these are usually in better condition. There are joint indexes: many have been calendared (see **41.10**).

If you find that the heir was under age and did hold land from the crown in chief, then it is worth investigating the records of the Court of Wards and Liveries, which operated between 1540 and 1660. The right to wardship was often sold by the crown, by no means always to the next of kin: grants of wardship may be found in the Patent Rolls (C 66). The records of most potential value are the legal proceedings in WARD 3 and WARD 13: the Court of Wards used equity procedure (see **47.3**), and so the records are full, informative, and in English. The deeds and evidences, in WARD 2, go back as far as the twelfth century: there is a partial index to them in the *Deputy Keeper's Sixth Report*, Appendix II. For more information, consult H E Bell, *An Introduction to the History and Records of the Court of Wards and Liveries*.

41.7 Licences to alienate

There is one further valuable source for the period before 1660. Property held by tenure in chief, as much was, could only lawfully be sold with the crown's permission, which was granted in the form of a licence to alienate.

Copies of the licences were enrolled on the Patent Rolls (C 66): there are printed calendars for the period 1216 to 1582. A search through the indexes to the calendars is an easy and sometimes rewarding way of searching for early conveyances. After the printed calendars cease, it is as easy to leaf through the Entry Books of Licences and Pardons for Alienation, 1571-1650 (A 4) as to use the contemporary finding aids to the Patent Rolls.

41.8 Crown lands

Many properties have, at some time, been in the hands of the crown, and, especially in the sixteenth century, many people were tenants of crown properties. If there is any evidence to suggest that a piece of property was in the crown's hands or that a person was a crown tenant, it is worth exploring the records of the royal properties; but they are voluminous and difficult to use and specialist advice should be sought.

41.9 Chester, Durham and Lancaster

The palatinates of Chester (CHES), Durham (DURH) and Lancaster (PL and DL) had their own administrations which paralleled the central government. Fines, recoveries, enrolments and deeds relating to property in those areas should be sought among their records.

41.10 Land ownership: bibliography and sources

[An * means this work can be seen at Chancery Lane: a # means it can be seen at Kew.]

Published works

General works
J H Harvey, *Sources for the History of Houses* (British Records Association, 1968) *
Public Record Office, *Confiscations, Sales and Restorations of Crown and Royalist Lands, 1642-1660* (Information Leaflet) *#
Public Record Office, *Private Conveyances in the Public Record Office* (Information Leaflet) *#
A W B Simpson, *An Introduction to the History of the Land Law* (Oxford, 1961)

Court rolls
P D A Harvey, *Manorial Records* (Gloucester, 1984)
A Travers, 'Manorial Documents', *Genealogists' Magazine*, vol. XXI, pp. 1-10

Deeds
N W Alcock, *Old Title Deeds* (Chichester, 1986) *
Descriptive Catalogue of Ancient Deeds preserved in the Public Record Office (London, 1890-1915). (This covers parts of the Ancient Deeds Series A, B, C and D.) *
A A Dibben, *Title Deeds* (Historical Association, 1968)
List and Index Society, *Ancient Deeds, Series A* (vols. 151, 152: continues the *Descriptive Catalogue)*
List and Index Society, *Ancient Deeds, Series AS and WS* (vol. 158)
List and Index Society, *Ancient Deeds, Series B* (vols. 95, 101, 113, 124: continues the *Descriptive Catalogue)*

List and Index Society, *Ancient Deeds, Series BB* (vol. 137)
List and Index Society, *Ancient Deeds, Series DD* (vol. 200)
List and Index Society, *Ancient Deeds, Series E* (vol. 181)
F Sheppard and V Belcher, 'The Deed Registries of Yorkshire and Middlesex', *Journal of the Society of Archivists*, vol. VI, pp. 274-286

Inquisitions post mortem and wardships
H E Bell, *An Introduction to the History and Records of the Court of Wards and Liveries* (Cambridge, 1953) *
Calendar of Inquisitions Miscellaneous, Henry III to Henry VII (London, 1916-1968) *
Calendar of Inquisitions Post Mortem, Henry III to Henry IV, and *Henry VII* (London, 1898-1989) *
R F Hunnisett, 'The Reliability of Inquisitions as Historical Evidence', *The Study of Medieval Records*, ed. D A Bullough and R L Storey (Oxford, 1971)
R E Latham, 'Hints on Interpreting the Public Records: III, Inquisitions Post Mortem', *Amateur Historian*, vol. I, pp. 77-81
M McGuinness, 'Inquisitions Post Mortem', *Amateur Historian*, vol. VI, pp. 235-242
Public Record Office, *Index of Inquisitions Post Mortem, Henry VIII to Charles I* (Lists and Indexes, vols. XXII, XXVI, XXXII and XXXIII) *

Licences to alienate
Calendar of Patent Rolls, Henry III to Henry VII, and *Edward VI to 1582* (London, 1891-1986) *
Letters and Papers of Henry VIII (London, 1864-1932). (This includes a calendar of the Patent Rolls for Henry VIII.) *
List and Index Society, *Chancery Patent Rolls Calendar, James I* (vols. 97, 98, 109, 121, 122, 133, 134, 157, 164, 187, 193, 218, 229, 233; this is a reproduction of a contemporary calendar, arranged in letter order of grantees' names)

Rental and surveys
Public Record Office, *List of Rentals and Surveys and other analogous documents* (Lists and Indexes, vol. XXV) *
Public Record Office, *List of Special Commissions and Returns in the Exchequer* (Lists and Indexes, vol. XXXVIII) *

Unpublished finding aids

Catalogue of Lists and Indexes, sections relating to Exchequer, King's Bench and Common Pleas (for indexes to Plea and Recovery Rolls) *
Indexes to the Close Rolls *
Lists and indexes of ancient deeds, (not included in the published works) *
List of feet of fines *

Records

Alienation Office (at Chancery Lane)
A 4 Entry books of Licences and Pardons for Alienation. 1571-1650

Admiralty (at Kew)
ADM 74 Greenwich Hospital Court Rolls. 1473-1930

Chancery (at Chancery Lane)
C 54 Close Rolls. 1204-1903
C 66 Patent Rolls. 1202-1962
C 116 Masters' Exhibits, Court Rolls. 1294-1808
C 132 Inquisitions Post Mortem. Henry III
C 133 Inquisitions Post Mortem. Edward I
C 134 Inquisitions Post Mortem. Edward II
C 135 Inquisitions Post Mortem. Edward III
C 136 Inquisitions Post Mortem. Richard II
C 137 Inquisitions Post Mortem. Henry IV
C 138 Inquisitions Post Mortem. Henry V
C 139 Inquisitions Post Mortem. Henry VI
C 140 Inquisitions Post Mortem. Edward IV
C 141 Inquisitions Post Mortem. Richard III
C 142 Inquisitions Post Mortem. Henry VII to Charles II
C 143 Inquisitions Ad Quod Damnum. Henry III to Richard III
C 145 Miscellaneous Inquisitions. 3 Henry III to 2 Richard III
C 146 Ancient Deeds, Series C. c.1100-1627
C 147 Ancient Deeds, Series CC. c.1100 to Elizabeth I
C 148 Ancient Deeds, Series CS. Edward I to Elizabeth I
C 149 Modern Deeds. James I onwards

Court of Common Pleas (at Chancery Lane)
CP 25 Feet of Fines. Henry II to 1839
CP 40 Court of Common Pleas: *De Banco* Rolls. 1272-1875. (Indexes in IND 1/1-6605.)
CP 43 Recovery Rolls. 1582-1834. (Indexes in IND 1/17183-17216.)

Palatinate of Chester (at Chancery Lane)
CHES 2 Enrolments. 1307-1830
CHES 29 Plea Rolls Chester. 1255-1831
CHES 30 Plea Rolls Flint. 1283-1831
CHES 31 Fines and Recoveries. 1280-1831
CHES 32 Enrolments of Fines and Recoveries. 1585 to Anne

Crown Estate Commission (at Chancery Lane)
CRES 5 Court Rolls and Other Manorial Documents. 1441-1950

Duchy of Lancaster (at Chancery Lane)
DL 25 Deeds, Series L. 12th to 17th centuries
DL 26 Deeds, Series LL. 12th to 17th centuries
DL 27 Deeds, Series LS. 12th to 17th centuries
DL 30 Court Rolls. Edward I to 1925
DL 32 Parliamentary Surveys. Commonwealth
DL 42 Miscellaneous Books. John to 1894

DL 43 Rentals and Surveys. Henry III to George III
DL 44 Special Commissions and Returns. 1558-1853

Palatinate of Durham (at Chancery Lane)
DURH 12 Feet of Fines. 1535-1834
DURH 13 Judgment Rolls. 1344-1845
DURH 21 Deeds, Series G. 17th to 18th centuries

Exchequer (at Chancery Lane)
E 13 Plea Rolls. 1235-1875
E 40 Treasurer's Remembrancer: Ancient Deeds, Series A. 12th century to 1603
E 41 Treasurer's Remembrancer: Ancient Deeds, Series AA. 12th century to 1603
E 42 Treasurer's Remembrancer: Ancient Deeds, Series AS. 12th century to 1603
E 43 Treasurer's Remembrancer: Ancient Deeds, Series WS. 12th century to 1603
E 44 Treasurer's Remembrancer: Modern Deeds. 17th century
E 134 Depositions Taken by Commission. Elizabeth I to Victoria
E 142 Ancient Extents. John to Henry VI
E 149 Inquisitions Post Mortem: Series I. Henry III to Richard III
E 150 Inquisitions Post Mortem: Series II. Henry VII to James I
E 159 Memoranda Rolls. 1217-1959
E 164 Miscellaneous Books, Series I. Henry III to 1797
E 178 Special Commissions of Inquiry. Elizabeth I to Victoria
E 210 King's Remembrancer: Ancient Deeds, Series D. To 1603
E 211 King's Remembrancer: Ancient Deeds, Series DD. To 1603
E 212 King's Remembrancer: Ancient Deeds, Series DS. To 1603
E 213 King's Remembrancer: Ancient Deeds, Series RS. To 1603
E 315 Miscellaneous Books. 12th to 18th centuries
E 326 Augmentations Office: Ancient Deeds, Series B. 12th century to 1603
E 327 Augmentations Office: Ancient Deeds, Series BX. 12th century to 1603
E 328 Augmentations Office: Ancient Deeds, Series BB. 12th century to 1603
E 329 Augmentations Office: Ancient Deeds, Series BS. 12th century to 1603
E 330 Augmentations Office: Modern Deeds, Series B. After 1603
E 354 Pipe Office: Ancient Deeds, Series P. 16 Henry VIII to 5 James I
E 355 Pipe Office: Ancient Deeds, Series PP. 16th century
E 368 Memoranda Rolls. 1217-1835

Court of King's Bench (at Chancery Lane)
KB 26 Early Plea and Essoin Rolls. 1193-1272
KB 27 *Coram Rege* Rolls. 1273-1702
KB 122 Judgment Rolls. 1702-1875

Office of the Auditors of Land Revenue (at Chancery Lane)
LR 3 Land Revenue Court Rolls. 1286-1837
LR 14 Ancient Deeds, Series E. Henry III to Elizabeth I
LR 15 Ancient Deeds, Series EE. 1229-1720
LR 16 Modern Deeds, Series E. 17th to 18th centuries

Ministry of Agriculture, Fisheries and Food (at Kew)
MAF 5 Manor of Paglesham Manorial Documents. 1386-1926

MAF 9 Deeds and Awards of Enfranchisement. 1841-1925
MAF 13 Extinguishment of Manorial Incidents Series I. 1926-1944
MAF 20 Manor Files. 1840-1900. (Arranged alphabetically by name of the manor.)
MAF 27 Extinguishment of Manorial Incidents Series II. 1936-1957

Palatinate of Lancaster (at Chancery Lane)
PL 2 Close Rolls. 1409-1470
PL 14 Chancery Miscellanea. Richard II to Victoria
PL 15 Court of Common Pleas: Plea Rolls. 1400-1848
PL 17 Court of Common Pleas: Fines. 1362-1834
PL 29 Deeds, Series H. c.1550-c.1850

Special Collections (at Chancery Lane)
SC 2 Court Rolls. c.1200-c.1900

Principality of Wales (at Chancery Lane)
WALE 29 Ancient Deeds, Series F. Edward I to Elizabeth I
WALE 30 Ancient Deeds, Series FF. c.1507-1633
WALE 31 Modern Deeds. James II to 19th century

Court of Wards and Liveries (at Chancery Lane)
WARD 2 Deeds and Evidences. c.1200 to Charles I
WARD 3 Depositions. Henry VIII to Charles I
WARD 7 Inquisitions Post Mortem. Henry VIII to Charles I
WARD 13 Pleadings. Edward VI to Charles I

42. Surveys of land and house ownership

42.1 Introduction

For most parishes of England and Wales there is either a tithe map and apportionment
or an enclosure award and map, generally dating from the nineteenth century. If you
are researching a particular village or group of villages, they provide a fascinating
source from which it is possible to find out exactly where an ancestor's dwelling was
and who his neighbours were. Less well known as yet are the records produced by the
Valuation Office, which provide a national survey of house ownership in 1910-1913,
useful for both urban and rural areas.

42.2 Tithe records

Tithes were a tax of a tenth of all produce, payable to the local clergyman by his
parishioners (hence tithe barns). After the Reformation many entitlements to receive
tithes passed into the hands of laymen. In 1836 the Tithe Commutation Act fixed
money payment for payment in kind. The maps and apportionments created by this

procedure supply names of land owners and occupiers for a large number of parishes and chapelries, with details of the holdings and a description of the state of cultivation. Copies of the tithe maps and apportionments are held in county record offices, as well as in the PRO (IR 29, IR 30).

For areas where tithes had already been commuted for land or money in the course of private enclosures there are, of course, no tithe maps or apportionments in these classes. Also, there were a good many districts in which, although the tithes were commuted under the provisions of the 1836 Act, no apportionment was made. This was either because the amount involved was negligible or because the land owners were themselves the tithe owners, and the agreement or award of a gross tithe rentcharge was followed by the redemption or merger of the tithe rentcharges. By this means the expense of a formal apportionment and the preparation of a map was avoided. In such cases the result of the proceedings will be recorded in a formal agreement or instrument of merger (TITH 3), and there should be a tithe file (IR 18) which is rarely informative.

42.3 Enclosure awards

The term enclosure, as applied to land, usually refers either to the fencing in of commons by land owners, or to the process of combining a number of small farmsteads or plots and converting them into pasture. Before embarking on research among the surviving records, you should consult W E Tate's book, *A Domesday of English Enclosure Acts and Awards*.

Enclosure on a large scale in the sixteenth century was effected by decree of the courts of equity, especially Chancery and Exchequer. In order to locate an enclosure ratified by this method, the names of the parties involved must be known. In the eighteenth century most enclosures were made by private act of Parliament. Once the bill had gone through Parliament, a commission investigated and surveyed the land. From this, they drew up a binding enclosure award, allotting the plots of land. Most of these were not published officially, and it may be necessary to trace them via the original acts in the House of Lords Record Office.

The General Inclosure Acts of 1801 and 1836 did not specify where the awards were to be kept. Some were enrolled at Westminster and are now at the PRO in C 54; others are to be found in the county record offices. In 1845 a third General Inclosure Act directed that the Enclosure Commissioners for England and Wales retain the original awards. Their successors, the Land Commissioners, the Board of Agriculture, and the Ministry of Agriculture and Fisheries, continued this obligation and records produced under the terms of this act are now found in MAF 1.

42.4 House surveys, 1910-1913

Under the Finance Act of 1910, a tax was attached to the profit of house sales, if part of the profit was judged to have occurred because of the provision of amenities at the public expense. For example, if a park was opened nearby, trees planted in the road, and the road paved, the house price might increase because the site had become more attractive, although the householder had given neither effort nor financial contribution to the improvements.

In order to establish a fixed point from which to measure subsequent increases in value, a huge (and expensive) valuation exercise took place, between 1910 and 1913, the largest since 1086 and Domesday Book. The valuers wrote detailed descriptions and valuations of each house, and details of owners and tenants (but not occupiers) in Field Books (IR 58). These have been available for some time, but until recently they have been difficult to use, because the individual entries were made in a numerical sequence unrelated to location on the ground. Now, however, the 55,000 Valuation Office Record Maps (IR 121/1-IR 135/9) are largely available for inspection: on these, each house has a number as a key to the Field Books. As a result, the Field Books are now becoming widely used.

A second set of books, known as Domesday Books, was also made: these included the actual occupiers as well as owners and tenants; these are particularly useful as most people lived in rented accommodation. Most of these Domesday Books are to be found in county record offices, which may also have duplicates of the Record Maps. The PRO has the Domesday Books for the City of London and for Paddington (IR 91).

As an exercise in raising money, the whole operation proved to be an expensive failure: it was called off in 1920.

42.5 Surveys of land and house ownership: bibliography and sources

[An * means this work can be seen at Chancery Lane: a # means it can be seen at Kew.]

Published works

G Beech, 'Maps for Genealogy and Local History', *Genealogists' Magazine*, vol. XXII, pp. 197-202
J H Harvey, *Sources for the History of Houses* (British Records Association, 1968) *
R J P Kain, *An Atlas and Index of Tithe Files of mid-nineteenth century England and Wales* (Cambridge, 1980)
A Parliamentary Return of Inclosure Awards (House of Commons Sessional Papers, 1904 (50) LXXVIII, 545)
Public Record Office, *Enclosure Awards* (Information Leaflet) *#
Public Record Office, *Tithe Records in the PRO* (Information Leaflet) *#
Public Record Office, *Valuation Records Created Under the Finance (1909-1910) Act* (Information Leaflet) *#
W E Tate, *A Domesday of English Enclosure Acts and Awards* (Reading, 1978) *

Records

Chancery (at Chancery Lane)
C 54 Close Rolls. 1204-1903

Court of Common Pleas (at Chancery Lane)
CP 40 Court of Common Pleas: *De Banco* Rolls. 1272-1875
CP 43 Court of Common Pleas: Recovery Rolls. 1582-1837

Exchequer (at Chancery Lane)
E 13 Exchequer of Pleas, Plea Rolls. 1235-1875
E 159 King's Remembrancer Memoranda Rolls. 1217-1959

Inland Revenue (at Kew)
IR 18 Tithe Files. 1836-c.1870
IR 29 Tithe Redemption Office: Tithe Apportionments. Victoria. (On microfilm.)
IR 30 Tithe Redemption Office: Tithe Maps. Victoria. (On microfilm.)
IR 58 Valuation Office: Field Books. 1910
IR 91 Valuation Office: Domesday Books. 1910
IR 121/1-IR 121/22 Valuation Office: Finance Act 1910, Record Sheet Plans: London
    Region. c.1910
IR 124/1-IR 124/9 Valuation Office: Finance Act 1910, Record Sheet Plans: South
    East Region. c.1910
IR 125/1-IR 125/11 Valuation Office: Finance Act 1910, Record Sheet Plans: Wessex
    Region. c.1910
IR 126/1-IR 126/10 Valuation Office: Finance Act 1910, Record Sheet Plans: Central
    Region. c.1910
IR 127/1-IR 127/9 Valuation Office: Finance Act 1910, Record Sheet Plans: East
    Anglia Region. c.1910
IR 128/1-IR 128/10 Valuation Office: Finance Act 1910, Record Sheet Plans:
    Western Region. c.1910
IR 129/1-IR 129/9 Valuation Office: Finance Act 1910, Record Sheet Plans: West
    Midlands Region. c.1910
IR 130/1-IR 130/9 Valuation Office: Finance Act 1910, Record Sheet Plans: East
    Midland Region. c.1910
IR 131/1-IR 131/11 Valuation Office: Finance Act 1910, Record Sheet Plans: Welsh
    Region. c.1910
IR 132/1-IR 132/8 Valuation Office: Finance Act 1910, Record Sheet Plans:
    Liverpool Region. c.1910
IR 133/1-IR 133/8 Valuation Office: Finance Act 1910, Record Sheet Plans:
    Manchester Region. c.1910
IR 134/1-IR 134/10 Valuation Office: Finance Act 1910, Record Sheet Plans:
    Yorkshire Region. c.1910
IR 135/1-IR 135/9 Valuation Office: Finance Act 1910, Record Sheet Plans:
    Northern Region. c.1910

Court of King's Bench (at Chancery Lane)
KB 122 Court of King's Bench: Plea Side: Plea Rolls.1702-1875

Tithe Commission (at Kew)
TITH 1 Boundary Awards. 1839-1842, 1860
TITH 2 Awards and Agreements: Sealed Originals. 1836-1866
TITH 3 Tithes and Tithe Rentcharge: Declarations of Merger. 1837-1937

43. Taxation

43.1 Poll taxes, hearth taxes, subsidies and other early sources

Most tax records until the late seventeenth century are in the Subsidy Rolls (E 179). The list to this very large class is arranged first by county, and then by date.

The tax records of most use to the genealogist are the hearth tax returns and assessments of 1662-1674. These relate to the levy of two shillings on every hearth. The most complete hearth tax records are those for 25 March 1664. Information supplied includes names of householders, sometimes their status, and the number of hearths for which they are chargeable. The number of hearths is a clue to wealth and status. Over seven hearths usually indicates gentry and above; between four and seven hearths, wealthy craftsmen and tradesmen, merchants and yeomen. Between two and three hearths suggests craftsmen, tradesmen, and yeomen; the labouring poor, husbandmen and poor craftsmen usually only had one hearth. There are many gaps in the records, partly because of the loss of documentation, but partly also because of widespread evasion of this most unpopular tax. Hearth tax returns for particular areas have been published by many local record societies (see the card index of records in print), and some records are to be found in county record offices, among the quarter session records.

The same class of Subsidy Rolls (E 179) also contains records of other taxes from the twelfth to the early eighteenth centuries. Some of the earlier tax returns and assessments, especially the poll taxes of the reign of Richard II and the subsidies of the reign of Henry VIII, include lists of names; where they do, the fact is noted in the class list. The list of contributors to the 'Free and Voluntary Present' to Charles II in 1662 provides names and occupations or status of the wealthier members of society. About half the numbers who paid hearth tax subscribed to the 'Present'. Returns for Surrey have been published.

The parish lists of contributors to the fund for the relief of Protestant refugees for Ireland in 1642 provide a number of names; but survival is patchy (SP 28/191-195, E 179). The Surrey lists are very good and a typescript list and index is available.

43.2 Land taxes

From 1689 to 1830 there are records of land and assessed taxes in E 181-E 184, but they do not in general give lists of names, although defaulters may be listed. Land tax assessments may be found in county record offices for the period 1780-1832. In the PRO are the Land Tax Redemption Office Quotas and Assessments (IR 23). They list all owners of property subject to land tax in England and Wales in 1798-1799. The arrangement is by land tax parish and there is no index of names. In 1798 the land tax became a fixed annual charge and many people purchased exemption. The records of these transactions are also useful and may include maps and plans (IR 22, IR 24). The arrangement is by parish. See the book by Gibson and Mills for lists of records in the PRO and elsewhere, arranged by county.

43.3 Income taxes

Income tax returns are not transferred to the PRO and they are not available for public inspection.

43.4 Taxation: bibliography and sources

[An * means this work can be seen at Chancery Lane: a # means it can be seen at Kew.]

Published works

M W Beresford, 'Lay Subsidies', *Amateur Historian*, vol. III pp. 325-328 and vol. IV pp.101-109

M W Beresford, 'Poll Taxes of 1377, 1379 and 1381', *Amateur Historian*, vol. III pp. 271-278

J S W Gibson, *Hearth Tax Returns, other later Stuart Tax Lists, and the Association Oath Rolls* (FFHS, 1985) *

J S W Gibson and D Mills, *Land Tax Assessments, c.1690-c.1950* (FFHS, 1984) *

L M Marshall, 'The Levying of the Hearth Tax; 1662-1668', *English Historical Review*, vol. LI, pp. 628-646

C A F Meekings, *Introduction to the Surrey Hearth Tax, 1664* (Surrey Record Society, vol. XVII) *

Public Record Office, *Tax Records as a Source for Local and Family History*, (Information Leaflet) *#

C Webb, *Calendar of the Surrey Portion of the Free and Voluntary Present to Charles II* (West Surrey Family History Society, 1982) *

C Webb and East Surrey Family History Society, *Surrey Contributors to the Relief of Protestant Refugees from Ireland, 1642*

Unpublished finding aids

PRO card index of records in print

Records

Exchequer (at Chancery Lane)
E 179 Subsidy Rolls. c. Henry II to William and Mary

Inland Revenue (at Kew)
IR 22 Land Tax Redemption Office, Parish Books of Redemptions. 1799-1953
IR 23 Land Tax Redemption Office, Quotas and Assessments. 1798-1801, 1828-1914
IR 24 Land Tax Redemption Office, Registers of Redemption Certificates. 1799-1963

Secretaries of State (at Chancery Lane)
SP 29/191-195: contributors to the relief of Protestant refugees in Ireland, 1642

44. Tontines and annuity records

44.1 Tontines and annuity records

Tontines were government schemes for raising money. There were eleven tontines between 1693 and 1789. In return for an original investment, participants were guaranteed a yearly income for the life of a living nominee chosen by the investor. People usually nominated their youngest relative. As the nominees died off, the central fund was distributed between fewer and fewer people and the annuity therefore became more valuable as the years passed. There were in all about 15,000 participants. The records (NDO 1-NDO 3) may give details concerning the marriages, deaths and wills of contributors and nominees. Contributors were usually substantial people and chiefly from the south of England. Many were spinsters. The registers have integral indexes.

The records of the Irish Tontines (NDO 3) can be useful given the general dearth of Irish material.

44.2 Tontines and annuity records: bibliography and sources

[An * means this work can be seen at Chancery Lane: a # means it can be seen at Kew.]

Published works

F Leeson, *A Guide to the Records of the British State Tontines and Life Annuities of the 17th and 18th Centuries* (Shalfleet Manor, 1968)

Records

National Debt Office (at Kew)
NDO 1 Life Annuities (1745-1757) and Tontine (1789). 1745-1888
NDO 2 Life Annuities (1766-1779) and Tontine (1789). 1776-1888
NDO 3 Irish Tontines (1773-1777). 1773-1871

45. Business records

45.1 Company records and companies' registration

Until the mid nineteenth century, companies could only be incorporated by Royal Charter or special Act of Parliament. Registration between 1844 and 1856 enabled companies to be formed cheaply and easily, and successive Companies Acts have specified that certain documents (such as lists of directors and annual balance sheets) should be registered. Some information about the business activities of directors and shareholders of registered companies can be found in the records which have been so created.

For records relating to live companies and to those which have ceased to function within the last 20 years, apply to the Companies Registration Office, in London, Edinburgh, or Cardiff (addresses in **48.7**). For a small fee the Offices will produce a microfiche copy which contains all the required documents relating to any one company. Other company registration records are held in the PRO as listed below. However, to search the records at the PRO, you really need to get the company number from the Companies Registration Offices first. At the London Office, there are unique card indexes of all companies registered from 1856.

From 1916 people running businesses under names other than their own were required to register with the Board of Trade. These records are in the registry of business names (BT 253) but contain no genealogical information.

Share certificates of companies formed after 1844 are in the files of returns made to the Registrar of Companies (BT 31 and BT 41). These contain names, addresses and occupations of shareholders. Notices of receiverships, liquidations and bankruptcies appear in the *London Gazette*, available at Kew in ZJ 1.

The PRO has the records of canal and railway companies nationalised in 1947 (in RAIL: see **26.1**). There are numerous records of various companies and other commercial undertakings among the exhibits used in litigation (see **47.3**) and bankruptcy (see **46**). Otherwise, for records of companies themselves, advice may be obtained from the Business Archives Council (address in **48.6**).

45.2 Business records: bibliography and sources

[An * means this work can be seen at Chancery Lane: a # means it can be seen at Kew.]

Published works

J Armstrong, *Business Documents: their origins, sources and uses in historical research* (London, 1987)

H A L Cockerell and E Green, *The British Insurance Business, 1547-1970* (London, 1976)

D J Jeremy, *Dictionary of Business Biography: Biographical Dictionary of Business Leaders active in Britain in the Period 1860-1980* (London, 1984-1986)

Public Record Office, *Registration of Companies and Businesses* (Information Leaflet) *#

C T and M J Watts, 'Company Records as a source for the Family Historian', *Genealogists' Magazine*, vol. XXI, pp. 44-54.

Records

Board of Trade (at Kew)

BT 31 Companies Registration Office: Files of Dissolved Companies. 1855-1963. (Only a 1% sample of files of private companies have been retained. The records in this class are open after five years.)

BT 34 Companies Registration Office: Dissolved Companies, Liquidators' Accounts. 1890-1932
BT 41 Companies Registration Office: Files of Joint Stock Companies Registered under the 1844 and 1856 Acts. 1844-c.1860. (Alphabetically arranged.)
BT 253 Register of Business Names. 1916-1982. (Sample years.)

Supreme Court of Judicature (at Chancery Lane)
J 13 Companies (Winding-up) Proceedings. 1891-1951 (Samples only from 1949. Card index available.)

British Transport Historical Records (at Kew)
RAIL 1-RAIL 1180. (These classes contain records of pre-nationalisation railway, canal and related companies, the London Passenger Transport Board and successors.)

London Gazette (at Kew)
ZJ 1 *London Gazette*. 1665-1986

46 Debtors and bankrupts

46.1 Introduction

The court and prison records held in the PRO and locally (see **38, 39** and **47**) include very many references to legal proceedings against debtors and to the imprisonment of those convicted of being unable or unwilling to pay their debts. From 1543 to 1861 debtors who were traders and who owed large sums were usually exempt from the laws relating to debtors and from consequential imprisonment. They were subject instead to bankruptcy proceedings, for which separate records were kept (see **46.3**). From 1862 bankruptcy proceedings were extended to all insolvent debtors (i.e. those unable to pay), although some continued to be imprisoned for debt until 1970.

46.2 Debtors

Among the court and gaol records in the PRO are some which relate particularly to debtors. The records of the Palace Court, 1630-1849, mainly concern the recovery of small debts in the London area (PALA 1-PALA 9). Debtors gaoled by the central courts may appear in the records of the Fleet, King's Bench, Marshalsea and Queen's prisons for debtors, 1685-1862 (PRIS 1-PRIS 11), in the returns of imprisoned debtors made to the Court of Bankruptcy, 1862-1869 (B 2/15-32), or in the Palace Court's lists of prisoners, 1754-1842 (PALA 2).

Petitions for the discharge of prisoners for debt in England and Wales, 1813-1862, were registered by the Court for the Relief of Insolvent Debtors (B 6/45-71). Petitions by debtors who were not traders or who were traders owing small amounts, for protection orders against the laws relating to debtors, were registered by the Court of

Bankruptcy, 1842-1847, and the Court for the Relief of Insolvent Debtors, 1847-1861 (B 6/88-89, 94-96), and also by local courts of bankruptcy jurisdiction: see **46.3**. Proposals for repayments by insolvent debtors were recorded by the Court of Bankruptcy, 1848-1862 (B 6/97-98). From 1712 official notices relating to many insolvent debtors in England and Wales, were placed in the *London Gazette* (ZJ 1), which was indexed from 1790. Details were also published in *Perry's Bankruptcy and Insolvent Weekly Gazette* (later *Perry's Gazette*), from 1827.

These records and publications relating to debtors rarely give more than their names, addresses and occupations and sometimes those of their creditors, with formal details of conviction and imprisonment, where appropriate. Additional information can sometimes be found in the court records of legal actions against them: see **46.1**.

46.3 Bankrupts

From 1543, debtors who were 'traders' and who had substantial debts were usually exempt from the laws relating to debtors, and were subject instead to bankruptcy proceedings. The term 'traders' was quite narrowly defined, but in practice included persons engaged in most forms of business activity. The relevant amount of indebtedness varied from time to time, but was always high enough to exclude small traders in most circumstances. Bankruptcy was a process whereby a court official declared qualifying debtors bankrupt, took over their property, and distributed it to their creditors in proportion to what they were owed. Subject to certain procedures, bankrupts could then usually be discharged from their debts and escape imprisonment. Bankrupts included individuals, partnerships and, until 1844, joint stock companies. Their annual numbers increased from a few hundreds to many thousands between the eighteenth and twentieth centuries.

The PRO holds records of bankruptcy proceedings in England and Wales from 1710 (B 1-B 12, BT 39, BT 40, BT 221, BT 226, C 217), although their coverage is incomplete until 1821 and some of the more recent ones are closed for 75 years. Occasional earlier references to bankruptcy proceedings can be found in the records of the courts of Common Pleas and King's Bench until 1751 (see **47.2**); in the State Papers Domestic (SP classes), the Registers of the Privy Council (PC 2) and the Patent Rolls (C 66), for the sixteenth and seventeenth centuries; and in the Supplementary Patent Rolls (C 67), 1642-1654. From 1571 some conveyances of bankrupts' estates were entered on the Close Rolls (C 54).

From 1842 separate records of bankruptcy proceedings outside the London area were kept by district bankruptcy courts (1842-1869) and by county courts with bankruptcy jurisdiction (from 1861), and they are now held locally. Registers of petitions in bankruptcy in England and Wales from 1912 to date are held in the Thomas More Building, Royal Courts of Justice, where searches may be made on payment of a fee. Throughout, legal issues relating to bankruptcy were heard separately in local and central courts, and especially in Chancery. Bankrupts guilty of fraud, dishonesty or misconduct remained liable to imprisonment and may be found in the gaol records referred to in **46.1**. Records relating to Scottish bankruptcies ('sequestrations') are held in the Scottish Record Office.

Bankruptcy records usually give only the name, address and occupation of the debtors and of their creditors, and a formal summary of court proceedings. In some instances, where case papers survive (B 3, B 9, BT 221, BT 226) or where the proceedings were subjected to legal review (B 1, B 7), they may also provide interesting information about the bankrupts' family and business links, trading activities and economic circumstances.

From 1684 official notices relating to bankruptcy proceedings in England and Wales were placed in the *London Gazette*, which was indexed from 1790; however before about 1830 they include some names not found in the records and omit some names which are. Scottish notices were placed in the *Edinburgh Gazette*, although a few are found in the *London Gazette*. From 1862 official notices relating to county court proceedings were placed in local newspapers. There have been many other published lists of bankrupts, the most useful of which are listed below.

46.4 Debtors and bankrupts: bibliography and sources

[An * means this work can be seen at Chancery Lane: a # means it can be seen at Kew.]

Published works

W Bailey, *List of Bankrupts, Dividends and Certificates, 1772-1793* (London, 1794).
Edinburgh Gazette (Edinburgh, 1699 continuing)
London Gazette (London, 1665 continuing) #
S Marriner, 'English Bankruptcy Records and Statistics before 1850', *Economic History Review*, 2nd series, vol. XXXIII, pp. 351-366
Perry's Bankrupt and Insolvent Weekly Gazette (London, 1827-1881)
Perry's Gazette (London, 1882 continuing)

Records

Commissioners of Bankrupts, Court of Bankruptcy, London Court of Bankruptcy and High Court of Justice in Bankruptcy (at Chancery Lane)
B 1 Bankruptcy Order Books. 1710-1877
B 2/15-32: gaolers' records of imprisoned debtors, 1862-1869
B 3 Bankruptcy Commission Files. 1759-1911
B 4 Bankruptcy Commission Docket Books. 1710-1849
B 5 Bankruptcy Enrolment Books. 1710-1859
B 6/1-44, 72-87, 90, 99-223: registers of bankruptcy proceedings, 1733-1925
B 6/88-89: registers of the petitions of insolvent debtors for protection orders, 1842-1847
B 6/97-98: registers of proposals for repayments by insolvent debtors, 1848-1862
B 7 Bankruptcy Minute Books. 1714-1875
B 8 Index to Bankruptcy Enrolment Books and Registers. 1820-1870
B 9 Proceedings under Bankruptcy Acts. 1832-1958. (Some subject to 75 year closure.)
B 11 Registers of Petitions. 1884-1925
B 12 Registers of Receiving Orders. 1887-1925

Court for the Relief of Insolvent Debtors (at Chancery Lane)
B 6/45-71: registers of petitions for the discharge of prisoners for debt, 1813-1862
B 6/94-96: registers of petitions of insolvent debtors for protection orders, 1847-1862

Board of Trade, Bankruptcy Department (at Kew)
BT 39 Register of Deeds of Arrangement. 1888-1947
BT 40/25-52: register of bankruptcies in London (1870-1886) and county courts (1870-1884)
BT 221 Bankruptcy Division: Records. 1879-1972.
BT 226 Bankruptcy Cases: High Court Papers. 1891-1988

Chancery (at Chancery Lane)
C 54 Close Rolls. 1204-1903
C 66 Patent Rolls. 1201-1962
C 67 Supplementary Patent Rolls. 1275-1749
C 217 Miscellaneous Papers, Exhibits, etc. (Petty Bag Office). (Includes bankruptcy proceedings, 1774-1830.)

Palace Court (at Chancery Lane)
PALA 1 Bail Books. 1692-1836
PALA 2 Custody Books. 1754-1842
PALA 3 Docket Books. 1802-1849
PALA 4 Habeas Corpus Books. 1700-1849
PALA 5 Plaint Books. 1686-1849
PALA 6 Plea Rolls. 1630-1849
PALA 7 Profit Books. 1644-1846
PALA 8 Rule Books. 1666-1833
PALA 9 Miscellanea. Charles I - Victoria

Privy Council (at Chancery Lane)
PC 2 Registers. 1540-1978

Fleet Prison (at Chancery Lane)
PRIS 1 Commitment Books. 1685-1748 (incomplete) and 1778-1842
PRIS 3 Discharges. 1775-1842

King's (Queen's) Bench and Queen's Prisons (at Chancery Lane)
PRIS 4 Commitment Books. 1719-1721 and 1747-1862
PRIS 7 Discharges. 1776-1862

Marshalsea Prison (at Chancery Lane)
PRIS 11/1-3: commitment books, 1812-1842

Secretaries of State (at Chancery Lane)
SP 1-SP 17 State Papers Domestic, Henry VIII - Charles I

London Gazette (at Kew)
ZJ 1 *London Gazette*. 1665-1986

47. Civil litigation

47.1 Introduction

Civil litigation (law suits between two parties) makes up a large part of the PRO's holdings at Chancery Lane, covering disputes about land, property rights, debts, inheritance, trusts, frauds, etc. Records of civil litigation differ according to the kind of law and procedure used by the court in which they were heard.

The main body of law in use in England was the common law, supplemented by statute law. This law was used by the ancient royal courts of Common Pleas and King's Bench, in the civil actions heard at the assizes, and in the Exchequer of Pleas and the common law side of the Chancery. Unfortunately for the family historian, common law records (although extensive) are very largely composed of standard legal formulae, and do not contain much detail of any kind.

The faults of the common law, including its failure to enforce trusts and wills, were partly rectified by the use of equity courts, where the king's representatives were required to provide a judgement according to conscience and justice, that would not be obtainable in a common law court. The records of the equity courts form a wonderful source of social history, but it can be difficult to search them for a particular case. The main equity court was the Chancery, where the Chancellor acted as the king's deputy. Other courts, such as the Court of Requests (supposedly for poor plaintiffs) and Star Chamber grew out of the king's council; Star Chamber applied common law, but used equity procedure.

In addition to these royal courts, there were similar common law and equity courts in the palatinates of Chester, Durham and Lancaster, and in Wales: the records of Welsh courts are now in the National Library of Wales. The duchy (as opposed to the palatinate) of Lancaster had its own courts, available to tenants of duchy lands throughout the kingdom.

Three other systems of law also operated in England. Civil law (a branch of Roman law) was used in the High Court of Admiralty and in the High Court of Delegates; ecclesiastical law (another branch of Roman law) was used in the church courts; and customary law was used in other local courts based on the jurisdiction of the lord rather than the king.

All these legal systems (except for the ecclesiastical and local courts) were brought together in a series of mid nineteenth century reforms, which resulted in a single Supreme Court of Judicature, with separate Divisions of Chancery, Common Pleas, Exchequer, King's Bench, and Probate, Divorce and Admiralty.

47.2 Records of the common law courts

Records of civil cases in the common law courts are difficult to find and are generally uninformative for family history. The records themselves are astonishing in quantity and are in Latin until 1733: they were also enrolled in a special 'court hand', quite unlike other contemporary handwriting styles. However, there are considerable numbers of contemporary finding aids to the records, so that it is possible to trace cases, if you wish to follow a particular known dispute.

47.3 Records of the equity courts

In contrast to the common law courts, the amount of detail given in equity cases is almost overwhelming. The records abound in vivid sketches of daily life, particularly of disputes among families: they are also in English. Because the procedure was so similar for all equity courts, references to the records of each court are given in **47.7**.

The normal procedure in all the equity courts was for the plaintiff to submit a written bill of complaint to the court, detailing all the various wrongs alleged to have been committed against him. The defendant would submit a similar document, the answer, refuting the allegations of the bill. The plaintiff would respond with a replication, and the defendant with a rejoinder. By this time, the points of issue should have been whittled down considerably from those first alleged. A series of set questions relating to the points at issue was drawn up (the interrogatory), which was put to witnesses, by local commissioners if they lived at a distance. Their answers, the depositions, can be very full and helpful. Other evidence might include affidavits (voluntary statements made on oath) and exhibits (documents belonging to the parties, not necessarily relating to specific points at issue).

In Chancery (the main equity court), pleadings, evidences and exhibits were sent to one of the Masters in Chancery for consideration and a report back to the Chancellor. By the eighteenth century, Chancery cases could take up to thirty years to decide, with long delays caused by the dependence on one judge: as a result, some cases were remitted to the civil side of the assizes for a local hearing after the issues had been defined. Orders and decrees made by the Chancellor, or by the judges in the other equity courts, were generally enrolled in some fashion: for some courts, such as the early Chancery and the Star Chamber, they no longer exist.

One of the main problems with using equity records is that the documents relating to a single case were not all filed together, but were filed with other documents of the same type: pleadings, depositions, orders etc. were filed in separate series. This is where it can be helpful to consult the Masters' papers in Chancery, because they generally copied everything (at vast expense to the litigants) to bring it together. However, searching in the equity records of Chancery can be a protracted business, because of the huge volume of cases handled by the court, and the large bureaucracy that became attached to it. The Bernau Index (available on microfilm at the Society of Genealogists) is worth consulting for equity type proceedings in Chancery, Exchequer, Requests and Star Chamber, although its coverage is not complete.

Equity records of the Chancery run from the late fourteenth century to 1875: after 1875, similar records can be found among the records of the Supreme Court of Judicature. The equity jurisdiction of the Exchequer ran from the mid sixteenth century to 1841, when it was taken over by the Chancery. There are PRO information leaflets on using the records of both these courts, which should be consulted.

The Court of Requests and Star Chamber only lasted from the early sixteenth century to the 1640s. In the palatinates, the Chancery of Durham and the Chancery of the County Palatine of Lancaster lasted from the fifteenth century to 1971: the Chester equity court, known as the Exchequer, lasted from the fifteenth century to 1830. The equity court of the Duchy of Lancaster, known as the Duchy Chamber, started in the fourteenth century and still exists in theory.

47.4 Records of the civil law courts

There were also various civil law courts (generally applying Roman or 'civil' international law). Disputes concerning ships or cargoes were normally heard in the High Court of Admiralty (HCA classes). Appeals in maritime, ecclesiastical, testamentary and divorce cases went to the High Court of Delegates (DEL) until 1834 and to the Judicial Committee of the Privy Council (PCAP) between 1834 and 1858 (1879 for maritime cases). The records of these courts can be very informative.

47.5 Chancery: unclaimed money (dormant funds)

Many families have stories of money 'in Chancery'. This may refer to money deposited by solicitors (from 1876) when they were unable to trace legatees or next of kin. Since 1876, annually-prepared accounts have been produced: they can be inspected, free of charge, at the Court Funds Office (address in **48.7**). Evidence of beneficial interest is required. Lists of funds published as supplements to the *London Gazette* (1893-1974), can be consulted in the PRO, Chancery Lane. Successful claims are extremely rare.

47.6 Chancery and Chancery Division: pedigrees

Pedigrees were frequently produced as evidence in law suits but, except in a few classes, it is very difficult to find them. For the eighteenth and nineteenth centuries there are manuscript indexes of pedigrees in some classes of Chancery Masters Exhibits (C 103-C 114) on the open shelves. Most of these pedigrees relate to disputed wills and administrations. A typed index to pedigrees among various papers of the Chancery Division of the Supreme Court is available, which gives the names of the principal persons shown in the pedigrees and a separate index to the names mentioned in the titles to suits.

47.7 Civil litigation: bibliography and sources

[An * means this work can be seen at Chancery Lane: a # means it can be seen at Kew.]

Published works

J H Baker, *An Introduction to English Legal History* (London, 3rd edn 1990)

P W Coldham, 'Genealogical Resources in Chancery Records', *Genealogists' Magazine*, vol. XIX, pp. 345-347 and vol. XX, pp. 257-260

R E F Garrett, *Chancery and Other Legal Proceedings* (Shalfleet Manor, 1968)

Public Record Office, *An Introduction to Chancery Proceedings* (Information Leaflet) *#

Public Record Office, *Equity Proceedings in the Court of Exchequer* (Information Leaflet) *#

Finding aids

Bernau Index: Society of Genealogists. This covers C 11, C 12, C 21, C 24, 8% of C 22, and parts of other classes.

At the PRO, Chancery Lane, there is an extensive collection of published and unpublished indexes to plaintiffs, defendants, deponents etc. for a large number of classes and parts of classes of equity and equity-type proceedings: ask in the search rooms.

Records

Chancery (at Chancery Lane)

C 1 Early Chancery Proceedings. Richard II to Philip and Mary
C 2 Chancery Proceedings, Series I. Elizabeth I to Charles I
C 3 Chancery Proceedings, Series II. Elizabeth I to Commonwealth
C 5-C 10 Chancery Proceedings, Before 1714. James I to 1714
C 11 Chancery Proceedings, Various Six Clerks, Series I. 1714-1758
C 12 Chancery Proceedings, Various Six Clerks, Series II. 1758-1800
C 13 Chancery Proceedings, Various Six Clerks, Series III. 1800-1842
C 14 Chancery Proceedings, Modern, Series I. 1842-1852
C 15 Chancery Proceedings, Modern, Series II. 1853-1860
C 16 Chancery Proceedings, Modern, Series III. 1861-1875
C 21 Country Depositions, Series I. Elizabeth I to Charles I
C 22 Country Depositions, Series II. 1649-1714
C 23 Unpublished Depositions. Elizabeth I to Victoria
C 24 Town Depositions. 1534-1853
C 25 Chancery Interrogatories. 1598-1852
C 31 Chancery Affidavits. 1611-1875
C 32 Chancery Cause Books. 1842-1880
C 33 Chancery Entry Books of Decrees and Orders. 1544-1875
C 38 Masters' Reports and Certificates. 1544-1875
C 39 Masters' Reports (Supplementary). 1580-1892
C 78 Decree Rolls.1534-1903
C 79 Supplementary Decree Rolls. 1534-1903
C 103-C 114 Masters' Exhibits. 1234-1860
C 117-C 126 Masters' Documents. 17th to 19th centuries

Palatinate of Chester (at Chancery Lane)
CHES 9 Papers in Causes. 1501-1830

CHES 11 Exhibits. Henry III to Charles II
CHES 12 Unpublished Depositions. Elizabeth I
CHES 13 Original or Draft Decrees and Orders. 1559-1790
CHES 14 Entry Books. 1562-1830
CHES 15 Exchequer Pleadings. Henry VIII to 1830. (These relate to real property, i.e. land.)
CHES 16 Exchequer Pleadings (Paper). 1559-1762. (These relate to debts and personal property.)

High Court of Delegates (at Chancery Lane)
DEL 1 Processes. 1609-1834
DEL 2 Cause Papers. c.1600-1834
DEL 3 Examinations. 1557-1735
DEL 7 Case Books. 1796-1834
DEL 11 Miscellaneous Lists and Indexes, etc. 1538-1868

Duchy of Lancaster (at Chancery Lane)
DL 3 Depositions and Examinations, Series I. Henry VII to Philip and Mary.
DL 4 Depositions and Examinations, Series II. 1558-1818
DL 5 Entry Books of Decrees and Orders. 1472-1872
DL 6 Draft Decrees. Henry VIII to 1810
DL 8 Draft Injunctions. 1614-1794
DL 9 Affidavits, Reports, Certificates, Orders, Petitions, etc. 1560-1857
DL 48 Sealed Depositions. 1695-1739
DL 49 Papers in Law Suits. 1502-1853

Palatinate of Durham (at Chancery Lane)
DURH 1 Affidavits. 1657-1812
DURH 2 Bills, Answers, etc. 1576-1840
DURH 4 Entry Books of Decrees and Orders. 1633-1958
DURH 5 Original Decrees, Orders and Reports. 1613-1778
DURH 6 Draft Decrees, Orders and Reports. 1749-1829
DURH 7 Interrogatories, Depositions, Writs, etc. 1557-1804

Exchequer (at Chancery Lane)
E 103 Affidavits. 1774-1951
E 112 Bills, Answers, etc. Henry VIII to 1951
E 123-E 127 Entry Books of Decrees and Orders. 1558-1841
E 128 Original Decrees and Orders. 1580-1662
E 129 Supplementary Original Decrees and Orders. c.1350-c.1840
E 130 Original Decrees. 1660-1841
E 131 Original Orders. 1660-1841
E 133 Barons' Depositions. Elizabeth I to 1841
E 134 Depositions Taken by Commission. Elizabeth I to Victoria
E 140 Exhibits. c.1650-c.1850
E 185 Equity Petitions. 1627-1841
E 193 Replications and Rejoinders. 1558-1841
E 194 Reports and Certificates. 1648-1841

E 207 *Bille*. (Includes affidavits in equity causes, Elizabeth I to 1774.)

Supreme Court of Judicature (at Chancery Lane)
For records of the various Divisions of this court, see the *Current Guide* Part 2, under the lettercode J.
J 40 Master Keen's Papers and Pedigrees. 1850-1929
J 63 Master Mosse's Papers and Pedigrees. c.1852-1917
J 64 Master Hawkins' Pedigrees. 1849-1925
J 66 Master Hulbert's Pedigrees. 1849-1926
J 67 Master Newman's Papers and Pedigrees. 1893-1931
J 68 Various Masters' Pedigrees. 1852-1974

High Court of Admiralty (at Chancery Lane)
For records of this court, see the *Current Guide* Part 2.

Judicial Committee of the Privy Council (at Chancery Lane)
PCAP 1 Appeals Processes. 1834-1879
PCAP 3 Appeals Case Books. 1834-1870

Palatinate of Lancaster (at Chancery Lane)
PL 6 Bills. 1485-1853
PL 7 Answers. 1474-1858
PL 8 Replications, etc. 1601-1856
PL 9 Affidavits. 1610-1678, 1793-1836
PL 10 Depositions. 1581-1854
PL 11 Entry Books of Decrees and Orders. 1524-1848
PL 12 Exhibits. 1795-1860
PL 30 Reports and Certificates. 1813-1849

Court of Requests (at Chancery Lane)
REQ 2 Proceedings. Henry VII to Charles I

Court of Star Chamber (at Chancery Lane)
STAC 1 Proceedings, Henry VII. Henry VII
STAC 2 Proceedings, Henry VIII. Henry VIII
STAC 3 Proceedings, Edward VI. Edward VI
STAC 4 Proceedings, Mary I. Mary I
STAC 5 Proceedings, Elizabeth I. Elizabeth I
STAC 7 Proceedings, Elizabeth I (Addenda). Elizabeth I
STAC 8 Proceedings, James I. James I
STAC 9 Proceedings, Charles I. Charles I

48. Useful addresses

48.1 Genealogical societies and organisations in the United Kingdom and Channel Islands

Association of Genealogists and Record
Agents
Honorary Secretary
1 Woodside Close
Stanstead Road
Caterham
Surrey CR3 6AU

Association of Scottish Genealogists
and Record Agents
PO Box 174
Edinburgh EH3 5QZ

Channel Islands Family History Society
PO Box 507
St Helier
Jersey
Channel Islands

Federation of Family History Societies
Administrator
c/o Benson Room
Birmingham and Midland Institute
Margaret Street
Birmingham B3 3BS

Genealogical Society of Utah
751 Warwick Road
Solihull
Birmingham B91 3DQ

Guild of One Name Studies
Box G
c/o 14 Charterhouse Buildings
Goswell Road
London EC1M 7BA

The Manager
Church of Jesus Christ of Latter Day
Saints
Hyde Park Family History Centre
64-68 Exhibition Road
London SW7 2PA

Institute of Heraldic and Genealogical
Studies
Northgate
Canterbury
Kent CT1 1BA

Irish Genealogical Research Society
c/o The Challoner Club
59-61 Pont Street
London SW1X 0BG

Scots Ancestry Research Society
3 Albany Street
Edinburgh EH1 3PY

Scottish Genealogical Society
21 Howard Place
Edinburgh EH3 5JY

Scottish Tartan Society
Davidson House
Drummond Street
Comrie
Crieff
Perthshire PH6 2DW

Society of Genealogists
14 Charterhouse Buildings
Goswell Road
London EC1M 7BA

Ulster Historical Foundation
68 Balmoral Avenue
Belfast BT9 6NY

48.2 Genealogical societies and organisations abroad

Australian Federation of Family History
Organisations
PO Box 30
Blackburn
Victoria 3130
Australia

Australian Genealogists, Society of
Richmond Villa
120 Kent Street
Observatory Hill
Sydney
NSW 2000
Australia

Centraal Bureau voor Genealogie
Prins Willem Alexander hof 22
2595 BE DEN HAAG
The Netherlands
Mailing address:
PO Box 11755
2502 AT DEN HAAG
The Netherlands

Centre d'Entaide Généalogique de
France
69 rue du Cardinal Renoire
F-75005
Paris
France

The Family History Association of
Canada
PO Box 398
West Vancouver
British Columbia V7V 3P1
Canada

The Genealogical Publishing Co. Inc.
111 Water Street
Baltimore
Maryland 21201
U S A

Genealogical Society of South Africa
PO Box 4839
Capetown
South Africa 800D

Family History Department
Genealogical Library
35 North West Temple Street
Salt Lake City
Utah 84150
U S A

International Society for British
Genealogy and Family History
PO Box 20425
Cleveland
Ohio 44120
U S A

Irish Family History Society
1 Charleville Road
Tullamore
Co. Offaly
Eire

National Genealogical Society
4527 17th St North
Arlington
Virginia 22207-2363
U S A

New Zealand Society of Genealogists
Inc.
PO Box 8795
Symonds Street
Auckland 3
New Zealand

48.3 Historical associations

British Association for Cemeteries in
South Asia
76½ Chartfield Avenue
London SW15 6HQ

Business Archives Council
First Floor
185 Tower Bridge Road
London SE1 2UF

Business Archives Council of Scotland
Glasgow University Archives
The University
Glasgow G12 8QQ

Friends of the Public Record Office
c/o Public Record Office
Chancery Lane
London WC2A 1LR

Honourable Society of Cymmrodorion
30 East Castle Street
London W1N 7PD

Royal Air Force Association
43 Grove Park Road
London W4 3RV

Société Jersiaise
The Museum
Pier Road
9 St Helier
Jersey
Channel Islands

48.4 Religious libraries and archives

Anglo-Jewish Archives
The Mocatta Library
University College
Gower Street
London WC1E 6BT

Canterbury Cathedral, City and
Diocesan Record Office
The Precincts
Canterbury CT1 2EG

Catholic Central Library
47 Francis Street
London SW1P 1QR

Dr Williams's Library
14 Gordon Square
London WC1H 0AG

Genealogical Library
Church of Jesus Christ of Latter Day
Saints
Hyde Park Chapel
64-68 Exhibition Road
London SW7 2PA

Huguenot Library
University College
Gower Street
London WC1E 6BT

The Incumbent
The Chapel Royal
St James's Palace
London SW1

Jewish Museum
Woburn House
Upper Woburn Place
London WC1H 0EP

Lambeth Palace Library
London SE1 7JU

Methodist Archives and Research
Centre
John Rylands University Library of
Manchester
Deansgate
Manchester M3 3EH

Religious Society of Friends
The Librarian
Friends House
Euston Road
London NW1 2BJ

Scottish Catholic Archives
Columba House
16 Drummond Place
Edinburgh EH3 6PL

Spanish and Portuguese Synagogue
Honorary Archivist
9 Lauderdale Road
Maida Vale
London W9 1LT

United Synagogue, Office of the
The Archives
Woburn House
Upper Woburn Place
London WC1H 0EZ

48.5 Religious historical societies

Baptist Historical Society
Secretary
15 Fenshurst Gardens
Long Ashton
Bristol BS18 9AV

Catholic Record Society
c/o Miss R Rendel
114 Mount Street
London W1Y 6AH

Huguenot Society of Great Britain
and Ireland
c/o Malmaison
Church Street
Great Bedwyn
Wiltshire SN8 3PE

Presbyterian Historical Society of
Northern Ireland
Church House
Fisherwick Place
Belfast BT1 6DU

United Reformed Church History
Society
86 Tavistock Place
London WC1H 9RT

48.6 Museums, libraries and record offices

The Borthwick Institute of Historical
Research
St Anthony's Hall
Peaseholme Green
York YO1 2PW

British Library, Newspaper Library
Colindale Avenue
Colindale
London NW7 5HE

Business Archives Council
185 Tower Bridge Road
London SE1 2UF

British Library, Reference Division
Great Russell Street
London WC1B 3DG

City of London Police Record Office
26 Old Jewry
London EC2R 8OJ

College of Arms
Queen Victoria Street
London EC4V 4BT

Corporation of London Record Office
Guildhall
London EC2P 2EJ

Gray's Inn Library
South Square
Gray's Inn
London WC1R 5EU

Greater London Record Office
40 Northampton Road
London EC1R 0HB

Guildhall Library
Aldermanbury
London EC2P 2EJ

HMS *Belfast*
Symons Wharf
Vine Lane
Tooley Street
London SE1 2JH

HMS *Victory*
HM Naval Base
Portsmouth
Hampshire PO1 3PZ

Historic Ship Collection
East Basin
St Katherine's Dock
London E1 9AF

House of Lords Record Office
House of Lords
London SW1A 0PW

Imperial War Museum
Department of Documents
Lambeth Road
London SE1 6HZ

Imperial War Museum
Duxford Airfield
Duxford
Cambridgeshire CB2 4QR

India Office Library and Records
British Library
Orbit House
197 Blackfriars Road
London SE1 8NG

Inner Temple Library
Inner Temple
London EC4Y 7DA

Institute of Agricultural History and
Museum of English Rural Life
University of Reading
PO Box 229
Whiteknights
Reading RG6 2AG

The Law Society
Chancery Lane
London WC2A 1LR

The Law Society
Ipsley Court
Redditch
Hereford and Worcester BN8 0TD

Lincoln's Inn Library
Lincoln's Inn
London WC2A 3JN

Manx Museum
Kingswood Grove
Douglas
Isle of Man

Maritime Records Centre
Merseyside Maritime Museum
Pier Head
Liverpool L3 1DN

Metropolitan Police
Records Section
New Scotland Yard
Victoria Street
London SW1 0BG

Middle Temple Library
Middle Temple Lane
London EC4Y 98T

Modern Records Centre
University of Warwick Library
Coventry
West Midlands CV4 7AL

National Army Museum
Department of Records
Royal Hospital Road
London SW3 4HT

National Library of Wales
Aberystwyth
Dyfed SY23 3BU

National Maritime Museum
Manuscripts Section
Romney Road
Greenwich
London SE10 9NF

National Railway Museum Library
Leman Road
York YO2 4XJ

National Register of Archives
Quality House
Quality Court
Chancery Lane
London WC2A 1HF

National Register of Archives
(Scotland)
West Register House
Charlotte Square
Edinburgh EH2 4DF

The Priaulx Library
St Peter Port
Guernsey
Channel Islands

Public Record Office
Chancery Lane
London WC2A 1LR

Public Record Office
Ruskin Avenue
Kew
Richmond
Surrey TW9 4DU

Public Record Office of Northern
Ireland
66 Balmoral Avenue
Belfast BT9 6NY

Royal Air Force Museum
Department of Aviation Records
(Archives)
Hendon Aerodrome
London NW9 5LL

Royal Archives
Windsor Castle
Windsor
Berkshire SL4 1NJ

Royal Commission on Historical
Manuscripts
Quality House
Quality Court
Chancery Lane
London WC2A 1HF

Royal Marines Museum
Eastney
Southsea
Hampshire PO4 9PX

Royal Naval Museum
HM Naval Base
Portsmouth
Hampshire PO1 3LR

St Anthony's College
Middle East Centre
Oxford OX2 6JS

Scottish Record Office
PO Box 36
HM General Register House
Edinburgh EH1 3YY

Wapping Police Station Museum
98 Wapping High Street
London E1 9NE

48.7 Government departments

Air Historical Branch
Ministry of Defence
Lacon House
Theobalds Road
London WC1X 8RY

Army Medal Office
Government Office Buildings
Droitwich
Worcestershire WR9 8AU

Army Museums Ogilby Trust
Connaught Barracks
Duke of Connaught's Road
Aldershot
Hampshire GU11 2LR

Central Criminal Court
Courts' Administrator
Old Bailey
London EC4M 7EH

Chaplain of the Fleet
Ministry of Defence
Lacon House
Theobalds Road
London WC1X 8RY

Civil Service Commission
Management and Personnel Office
Treasury Chambers
Parliament Street
London SW1P 3AG

Clerk of the Court
Queen Elizabeth II Street
Alderney
Channel Islands

Companies Registration Office
Companies House
Crown Way
Maindy
Cardiff CF4 3UZ

Companies Registration Office
Companies House
102 George Street
Edinburgh EH2 3DJ

Companies Registration Office
Companies House
55-71 City Road
London EC1Y 1BB

Court Funds Office
22 Kingsway
London WC2B 6LE

Defence, Ministry of
CS(R)2a (Royal Naval Records)
Bourne Avenue
Hayes
Middlesex UB3 1RS

Defence, Ministry of
CS(R)2b (Army Personnel Records)
Bourne Avenue
Hayes
Middlesex UB3 1RS

Defence, Ministry of
CS(R)2c (Polish Service Personnel Records)
Bourne Avenue
Hayes
Middlesex UB3 1RS

Defence, Ministry of
CS(R)2e (Navy Personnel Records)
Bourne Avenue
Hayes
Middlesex UB3 1RS

Department of Social Security
Special Section 'A' Records Branch
Central Office
Longbenton
Newcastle upon Tyne NE98 1YX

General Register Office
St Catherine's House
10 Kingsway
London WC2B 6JP

General Register Office
(CA Section)
Segensworth Road
Titchfield
Fareham
Hampshire PO15 5RR

General Register Office (Northern Ireland)
Oxford House
49-55 Chichester Street
Belfast BT1 4HL

General Register Office (Scotland)
New Register House
Edinburgh EH1 3YT

General Registry
Finch Road
Douglas
Isle of Man

HM Greffier
The Greffe
Royal Court House
St Peter Port
Guernsey
Channel Islands

Home Office
Immigration & Nationality Department
Lunar House
40 Wellesley Road
Croydon CR9 2BY

Judicial Greffe (Jersey)
States Building
10 Hill Street
Royal Square
St Helier
Jersey
Channel Islands

Land Registry
Lincoln's Inn Fields
London WC2A 3PH

Naval Medal Office PP1B2
HMS *Centurion*
Grange Road
Gosport
Portsmouth PO13 9XA

Office of Population Censuses and
Surveys
St Catherine's House
10 Kingsway
London WC2B 6JP

Metropolitan Police
Pensions Branch
New Scotland Yard
Victoria Street
London SW1 0BG

Principal Registry of the Family
Division
Record Keeper
Correspondence Dept.
Somerset House
Strand
London WC2R 1LA

Public Record Office
Chancery Lane
London WC2A 1LR

Public Record Office
Ruskin Avenue
Kew
Richmond
Surrey TW9 4DU

Public Record Office of Northern Ireland
66 Balmoral Avenue
Belfast BT9 6NY

Registrar
La Vallette
Sark
Channel Islands

Registrar General of Northern Ireland
Fermanagh House
Ormeau Avenue
Belfast BT1 6DU

Registrar General of Scotland
New Register House
Prince's Street
Edinburgh EH1 3YT

Registrar General of Shipping and
Seamen
Llantrisant Road
Llandaff
Cardiff CF5 2YS

Registrar of the Guernsey Ecclesiastical
Court
12 New Street
St Peter Port
Guernsey
Channel Islands

Royal Air Force
Personnel Management Centre
PM(AR1b)
Eastern Avenue
RAF Barnwood
Gloucestershire GL4 7PN

Royal Air Force
Personnel Management Centre
P Man 3e(2)
RAF Innsworth
Gloucestershire GL3 1EZ

Royal Artillery
Record and Manning Office
Imphal Barracks
York YO1 4HD

Royal Courts of Justice
Strand
London WC2A 2LL

Royal Marines
Commandant General
Ministry of Defence
Main Building
Whitehall
London SW1A 2HB

Royal Marines
Drafting and Record Office
HMS *Centurion*
Grange Road
Gosport
Portsmouth PO13 9XA

Royal Military Police
Roussillon Barracks
Chichester
Sussex PO19 4BL

Royal Naval Medals OS10
Empress State Building
Lillie Road
London SW6 1TR

Scottish Record Office
PO Box 36
HM General Register House
Edinburgh EH1 3YY

Superintendent of Births, Marriages
and Deaths
The States Building
St Helier
Jersey
Channel Islands

Women's Land Army Benevolent
Association
c/o Mr D Roopnarine, Room 408
Ministry of Agriculture, Fisheries and
Food,
3-8 Whitehall Place,
London SW1A 2HH

48.8 Overseas organisations and archives

Genealogical Office
2 Kildare Street
Dublin 2
Republic of Ireland

General Register Office of Ireland
8-11 Lombard Street
Dublin 2
Republic of Ireland

Library of Congress
Washington DC 20540
U S A

Memorial University of Newfoundland
Maritime History Group
St John's
Newfoundland
Canada

National Library of Australia
Parkes Place
Canberra
ACT 2600
Australia

National Library of Ireland
Kildare Street
Dublin
Republic of Ireland

Public Archives of Canada
395 Wellington Street
Ottawa 4
Ontario K1A 0NA
Canada

Public Record Office of Ireland
The Four Courts
Dublin 7
Republic of Ireland

Registry of Deeds
King's Inn
Henrietta Street
Dublin
Republic of Ireland

48.9 International bodies

The Archivist
International Red Cross
British Red Cross Training Centre
Barnett Hill
Wonersh
Guildford
Surrey GU5 3PJ

British Red Cross Society
International Welfare Department
9 Grosvenor Crescent
London SW1X 7EJ

The Commonwealth War Graves
Commission
2 Marlow Road
Maidenhead
Berkshire SL6 7DX

The Salvation Army
(Investigating Officer)
105-109 Judd Street
London WC1H 9TS

INDEX

burial records 36-7
Burma
  births, marriages and deaths 50
Business Archives Council 224
business records
  bibliography and sources 224-5
  company records 223-4

calendars 16, 63, 64, 67-8, 84, 91, 163, 187, 188, 198
Cambridge
  prison registers 204
Canada
  Loyalist Regiment rolls 124
  muster rolls 92
  pension payments 92
  Public Archives 91
  see also North America
canal company records 172, 224
casualty returns 69, 106
  death registers 106
  naval officers 137
  other ranks 117
  see also General Register Office
catalogues 16
Catholic genealogy
  bibliography and sources 27, 188-90
  burials 188
  estates and possessions 188-9
  location of records 188
  persecution records 188-9
  registers of births, marriages and deaths 28, 32, 34
  see also oath rolls; recusant rolls
Cayman Islands
  births, marriages and deaths 46
cemetery records 34, 36-7
  see also burial grounds
census records
  bibliography and sources 26-7
  location of 15
census returns
  closure period 15, 25, 26
  colonial 26
  finding aids 25
  personal information 25, 26
  pre-1841 25

census returns (countries)
  Australia 26
  Barbados 26
  Channel Islands 25, 82
  England 25
  Ireland 26, 78
  Isle of Man 25, 80
  Scotland 26, 77
  Sierra Leone 26
  Surinam 26
  Wales 25, 74
Census Room (Public Record Office) 25, 26
censuses of population
  bibliography and sources 26-7
  census returns: England, Wales, Isle of Man and Channel Islands 25-6
  census returns: other places 26
Central Criminal Court (Old Bailey)
  jurisdiction 199-200
  records and sessions 199, 201-2
Chancery
  pedigrees 231
  records 40, 63-4, 69, 82, 85-6, 97, 100, 103, 147, 166, 179, 181, 182, 184, 185, 188, 189, 208, 211, 212, 215, 219, 228, 229, 230-1, 232
  solicitors' roll 178
  unclaimed money 231
Chancery Masters' exhibits 231
changes of name 102-3
Channel Islands
  association oath rolls 81, 99
  births, marriages and deaths 29, 37
  census returns 25, 82
  see also directory of useful addresses
Channel Islands genealogy
  bibliography and sources 82
  Guernsey, Alderney and Sark 81-2
  Jersey 81, 99
  societies 81
chapels, nonconformist 186
chapels royal 33, 36
chaplains
  army 113-14
  navy 133
charities 186

Royal Marines *cont.*
 other ranks 150-1
 pensions 151-2
 prisoners of war 192-3
 service records 150, 151
 warrant officers 150
 wills 69, 151
Royal Marines Museum 149
Royal Military Asylum 121
Royal Military Police 104, 161
Royal Mint 128
Royal Naval Air Service 153
Royal Naval Asylum, Greenwich 137,
 143, 175
Royal Naval Museum 131
Royal Naval Reserve 138-9, 167
Royal Naval Volunteer Reserve 139
Royal Navy *see* Navy
royal warrant holders 163
Russia
 births, marriages and deaths 58-9
 English Independent congregation of
 St Petersburg 30
 prisoners of war 192
 Russian Orthodox church records 33,
 190, 192

St Catherine's House *see* General
 Register Office
sailors *see* seamen
sailmakers 135
sacrament certificates 99, 184
Salvation Army 22-3
Sark *see* Channel Islands; Channel
 Islands genealogy
school records 181-2
schools
 for sailors' children 137, 138, 141-2,
 142-3, 175
 for soldiers' children 121-2, 175
Scotland
 births, marriages and deaths 29, 43, 77
 census returns 26, 77
 Customs officers 164
 Foreign Office registers 45
 foreign registers 77
 genealogical bibliographies 23

Scotland *cont.*
 heraldic authorities 22
 legal system 197
 see also directory of useful
 addresses; *entries beginning* Scottish...
Scottish bankruptcies ('sequestrations')
 226, 227
Scottish Excise 165
Scottish genealogical societies 77
Scottish genealogy
 bibliography and sources 77
 location of records 77, 172
Scottish Record Office 77, 172, 197, 226
Sea Fencibles 138
seamen
 disabled 140, 141
 prisoners of war 193
 see also merchant seamen; Navy;
 Navy: commissioned officers; Navy:
 naval ratings; Navy: warrant officers;
 Registrar General of Shipping and
 Seamen; Royal Greenwich Hospital;
 Sea Fencibles
seamen's families *see* Navy; Royal
 Greenwich Hospital
Seamen's Fund Winding-up Act 169
Secretaries of State 89, 129, 148, 190,
 209, 222, 228
sentences
 court judgements 68
 pardons 203, 205, 206
 see also petitions
sequestrations *see* Scottish bankruptcies
serjeants-at-law *see* lawyers
share certificates and shareholders 224
ships, museum
 HMS *Belfast* 131
 HMS *Victory* 131
 see also Historic Ships Collection
ships and shipping *see* fishing vessels;
 Lloyds Register of Shipping; maritime
 court cases; *Mercantile Navy List*
 passenger lists and registers; prison
 ships; Registrar General of Shipping
 and Seamen; transportation contracts
ships logs 135
ships' numbers 168, 169

Welsh genealogy
  bibliography and sources 75-6
  guides 74
  location of records 74-5
  see also directory of useful addresses;
    Wales
Wesleyan Methodist Metropolitan
  Registry 31, 46
West Indies
  bibliography 95-6
  births, marriages and deaths 62
  emigrants to:
    British 91-2
    foreign 93
    location of records 26, 90-1
    naturalisation 93
  prisoners transported to 206-7, 208-9
  slave owners 92
wills
  after 1858 65
  as sources for genealogists 66-7, 70
  before 1858 66

wills *cont.*
  bibliography and sources 70-3
  Channel Islands 81
  death duty registers 66, 69-70
  indexes and finding aids 67-8
  inventories and accounts 68
  Irish 78
  litigation 68-9
  location 63, 65, 66
  military 69, 124
  other probate records 69
  PCC and grants of administration 66-8
  persons dying overseas 66, 92
  Royal Marines 151
  Scottish 77
  seamen's 66, 143, 170
  Wales 66

Yorkshire 64, 211

Zanzibar
  births, marriages and deaths 62

Printed in the United Kingdom for HMSO
Dd294209 6/91 C60 G3390 10170